PowerScore Test Preparation

LSAT Reading Comprehension Passage Type Training II:

LSAT PrepTests 21 through 40

The complete text of every LSAT Reading Comprehension Question from PrepTest 21 through 40 sorted according to PowerScore's famous LSAT Reading Comprehension Bible system.

Copyright © 2012 by PowerScore Incorporated.

All Rights Reserved. No part of this publication may be reproduced, stored in a retrieval system, or transmitted in any form or by any means electronic, mechanical, photocopying, recording, scanning, or otherwise, without the prior written permission of the Publisher. Parts of this book have been previously published in other PowerScore publications and on the powerscore.com website.

All actual LSAT questions printed within this work are used with the permission of Law School Admission Council, Inc., Box 2000, Newtown, PA 18940, the copyright owner. LSAC does not review or endorse specific test preparation materials or services, and inclusion of licensed LSAT questions within this work does not imply the review or endorsement of Law Services. LSAT is a registered trademark of Law Services.

LSAT and Law Services are registered trademarks of the Law School Admission Council, Inc.

PowerScore® is a registered trademark. The Reading Comprehension Bible™, The Logic Games Bible™, The Games Bible™, The Logical Reasoning Bible™, VIEWSTAMP™, The Conclusion Identification Method™, The Fact Test™, Traps of Similarities and Distinctions™, Trap of Separation™, Trap of Proximity™, Trap of Inserted Alternate Viewpoint ™, Traps of Chronology™, Passage Topic Traps™, The Location Element™, The Uniqueness Rule of Answer Choices™, the Agree/Disagree Test™, Passage Commonality™, Passage Exclusivity™, and Passage Aggregate™ are the exclusive service marked property of PowerScore. Any use of these terms without the express written consent of PowerScore is prohibited.

Published by
PowerScore Publishing, a division of PowerScore Incorporated
57 Hasell Street
Charleston, SC 29401

Authors: David M. Killoran
    Steven G. Stein

Manufactured in Canada
August 2012

ISBN: 978-0-9846583-0-5

PowerScore PUBLICATIONS

LSAT Preparation Guides

PowerScore LSAT Logic Games Bible
- Ultimate guide for attacking the Logic Games section of the test
- Multiple drills with in-depth explanations and detailed methodology
- 30 real LSAT Logic Games, diagrammed with detailed analyses

PowerScore LSAT Logical Reasoning Bible
- Definitive guide to the Logical Reasoning section of the test
- Detailed discussions of the ideal approach to each Logical Reasoning question type
- Over 100 real LSAT questions analyzed and explained

PowerScore LSAT Reading Comprehension Bible
- Comprehensive guide to the Reading Comprehension section of the test
- Extensive discussions of both standard and comparative reading passages
- Detailed explanations of actual LSAT passages and question sets

LSAT Question Collections

PowerScore LSAT Reading Comprehension Passage Type Training
- Includes every reading passage and question from LSAT PrepTests 1 through 20
- Passage types divided by category; answer keys provide line references

PowerScore LSAT Game Type Training
- Includes every Logic Game and question from LSAT PrepTests 1 through 20
- 80 Logic Games games sorted according to the games classification system used in the *PowerScore LSAT Logic Games Bible*.

Available at PowerScore.com

PowerScore LSAT Reading Comprehension Bible Workbook

- The ideal complement to PowerScore's renowned *LSAT Reading Comprehension Bible*
- An entire chapter of drills to practice and apply concepts from the *Reading Comprehension Bible*
- Twenty complete reading comprehension passages followed by complete explanations

PowerScore LSAT Logic Games Bible Workbook

- The ideal complement to PowerScore's renowned *LSAT Logic Games Bible*
- An entire chapter of drills to practice and apply concepts from the *Logic Games Bible*
- Thirty complete games with each rule and inference discussed and diagrammed

PowerScore LSAT Logical Reasoning Bible Workbook

- A perfect complement to the renowned *PowerScore LSAT Logical Reasoning Bible*
- Multiple drills to apply the concepts and approaches from the *Logical Reasoning Bible*
- Six full sections (over 150 Logical Reasoning questions), followed by complete explanations

Test and Question Explanations

PowerScore LSAT Logic Games Setups Encyclopedias

- Extensive discussions of every game from LSAT PrepTests 1 through 20
- Includes complete setups, and analyses of every rule, inference, and diagram
- Volume 2 (PrepTests 21-40), and Volume 3 (Preptests 41-60) are also available

PowerScore LSATs Deconstructed Series

- Provides original LSAC-released PrepTests, followed by comprehensive discussion and analysis
- Includes complete game setups, passage breakdowns, and every question and answer explained

Need LSAT Help?
You're not alone.

Visit powerscore.com to learn more about our Full-Length, Weekend, and Live Online courses.

Contents

Chapter One: Introduction

Introduction 1
A Brief Overview of the LSAT 3
The LSAT Scoring Scale 4
The LSAT Percentile Table 5
The Use of the LSAT 6
The Reading Comprehension Section 7
Approaching the Passages 10
Reading Comprehension Classifications Explained 14
Diversity Passages 14
Law-Related Passages 16
Science Passages 17
Humanities Passages 18

Chapter Two: Diversity

Diversity I: Affirming Underrepresented Groups

Passage #1: June 1997 Questions 1-8 20
Passage #2: December 1997 Questions 7-13 22
Passage #3: June 1998 Questions 14-21 24
Passage #4: September 1998 Questions 22-27 26
Passage #5: December 1998 Questions 8-14 28
Passage #6: October 1999 Questions 8-15 30
Passage #7: December 1999 Questions 22-27 32
Passage #8: June 2000 Questions 6-12 34
Passage #9: June 2000 Questions 13-20 36
Passage #10: October 2000 Questions 14-19 38
Passage #11: December 2000 Questions 8-14 40
Passage #12: October 2001 Questions 1-6 42
Passage #13: October 2001 Questions 7-14 44
Passage #14: June 2002 Questions 14-21 46
Passage #15: October 2002 Questions 1-8 48
Passage #16: December 2002 Questions 1-8 50
Passage #17: June 2003 Questions 6-12 52

Diversity II: Undermining Overrepresented Groups

Passage #1: December 2002 Questions 9-16 54

Diversity III: Mixed Group Passages

Passage #1: December 1996 Questions 22-27 56
Passage #2: October 1997 Questions 19-26 58
Passage #3: September 1998 Questions 6-13 60
Passage #4: October 2000 Questions 8-13 62

Chapter Three: Law Related Passages

Law Passages

Passage #1: December 1996 Questions 9-16 66
Passage #2: June 1997 Questions 9-16 68
Passage #3: October 1997 Questions 6-13 70
Passage #4: June 1998 Questions 1-7 72
Passage #5: December 1998 Questions 1-7 74
Passage #6: June 1999 Questions 1-5 76
Passage #7: October 1999 Questions 22-27 78
Passage #8: December 1999 Questions 15-21 80
Passage #9: October 2000 Questions 1-7 82
Passage #10: December 2000 Questions 23-28 84
Passage #11: October 2001 Questions 21-26 86
Passage #12: June 2002 Questions 1-7 88
Passage #13: October 2002 Questions 9-14 90
Passage #14: June 2003 Questions 20-27 92

Regulation Passages

Passage #1: December 2001 Questions 21-26 94
Passage #2: December 2002 Questions 24-28 96

Chapter Four: Social Science Passages

Passage #1: June 1997 Questions 22-26 100
Passage #2: December 1997 Questions 1-6 102
Passage #3: December 1997 Questions 14-20 104
Passage #4: June 1998 Questions 22-26 106
Passage #5: December 1998 Questions 22-26 108
Passage #6: June 2000 Questions 1-5 110
Passage #7: June 2002 Questions 22-26 112
Passage #8: October 2002 Questions 15-20 114

Chapter Five: Hard Science Passages

Passage #1: December 1996 Questions 17-21 118
Passage #2: September 1998 Questions 14-21 120
Passage #3: December 1998 Questions 15-21 122
Passage #4: June 1999 Questions 6-13 124
Passage #5: October 1999 Questions 16-21 126
Passage #6: December 1999 Questions 1-6 128
Passage #7: October 2000 Questions 20-27 130
Passage #8: December 2000 Questions 15-22 132
Passage #9: June 2001 Questions 13-18 134
Passage #10: October 2001 Questions 15-20 136
Passage #11: December 2001 Questions 15-20 138
Passage #12: June 2002 Questions 8-13 140
Passage #13: December 2002 Questions 17-23 142
Passage #14: June 2003 Questions 13-19 144

Chapter Six: Humanities Passages

Passage #1: December 1996 Questions 1-8 148
Passage #2: June 1997 Questions 17-21 150
Passage #3: October 1997 Questions 1-5 152
Passage #4: October 1997 Questions 14-18 154
Passage #5: December 1997 Questions 21-27 156
Passage #6: June 1998 Questions 8-13 158
Passage #7: September 1998 Questions 1-5 160
Passage #8: June 1999 Questions 14-21 162
Passage #9: June 1999 Questions 22-26 164
Passage #10: October 1999 Questions 1-7 166
Passage #11: December 1999 Questions 7-14 168
Passage #12: June 2000 Questions 21-28 170
Passage #13: December 2000 Questions 1-7 172
Passage #14: June 2001 Questions 1-6 174
Passage #15: June 2001 Questions 7-12 176
Passage #16: June 2001 Questions 19-26 178
Passage #17: December 2001 Questions 1-6 180
Passage #18: December 2001 Questions 7-14 182
Passage #19: October 2002 Questions 21-27 184
Passage #20: June 2003 Questions 1-5 186

Answer Key and Line Reference Notes

Answer Key and Line Reference Notes 189

Appendix

Test-by-Test Passage Location Identifier 207

Endnotes

Contacting PowerScore 211

About PowerScore

PowerScore is one of the nation's fastest growing test preparation companies. Founded in 1997, PowerScore offers LSAT, GMAT, GRE, SAT, and ACT preparation classes in over 150 locations in the U.S. and abroad. Preparation options include Full-length courses, Weekend courses, Virtual courses, private tutoring, and admissions counseling services. For more information, please visit our website at www.powerscore.com or call us at (800) 545-1750.

For supplemental information about this book, please visit the *LSAT Reading Comprehension: Passage Type Training* website at www.powerscore.com/lsatbibles.

Chapter One: Introduction

Introduction

Welcome to *LSAT Reading Comprehension: Passage Type Training II* by PowerScore. In this book you will find every Reading Comprehension passage from LSAT PrepTests 21 through 40, arranged in groups according to the classification system used in the renowned *PowerScore LSAT Reading Comprehension Bible*.

Grouping each passage by type provides a number of practical benefits:

- The 80 passages in this book are an excellent practice resource, and an ideal supplement to the *LSAT Reading Comprehension Bible*.

- By examining passages with certain basic similarities, you can analyze the features of each passage type in order to better understand how passages are constructed, how they can be most quickly recognized, and how they can be most easily solved. This is especially the case if you have already read the *PowerScore LSAT Reading Comprehension Bible*.

- Alternatively, for more general practice with games of all types, you can use the appendix in the back of the book and do complete passage sections from individual tests. The appendix on page 207 gives directions for taking that approach.

- Even if you have not already read the *LSAT Reading Comprehension Bible*, this book provides an excellent practice resource, allowing you to develop your familiarity with various passage types and with the Reading Comprehension section in general.

At the end of this book a complete answer key is provided. While complete explanations of each passage and question are not provided, each answer key is accompanied by Line Reference Notes that indicate the location in the passage where the source for the correct answer can be found.

If you are looking to further improve your LSAT score, we also recommend that you pick up copies of the PowerScore LSAT Logic Games Bible and PowerScore LSAT Logical Reasoning Bible.

In our LSAT courses, our admissions counseling programs, and our publications, we always strive to present the most accurate and up-to-date information available. Consequently, we have devoted a section of our website to *LSAT Reading Comprehension: Passage Type Training II* students. This free online resource area offers supplements to the book material, answers questions posed by students, offers study plans, and provides updates as needed. There is also an official book evaluation form that we strongly encourage you to use. The exclusive *LSAT Reading Comprehension: Passage Type Training II* online area can be accessed at:

www.powerscore.com/lsatbibles

If you would like to discuss the LSAT with our experts, please visit our free LSAT discussion forum at:

forum.powerscore.com/lsat

If we can assist you in your LSAT preparation in any way, or if you have any questions or comments, please do not hesitate to email us at lsatbibles@powerscore.com. Additional contact information is provided at the end of this book. We look forward to hearing from you!

A Brief Overview of the LSAT

The Law School Admission Test is administered four times a year: in February, June, September/October, and December. This standardized test is required for admission to any American Bar Association-approved law school. According to Law Services, the producers of the test, the LSAT is designed "to measure skills that are considered essential for success in law school: the reading and comprehension of complex texts with accuracy and insight; the organization and management of information and the ability to draw reasonable inferences from it; the ability to think critically; and the analysis and evaluation of the reasoning and arguments of others." The LSAT consists of the following five sections:

- 2 Sections of Logical Reasoning (short arguments, 24-26 questions each)
- 1 Section of Reading Comprehension (3 long reading passages, 2 short comparative reading passages, 26-28 total questions)
- 1 Section of Analytical Reasoning (4 logic games, 22-24 total questions)
- 1 Experimental Section of one of the above three section types.

You are given 35 minutes to complete each section. The experimental section is unscored and is not returned to the test taker. A break of 10 to 15 minutes is given between the 3rd and 4th sections.

The five-section test is followed by a 35-minute writing sample.

The Logical Reasoning Section

Each Logical Reasoning Section is composed of approximately 24 to 26 short arguments. Every short argument is followed by a question such as: "Which one of the following weakens the argument?", "Which one of the following parallels the argument?", or "Which one of the following must be true according to the argument?". The key to this section is time management and an understanding of the reasoning types and question types that frequently appear.

Since there are two scored sections of Logical Reasoning on every LSAT, this section accounts for approximately 50% of your score.

The Analytical Reasoning Section

This section, also known as Logic Games, is often the most difficult for students taking the LSAT for the first time. The section consists of four games or puzzles, each followed by a series of five to eight questions. The questions are designed to test your ability to evaluate a set of relationships and to make inferences about those relationships. To perform well on this section you must understand the types of games that frequently appear and develop the ability to properly diagram the rules and make inferences.

At the conclusion of the LSAT, and for five business days afterwards, you have the option of cancelling your score. Unfortunately, there is no way to determine exactly what your score would be before cancelling.

CHAPTER ONE: INTRODUCTION

3

The Reading Comprehension Section

This section is composed of three long reading passages, each approximately 450 words in length, and two shorter comparative reading passages. The passage topics are drawn from a variety of subjects, and each passage is followed by a series of five to eight questions that ask you to determine viewpoints in the passage, analyze organizational traits, evaluate specific sections of the passage, or compare facets of two different passages.

The Experimental Section

Each LSAT contains one undesignated experimental section, and it does not count towards your score. The experimental can be any of the three section types previously discussed, and the purpose of the section is to test and evaluate questions that will be used on *future* LSATs. By pretesting questions before their use in a scored section, the experimental helps the makers of the test determine the test scale.

The Writing Sample

> For many years the Writing Sample was administered before the LSAT.

A 35-minute Writing Sample is given at the conclusion of the LSAT. The Writing Sample is not scored, but a copy is sent to each of the law schools to which you apply. In the Writing Sample you are asked to write a short essay that defends one of two possible courses of action.

> You must attempt the Writing Sample! If you do not, Law Services reserves the right not to score your test.

Do not agonize over the Writing Sample; in law school admissions, the Writing Sample is not a major determining element for three reasons: the admissions committee is aware that the essay is given after a grueling three hour test and is about a subject you have no personal interest in; they already have a better sample of your writing ability in the personal statement; and the committee has a limited amount of time to evaluate each application.

The LSAT Scoring Scale

Each administered LSAT contains approximately 101 questions, and each LSAT score is based on the total number of questions a test taker correctly answers, a total known as the raw score. After the raw score is determined, a unique Score Conversion Chart is used for each LSAT to convert the raw score into a scaled LSAT score. Since June 1991, the LSAT has used a 120 to 180 scoring scale, with 120 being the lowest possible score and 180 being the highest possible score. Notably, this 120 to 180 scale is just a renumbered version of the 200 to 800 scale most test takers are familiar with from the SAT and GMAT. Just drop the "1" and add a "0" to the 120 and 180.

Although the number of questions per test has remained relatively constant over the last eight years, the overall logical difficulty of each test has varied. This is not surprising since the test is made by humans and there is no precise way to completely predetermine logical difficulty. To account for these variances in test "toughness," the test makers adjust the Scoring Conversion Chart for each LSAT in order to make similar LSAT scores from different tests mean the same thing. For example, the LSAT given in June may be logically more difficult than the LSAT given in December, but by making the June LSAT scale "looser" than the December scale, a 160 on each test would represent the same level of performance. This scale adjustment, known as equating, is extremely important to law school admissions offices around the country. Imagine the difficulties that would be posed by unequated tests: admissions officers would have to not only examine individual LSAT scores, but also take into account which LSAT each score came from. This would present an information nightmare.

The LSAT Percentile Table

It is important not to lose sight of what LSAT scaled scores actually represent. The 120 to 180 test scale contains 61 different possible scores. Each score places a student in a certain relative position compared to other test takers. These relative positions are represented through a percentile that correlates to each score. The percentile indicates where the test taker ranks in the overall pool of test takers. For example, a score of 165 represents the 93rd percentile, meaning a student with a score of 165 scored better than 93 percent of the people who have taken the test in the last three years. The percentile is critical since it is a true indicator of your positioning relative to other test takers, and thus law school applicants.

Since the LSAT has 61 possible scores, why didn't the test makers change the scale to 0 to 60? Probably for merciful reasons. How would you tell your friends that you scored a 3 on the LSAT? 123 sounds so much better.

Charting out the entire percentage table yields a rough "bell curve." The number of test takers in the 120s and 170s is very low (only 1.6% of all test takers receive a score in the 170s), and most test takers are bunched in the middle, comprising the "top" of the bell. In fact, approximately 40% of all test takers score between 145 and 155 inclusive, and about 70% of all test takers score between 140 and 160 inclusive.

The median score on the LSAT scale is approximately 151. The median, or middle, score is the score at which approximately 50% of test takers have a lower score and 50% of test takers have a higher score. Typically, to achieve a score of 151, you must answer between 56 and 61 questions correctly from a total of 101 questions. In other words, to achieve a score that is perfectly average, you can miss between 40 and 45 questions. Thus, it is important to remember that you don't have to answer every question correctly in order to receive an excellent LSAT score. There is room for error, and accordingly you should never let any single question occupy an inordinate amount of your time.

There is no penalty for answering incorrectly on the LSAT. Therefore, you should guess on any questions you cannot complete.

CHAPTER ONE: INTRODUCTION

The Use of the LSAT

The Law School Admission Council uses a variety of names that all refer to one or more portions of the entire operation that administers the LSAT and attendant services. These names include Law Services, LSAC, and LSAS.

The use of the LSAT in law school admissions is not without controversy. It is largely taken for granted that your LSAT score is one of the most important determinants of the type of school you can attend. At many law schools a multiplier made up of your LSAT score and your undergraduate grade point average is used to help determine the relative standing of applicants, and at some schools a sufficiently high multiplier guarantees your admission.

For all the importance of the LSAT, it is not without flaws. As a standardized test currently given in the paper-and-pencil format, there are a number of skills that the LSAT cannot measure, such as listening skills, note-taking ability, perseverance, etc. Law Services is aware of these limitations and as a matter of course they warn all law schools about overemphasizing LSAT results. Still, since the test ultimately returns a number for each student, it is hard to escape the tendency to rank applicants accordingly. Fortunately, once you get to law school the LSAT is forgotten. Consider the test a temporary hurdle you must leap in order to reach the ultimate goal.

For more information on the LSAT, or to register for the test, contact Law Services at (215) 968-1001 or at their website at www.lsat.com.

The Reading Comprehension Section

The focus of this book is on the Reading Comprehension section of the LSAT, and each Reading Comprehension section contains four passage sets with a total of 26 to 28 questions. Since you have thirty-five minutes to complete the section, you have an average of approximately eight minutes and forty-five seconds to complete each passage set. Of course, the amount of time you spend on each passage set will vary with the reading difficulty of the passage, the difficulty of the questions, and the total number of questions per passage set.

On average, you have 8 minutes and 45 seconds to complete each passage set.

Why Reading Comprehension?

Each section of the LSAT is designed to test abilities required in the study and/or practice of law. The Logical Reasoning sections measure your skills in argumentation and logic. The Logic Games section tests your ability to understand the interaction of different variables and the laws which govern their actions. Reading Comprehension, a section included in many standardized tests, provides a test of skills particularly important to both law students and attorneys. Law students are required to read significant portions of dense text throughout their legal studies, and lawyers must often be ready to do the same in their normal course of business; given that the misreading of a contract or legal judgment could lead to disastrous results for a lawyer's clients (not to mention the lawyer), it should not be surprising that Reading Comprehension is an integral part of the Law School Admission Test.

The Section Directions

Each Reading Comprehension section is prefaced by the same set of official directions. Because the directions that precede every Reading Comprehension section are the same, you should familiarize yourself with the basic directions now. Once the actual test begins, *never* waste time reading the directions for any section.

In the official directions, the test makers indicate that you are to use the statements of the author of the passage to prove and disprove answer choices. You do not need to bring in additional information aside from the typical ideas that the average American or Canadian would be expected to believe on the basis of generally known and accepted facts. For example, you would be expected to understand the *basics* of how the weather works, or how supply and demand works, but not the specifics of either. Please note that this does not mean that the LSAT cannot set up scenarios where they discuss ideas that are extreme or outside the bounds of common knowledge, such as a passage about a difficult scientific or legal concept. The test makers can and do discuss complex or extreme ideas; in these cases, they give you context for the situation by providing additional information.

The directions also explain that in some cases more than one of the choices provided *could* answer the question, but that you are to choose the best answer choice—you must choose the option that provides the most accurate, complete answer. By stating up front that more than one answer choice could suffice to answer the question, the makers of the test compel you to read every single answer choice before making a selection. If you read only one or two answer choices and then decide you have the correct one, you could end up choosing an answer that has some merit but is not as good as a later answer. One of the test makers' favorite tricks is to place a highly attractive wrong answer choice immediately before the correct answer choice in the hopes that you will pick the wrong answer choice and then move to the next question without reading any of the other answers.

The Two Passage Types

The section directions also state that "Each set of questions in this section is based on a single passage or a pair of passages." Prior to June 2007, all LSAT Reading Comprehension sections consisted of four total passages, each accompanied by a series of five to eight questions. Each passage and its accompanying questions are known as a "passage set."

Starting with the June 2007 LSAT, the test makers introduced a new element to the test known as a Comparative Reading passage set, wherein two passages generally addressing the same topic are presented, and a set of questions follows. Because Comparative Reading passage sets did not appear within LSAT PrepTests 1 through 20, there are none in this book. However, a complete discussion of Comparative Reading passage sets is found in Chapter Seven of the *LSAT Reading Comprehension Bible*.

Remember, the LSAT is used for admission to US and Canadian law schools, hence the test is geared towards those cultures.

You should read all five answer choices in each question.

Passage Topics

Reading Comprehension passages are drawn from a wide variety of disciplines, including science, law, and humanities. Thus, you will typically encounter four passage sets with widely varying topical matter. However, even though passage subject matter differs, most sections are constructed from the same consistent set of topics, as follows:

<u>4 Passage Sets</u>

1   Law-related passage
1   Science-based passage
1   Humanities passage featuring diversity
1   Random passage, often Humanities

So, even though the exact subject matter of each passage changes from test to test, the typical LSAT contains one science passage, one law passage, and one humanities passage featuring diversity. The remaining passage is usually drawn from a humanities field such as history or economics, but occasionally the passage comes from science or law.

For a typical example, consider the topics from the December 2007 LSAT:

<u>Topic</u>	<u>Subject Matter</u>
Humanities/Diversity	Asian-American Poetry of Wing Tek Lum
Law	British Common Law
Humanities	University Research Commercialization
Science	Natural Predation and Cyclamen Mites

Please note that the topic of the passage is not necessarily indicative of the level of difficulty. That is, some Science passages are easy, some are difficult. The same goes for Law passages, Humanities passages, etc. In the next chapter we will discuss how to attack any type of passage, and we will discuss how the underlying structure of passages can be analyzed regardless of the passage topic. Topic is examined here so that you understand the nature of what you will be reading. In some cases, knowing the topic can help you make informed decisions about the viewpoints that will be presented therein, and in many cases, students perform better on passages that contain a subject matter that is familiar to them. And, although our primary analysis will focus on viewpoints and structure, later in this chapter we will examine passages from the most commonly occurring topics as a way to calibrate your test radar to the types of mechanisms and viewpoints put forth by the makers of the test.

To locate passages written in the desired style, test makers draw from various sources, which they adapt for use in the Reading Comprehension section. Academic, scientific, and scholarly journals tend to be written in a fairly sophisticated manner, and thus routinely provide materials for the LSAT; recent passage sources have included The University of California, Scientific American Library, and Johns Hopkins University. Articles are also drawn from publications devoted to the arts, including recent offerings from the American Academy of Arts and Sciences, and Poetry in Review Foundation. While the passages are drawn from a wide variety of sources, including newspapers, magazines, books, and journals, they tend to be written in a recognizable, academic style that generally evades simple analysis.

CHAPTER ONE: INTRODUCTION

Approaching the Passages

Every Reading Comprehension passage set contains two separate parts: the passage(s) and the questions. When examining the two parts for the first time, students sometimes wonder about the best strategy for attacking the passages: Should I read the questions first? Should I skim the passage? Should I read just the first and last sentence of each paragraph of the passage? The answer is *Read the passage in its entirety and then attack the questions*. That is, first read the entire passage with an eye towards capturing the main ideas, viewpoints, tone, and structure of the passage, and then proceed to the questions, answering them in order unless you encounter a question too difficult to answer. Although this may seem like a reasonable, even obvious, approach, we mention it here because some LSAT texts advocate reading the questions first or skimming the passage. Let us take a moment to discuss some of the various reading approaches that you *might* consider using, but should avoid:

1. **DO NOT** skim the passage, then do each question, returning to the passage as needed.

    In theory, it might seem that skimming could add some degree of efficiency, but in practice this is not the case. In fact, this approach actually reflects a fundamental misunderstanding of the nature of the Reading Comprehension section.

    Skimming might be sufficient to absorb lighter materials, such as newspapers or magazines, but that is because those types of materials are written with simplicity in mind. A newspaper editor wants readers to know half the story by the time they have read the headline, and magazines put the most attention-grabbing pictures on their covers; these publications are trying to draw you in, to entice you to make a purchase. The makers of the LSAT, on the other hand, are well aware that they are dealing with a captive audience; they do not feel any pressure to entertain (as you may have noticed), and passages are chosen based on completely different criteria.

    For many, skimming is a natural reaction to a time-constrained test, but unfortunately the test-makers are well aware of this tendency—the passages they use are chosen in part because they evade quick and simple analysis. In practice, the time "saved" on the front end skimming a passage is more than lost on the back end. In the question section, the skimmer invariably finds the need to go back and re-read, and is often not sufficiently familiar with the passage structure to locate relevant reference points quickly.

2. **DO NOT** read just the first and last sentence of each paragraph of the passage, and then do each question, returning to the passage as needed.

This type of "super-skimming" may also sound good in theory; the idea of breezing through the passages, trying to pick up the big picture ideas, may sound appealing, but again, these passages unfortunately do not work that way. This shorthand and ineffective approach is based in part on the common misconception that the main idea of every paragraph appears in the first or last sentence. While this may often hold true, we will see that this is not always the case. After all, the makers of the LSAT are extremely sharp, and they are familiar with these common approaches as well. That may be why many passages will not follow this general rule—the test makers do not like for passages to follow such a simple prescribed formula.

This approach is basically an even more simplistic and ineffective variation of skimming that provides neither substantive knowledge of the information in the passage nor familiarity with the structure sufficient to locate important reference points.

3. **DO NOT** scan the questions first, then go to the passage and read it, answering questions as you come upon relevant information.

Like the two methods discussed previously, this approach may have some initial appeal. Proponents claim that a preview of the questions gives readers more direction when approaching the passage—if they know what will be asked, perhaps students can get a sense of what to look for when reading the passage. Then, proponents argue, students can save time and effort by skimming through the material that is not pertinent to any of the questions.

There are several problems with this approach: Because there are between five and eight questions per passage, students are forced to try to juggle a large amount of disparate information before even starting the passage. Not only does this make retaining the details of the questions challenging, but it also detracts from one's attention when reading the passage. Second, reading the questions first often wastes valuable time, since the typical student who applies this flawed approach will read and consider the questions, read the passage, and then go back and read each question again. This re-reading takes time without yielding any real benefit.

The bottom line is that your reading approach must be maximally effective for all passages. The flawed strategies above, although perhaps effective in some limited contexts, do not consistently produce solid results.

Having discussed some common practices to avoid, let us now consider the proper way to attack an LSAT passage:

1. Always read the passage first. Read for an understanding of structure and detail, for viewpoints and themes, and for the author's tone. Make notations as needed.

2. After reading the passage, consider the questions in the order given. Return to the passage when necessary to confirm your answers.

3. If you encounter a question too difficult to answer, skip it and return to the question after completing the other questions in the passage set.

These are the basic steps to a proper approach to the Reading Comprehension section.

Your Focus While Reading

Have you ever reached the second, or even third, paragraph of an article or reading passage and suddenly realized that you had no idea what you had just been reading? Many students have had this uncomfortable experience at some point. How are we able to read with our eyes while our minds are elsewhere? Ironically, it is our familiarity with the act of reading that has allowed many to develop the "skill" to do so without 100% focus. This approach might be fine for the morning newspaper or a favorite magazine, but these publications tend to be more simply written and they are unaccompanied by difficult questions. LSAT passages, on the other hand, are chosen for their tendency to elude this type of unfocused approach. Faced with this type of reading, many people "zone out" and lose concentration. Thus, your state of mind when approaching these passages is extremely important.

Giving yourself the simple instruction, "read the passage," allows your mind too much free reign to wander as your eyes gloss over the words. Instead, you should take a more active approach, breaking down the passage as you go, creating something of a running translation, and effectively outlining and notating, as we will discuss further. Yes, it can be difficult to focus for long stretches of time, but you must train yourself through practice to keep your concentration at as high a level as possible.

In our experience, virtually all high-scoring LSAT takers read the passage before looking at the questions.

LSAT reading is unlike the reading most people engage in on a day-to-day basis. For example, newspapers and magazines, and even most novels, are written with an eye towards presenting the material in the clearest and most interesting fashion possible. LSAT Reading Comprehension passages, on the other hand, are not written in this manner. They are often written in an academic style that is, at times, dense and complex.

When starting a section, keep the following mindset tips in mind:

- Channel any nervous energy into intensity.

- Enjoy reading the passages—make them into a game or learning exercise.

- If you lose focus, take a deep breath, refocus, and then return to the task at hand.

- Read aggressively, not passively. Actively engage the material and think about the consequences of what you are reading.

Note: Strong readers have many advantages on this test, but becoming an effective reader obviously has significant value in many contexts. As you practice applying the approaches discussed in this book, keep in mind that they are applicable to reading in general, and not meant solely to help you achieve a high LSAT score (although this is obviously one of the benefits of having an effective approach to reading).

Many passages in the Reading Comprehension section discuss conflicts between different viewpoints, and this makes the reading inherently more interesting. Getting involved in the argument will make the passage more enjoyable for you and will also allow you to focus more clearly on the material.

Your Attitude While Reading

Many students approach the Reading Comprehension section with anxiety, concerned about the prospect of reading dense passages with difficult structures and unfamiliar terminology. As is the case with every section of the LSAT, maintaining the proper mindset is vital; in this section, expectations of boredom or anxiety can become self-fulfilling prophecies. If you wish to perform well, you must approach the passages with a positive, energetic, and enthusiastic attitude.

It is vital that you avoid a negative attitude as you practice and improve your approach to reading. Some passages might cover topics that you do not find inherently interesting, but you should not resent the authors for it! These passages are presented not to delight and amuse, but rather to test your reading comprehension skills. Some students approach the passages as puzzles to solve, while others read the passages and try to learn new things from them. Either way, the truth of the matter is that if you do not try to enjoy reading the passages or get some value from them, you will be hard-pressed to perform well.

Some students get annoyed by the academic style of writing of the exam, but this is just part of the test. The passages in this section are not meant to be easy, and the test makers know that the way the passages are written and constructed can be off-putting to many students. You must simply ignore this situation, and take on the passages as a challenge.

A positive attitude is perhaps the most underrated factor in LSAT success. Virtually all high-scoring students expect to do well on the LSAT, and this mind set helps them avoid distractions during the exam, and it helps them overcome any adversity they might face.

CHAPTER ONE: INTRODUCTION

Reading Comprehension Classifications Explained

In the following chapters, the Reading Comprehension passages from PrepTests 21 through 40 are presented in groups by classification type. The classification system we use is explained in detail in the *PowerScore LSAT Reading Comprehension Bible*. The following is a brief description of each classification type.

Chapter Two—Diversity Passages

The LSAT Reading Comprehension section tends to include at least one passage about a group (or member of a group) that has been traditionally viewed as underrepresented. As these passages tend to deal with the merits of cultural diversity and the value associated with the representation of diverse perspectives, we term them Diversity passages. There are three primary types of Diversity passages, and they have been separated in this book within Chapter Two.

Diversity I—Affirming Underrepresented Groups

Given the history of bias in standardized testing, it is no surprise that Law Services is very careful to avoid any perceived bias in their representation of traditionally underrepresented groups. What is surprising is the consistency in the tone used by the test writers. In the dozens of passages addressing traditionally underrepresented groups that have appeared on the LSAT in the past 15+ years, every single passage has addressed these groups in a positive manner. That is, in each instance, the attitude of the author toward the person or group under discussion has been positive or encouraging. This type of consistency goes beyond mere chance, and reveals one of the core attitudes of the test makers. Knowing how the test makers will approach a traditionally underrepresented group then allows you to predict the general direction of certain answer choices.

Diversity II—Undermining Overrepresented Groups

Let us take a moment to examine the other side of the coin. If the test makers consistently take a positive attitude towards traditionally underrepresented groups, then what attitude would you expect the test makers to take towards traditionally overrepresented groups? As you might expect, the attitude is often critical—if not wholly, then at least partially. This does make some sense, of course. If a test has been historically biased in favor of a certain group, one method to reverse that bias is to present a greater number of passages critical of that group. On the LSAT, this criticism most frequently appears in passages devoted to assessing the work of scholars, who, under the description of the overrepresented group we used earlier, are typically Caucasian males versed in Western thinking.

While this assertion may seem surprising, an analysis of every released

---

Each passage type is explained here in basic terms. For a comprehensive discussion of each classification, and how to best solve each type, we recommend that you pick up a copy of the PowerScore LSAT Reading Comprehension Bible.

LSAT from the modern era (1991 to the present) shows that usually when the test makers are critical of an individual or viewpoint, that person or perspective belongs to an historically well-represented group, that of Caucasian male authors.

Diversity III—Mixed Group Passages

There are many passages based primarily on single groups, either traditionally underrepresented or traditionally overrepresented groups. What happens, though, when a passage contains both groups? How do the test makers handle a situation, for example, when one of the members from the overrepresented group addresses one of the traditionally underrepresented groups, or vice versa? Let us take a moment to briefly discuss each scenario:

1. Member of an underrepresented group addresses a member of an overrepresented group.

   These scenarios occur relatively rarely, and thus they are not the focus of this section. When they do occur, it is normally because the member of the overrepresented group was critical of the member of the underrepresented group. Thus, the member of the underrepresented group is typically presented as being somewhat dismissive of the member of the overrepresented group (which is quite reasonable—who wouldn't be dismissive toward someone who criticized them?).

2. Member of an overrepresented group addresses a member of an underrepresented group.

   Although we find passages where members of an overrepresented group criticize a member of an underrepresented group, the response in those passages is predictable: that group or individual is then attacked. More interesting—and the focus of this section— are passages where members of an overrepresented group praise or commend members of an underrepresented group. For example, how would you expect the test takers to treat a Western Caucasian male scholar who wrote a study about the positive developments within a native culture? Such a scenario presents a bit of a dilemma for the test makers. Because the scholar is writing in a positive manner about a traditionally underrepresented group, the test makers endorse that position. But, perhaps because of the source of the commentary, the test makers usually also insert at least some mild criticism of the scholar. Thus, passages of this type, which we term "Assessing the Scholars," contain a fascinating display of the competing values of the test makers.

Chapter Three—Law Related Passages

The LSAT Reading Comprehension section usually features one passage based on a law related issue, and these passages are presented in Chapter Three.

Many students assume that because the LSAT is the test to gain admission to law school, the makers of the test must defend the legal system at every turn in the passages they present. This assumption is incorrect. Instead, the test makers treat the Law as a positive, benevolent, dynamic, and at times flawed system.

Seeing the legal system as having flaws is not unreasonable. A system as complex as law is bound to have areas where confusion, uncertainty, or change arises. This uncertainty within law can come from the rules, the witnesses, the attorneys, or even the judges. The test makers are happy to engage in frank discussions of the issues related to improving any aspect of the judicial system, and passages have addressed the following issues:

- Inferential errors made by juries
- How the Web affects copyright holders
- The blandness of legal writing
- Possible bias introduced by computer displays in court
- Indeterminacy in legal outcomes

The above is just a small sampling of issues that the LSAT has addressed regarding the legal system.

On the other hand, the test makers show no hesitation in discussing the law as a positive force, and as a remedy to right social injustice. For example, passages have addressed some of the following topics where the law is used as a remedy or an aid:

- The benefits of bankruptcy law revisions
- Native American rights to property
- Regulation of international waters

There are also a number of passages that deal with legal theory, and "big picture" issues related to the legal system. Various passages have addressed how to interpret law, how to model legal reasoning on computers, and the basis for punishment within the legal system. These passages tend to be more theoretical in nature and focus less on real world examples.

The makers of the test also do not limit themselves to addressing just the U.S. system of law. A number of previous passages have addressed the legal systems of Canada and England, and even South Africa.

In short, the law is treated as the complicated, powerful system it is, and the test makers examine both the faults and benefits of the system, as well as the theoretical underpinnings. Given that the name of the company that produces the LSAT is Law Services, one would expect that they have a great deal of familiarity with law related elements.

Regulation Passages

The legal system is used to correct possible damage and to regulate actions and industries. On the LSAT, passages occasionally appear that address the legal regulation of marketplaces and borders. In almost all cases the viewpoint presented by the authors is the same: regulation is either needed or should be expanded if already in place. Considering that Law Services is an organization that ultimately assists in producing lawyers, and it is the law which regulates our society, the consistency of this viewpoint should come as no surprise.

Science Passages

The spectrum of topics covered in the Reading Comprehension section is quite broad, but one topic that consistently appears is Science. On average, each Reading Comprehension section contains one passage based on Science.

Chapter Four—Soft Science Passages

Up until the October 1991 LSAT, all LSAT Reading Comprehension Science passages addressed the topic in a social science environment. For example, a passage would discuss the effects of technology on society, and examine the social implications of the new technology. Passages of this type, which we term Soft Science passages, still appear on the LSAT today, and are presented in Chapter Four. These passages are relatively easy because they focus more on social impact, or alternatively, they address scientific ideas that the average person is somewhat familiar with, such as oil drilling or renewable energy resources.

Chapter Five—Hard Science Passages

Starting in October 1991 with the infamous "Waterbugs" passage, the makers of the LSAT began to introduce passages based on scientific topics that the average student had never previously encountered, or knew little about. These passages, which we term Hard Science passages, still appear on today's LSAT, and appear with greater frequency than Soft Science passages. These passages are presented in Chapter Five.

The introduction of Hard Science often increases the difficulty of the section and includes a broader variety of subject matter on the test. Consider some of the Science passages that have appeared on the LSAT:

> Embryos and the genetic mechanisms of early polarity
>
> Brain neurotransmitter theory
>
> Gravity, dark matter, and neutrinos
>
> Max Planck and radiation wave theory

To most students, those topics appear at least a bit intimidating. However, you should not be overly concerned about any individual Science passage, because you are neither required nor expected to possess any degree of real scientific expertise.

Chapter Six—Humanities Passages

Humanities passages appear frequently on the LSAT, often with topics drawn from the fields of history or economics or literature. Although Humanities passages as a whole have no consistent, definable structure or theme, The ViewSTAMP analysis approach allows you to attack any humanities passage effectively.

DIVERSITY

Diversity I: Affirming Underrepresented Groups

Passage #1: June 1997 Questions 1-8 20
Passage #2: December 1997 Questions 7-13 22
Passage #3: June 1998 Questions 14-21 24
Passage #4: September 1998 Questions 22-27... 26
Passage #5: December 1998 Questions 8-14 28
Passage #6: October 1999 Questions 8-15... 30
Passage #7: December 1999 Questions 22-27 32
Passage #8: June 2000 Questions 6-12 34
Passage #9: June 2000 Questions 13-20 36
Passage #10: October 2000 Questions 14-19... 38
Passage #11: December 2000 Questions 8-14 40
Passage #12: October 2001 Questions 1-6... 42
Passage #13: October 2001 Questions 7-14... 44
Passage #14: June 2002 Questions 14-21 46
Passage #15: October 2002 Questions 1-8... 48
Passage #16: December 2002 Questions 1-8 50
Passage #17: June 2003 Questions 6-12 52

Diversity II: Undermining Overrepresented Groups

Passage #1: December 2002 Questions 9-16 54

Diversity III: Mixed Group Passages

Passage #1: December 1996 Questions 22-27 56
Passage #2: October 1997 Questions 19-26... 58
Passage #3: September 1998 Questions 6-13... 60
Passage #4: October 2000 Questions 8-13... 62

Passage #1: June 1997 Questions 1-8

Painter Frida Kahlo (1910-1954) often used harrowing images derived from her Mexican heritage to express suffering caused by a disabling accident and a stormy marriage. Suggesting much
(5) personal and emotional content, her works—many of them self-portraits—have been exhaustively psychoanalyzed, while their political content has been less studied. Yet Kahlo was an ardent political activist who in her art sought not only to explore
(10) her own roots, but also to champion Mexico's struggle for an independent political and cultural identity.

Kahlo was influenced by Marxism, which appealed to many intellectuals in the 1920s and
(15) 1930s, and by Mexican nationalism. Interest in Mexico's culture and history had revived in the nineteenth century, and by the early 1900s, Mexican *indigenista* tendencies ranged from a violently anti-Spanish idealization of Aztec Mexico to an
(20) emphasis on contemporary Mexican Indians as the key to authentic Mexican culture. Mexican nationalism, reacting against contemporary United States political intervention in labor disputes as well as against past domination by Spain, identified the
(25) Aztecs as the last independent rulers of an indigenous political unit. Kahlo's form of *Mexicanidad*, a romantic nationalism that focused upon traditional art uniting all *indigenistas*, revered the Aztecs as a powerful pre-Columbian society that
(30) had united a large area of the Middle Americas and that was thought to have been based on communal labor, the Marxist ideal.

In her paintings, Kahlo repeatedly employed Aztec symbols, such as skeletons or bleeding hearts,
(35) that were traditionally related to the emanation of life from death and light from darkness. These images of destruction coupled with creation speak not only to Kahlo's personal battle for life, but also to the Mexican struggle to emerge as a nation—by
(40) implication, to emerge with the political and cultural strength admired in the Aztec civilization. *Self-Portrait on the Border between Mexico and the United States* (1932), for example, shows Kahlo wearing a bone necklace, holding a Mexican flag,
(45) and standing between a highly industrialized United States and an agricultural, preindustrial Mexico. On the United States side are mechanistic and modern images such as smokestacks, light bulbs, and robots. In contrast, the organic and ancient symbols on the
(50) Mexican side—a blood-drenched Sun, lush vegetation, an Aztec sculpture, a pre-Columbian temple, and a skull alluding to those that lined the walls of Aztec temples—emphasize the interrelation of life, death, the earth, and the cosmos.

(55) Kahlo portrayed Aztec images in the folkloric style of traditional Mexican paintings, thereby heightening the clash between modern materialism and indigenous tradition; similarly, she favored planned economic development, but not at the
(60) expense of cultural identity. Her use of familiar symbols in a readily accessible style also served her goal of being popularly understood; in turn, Kahlo is viewed by some Mexicans as a mythic figure representative of nationalism itself.

1. Which one of the following best expresses the main point of the passage?

(A) The doctrines of Marxist ideology and Mexican nationalism heavily influenced Mexican painters of Kahlo's generation.
(B) Kahlo's paintings contain numerous references to the Aztecs as an indigenous Mexican people predating European influence.
(C) An important element of Kahlo's work is conveyed by symbols that reflect her advocacy of indigenous Mexican culture and Mexican political autonomy.
(D) The use of Aztec images and symbols in Kahlo's art can be traced to the late nineteenth-century revival of interest in Mexican history and culture.
(E) Kahlo used Aztec imagery in her paintings primarily in order to foster contemporary appreciation for the authentic art of traditional Mexican culture.

2. With which one of the following statements concerning psychoanalytic and political interpretations of Kahlo's work would the author be most likely to agree?

   (A) The psychoanalytic interpretations of Kahlo's work tend to challenge the political interpretations.
   (B) Political and psychoanalytic interpretations are complementary approaches to Kahlo's work.
   (C) Recent political interpretations of Kahlo's work are causing psychoanalytic critics to revise their own interpretations.
   (D) Unlike the political interpretations, the psychoanalytic interpretations make use of biographical facts of Kahlo's life.
   (E) Kahlo's mythic status among the audience Kahlo most wanted to reach is based upon the psychoanalytic rather than the political content of her work.

3. Which one of the following stances toward the United States does the passage mention as characterizing Mexican nationalists in the early twentieth century?

   (A) opposition to United States involvement in internal Mexican affairs
   (B) desire to decrease emigration of the Mexican labor force to the United States
   (C) desire to improve Mexico's economic competitiveness with the United States
   (D) reluctance to imitate the United States model of rapid industrialization
   (E) advocacy of a government based upon that of the Marxist Soviet Union rather than that of the United States

4. In the context of the passage, which one of the following phrases could best be substituted for the word "romantic" (line 27) without substantially changing the author's meaning?

   (A) dreamy and escapist
   (B) nostalgic and idealistic
   (C) fanciful and imaginative
   (D) transcendental and impractical
   (E) overwrought and sentimental

5. The passage mentions each of the following as an Aztec symbol or image found in Kahlo's paintings EXCEPT a

   (A) skeleton
   (B) sculpture
   (C) serpent
   (D) skull
   (E) bleeding heart

6. Which one of the following best describes the organization of the third paragraph?

   (A) contrast of opposing ideas
   (B) reconciliation of conflicting concepts
   (C) interrelation of complementary themes
   (D) explication of a principle's implications
   (E) support for a generalization by means of an example

7. The passage implies that Kahlo's attitude toward the economic development of Mexico was

   (A) enthusiastic
   (B) condemnatory
   (C) cautious
   (D) noncommittal
   (E) uncertain

8. The main purpose of the passage is to

   (A) critique an artist's style
   (B) evaluate opposing theories
   (C) reconcile conflicting arguments
   (D) advocate an additional interpretation
   (E) reconsider an artist in light of new discoveries

Passage #2: December 1997 Questions 7-13

In April 1990 representatives of the Pico Korea Union of electronics workers in Buchon City, South Korea, traveled to the United States in order to demand just settlement of their claims from the
(5) parent company of their employer, who upon the formation of the union had shut down operations without paying the workers. From the beginning, the union cause was championed by an unprecedented coalition of Korean American groups
(10) and deeply affected the Korean American community on several levels.

First, it served as a rallying focus for a diverse community often divided by generation, class, and political ideologies. Most notably, the Pico cause
(15) mobilized many young second-generation Korean Americans, many of whom had never been part of a political campaign before, let alone one involving Korean issues. Members of this generation, unlike first-generation Korean Americans, generally fall
(20) within the more privileged sectors of the Korean American community and often feel alienated from their Korean roots. In addition to raising the political consciousness of young Korean Americans, the Pico struggle sparked among them new interest
(25) in their cultural identity. The Pico workers also suggested new roles that can be played by recent immigrants, particularly working-class immigrants. These immigrants' knowledge of working conditions overseas can help to globalize the
(30) perspective of their communities and can help to establish international ties on a more personal level, as witnessed in the especially warm exchange between the Pico workers and recent working-class immigrants from China. In addition to broadening
(35) the political base within the Korean American community, the Pico struggle also led to new alliances between the Korean American community and progressive labor and social justice groups within the larger society—as evidenced in the
(40) support received from the Coalition of Labor Union Women and leading African American unionists.

The reasons for these effects lie in the nature of the cause. The issues raised by the Pico unionists had such a strong human component that
(45) differences within the community became secondary to larger concerns for social justice and workers' rights. The workers' demands for compensation and respect were unencumbered with strong ideological trappings. The economic exploitation faced by the
(50) Pico workers underscored the common interests of Korean workers, Korean Americans, the working class more inclusively, and a broad spectrum of community leaders.

The Pico workers' campaign thus offers an
(55) important lesson. It demonstrates that ethnic communities need more than just a knowledge of history and culture as artifacts of the past in order to strengthen their ethnic identity. It shows that perhaps the most effective means of empowerment
(60) for many ethnic communities of immigrant derivation may be an identification with and participation in current struggles for economic and social justice in their countries of origin.

7. Which one of the following best describes the main topic of the passage?

   (A) the contribution of the Korean American community to improving the working conditions of Koreans employed by United States companies
   (B) the change brought about in the Korean American community by contacts with Koreans visiting the United States
   (C) the contribution of recent immigrants from Korea to strengthening ethnic identity in the Korean American community
   (D) the effects on the Korean American community of a dispute between Korean union workers and a United States company
   (E) the effect of the politicization of second-generation Korean Americans on the Korean American community as a whole

8. The passage suggests that which one of the following was a significant factor in the decision to shut down the Pico plant in Buchon City?

   (A) the decreasing profitability of maintaining operations in Korea
   (B) the failure to resolve long-standing disputes between the Pico workers and management
   (C) the creation of a union by the Pico workers
   (D) the withholding of workers' wages by the parent company
   (E) the finding of an alternate site for operations

9. Which one of the following is NOT mentioned in the passage as a recent development in the Korean American community?

   (A) Young second-generation Korean Americans have begun to take an interest in their Korean heritage.
   (B) Recent Korean American immigrants of working-class backgrounds have begun to enter the more privileged sectors of the Korean American community.
   (C) Korean Americans have developed closer ties with activist groups from other sectors of the population.
   (D) Previously nonpolitical members of the Korean American community have become more politically active.
   (E) The Korean American community has been able to set aside political and generational disparities in order to support a common cause.

10. It can be inferred that the author of the passage would most likely agree with which one of the following statements about ethnic communities of immigrant derivation?

    (A) Such communities can derive important benefits from maintaining ties with their countries of origin.
    (B) Such communities should focus primarily on promoting study of the history and culture of their people in order to strengthen their ethnic identity.
    (C) Such communities can most successfully mobilize and politicize their young people by addressing the problems of young people of all backgrounds.
    (D) The more privileged sectors of such communities are most likely to maintain a sense of closeness to their cultural roots.
    (E) The politicization of such a community is unlikely to affect relations with other groups within the larger society.

11. In the second paragraph, the author refers to immigrants from China most probably in order to do which one of the following?

    (A) highlight the contrast between working conditions in the United States and in Korea
    (B) demonstrate the uniqueness of the problem faced by the Pico workers
    (C) offer an example of the type of role that can be played by recent working-class immigrants
    (D) provide an analogy for the type of activism displayed by the Korean American community
    (E) compare the disparate responses of two immigrant communities to similar problems

12. The primary purpose of the passage is to

    (A) describe recent developments in the Korean American community that have strongly affected other ethnic communities of immigrant derivation
    (B) describe a situation in the Korean American community that presents a model for the empowerment of ethnic communities of immigrant derivation
    (C) detail the problems faced by the Korean American community in order to illustrate the need for the empowerment of ethnic communities of immigrant derivation
    (D) argue against economic and social injustice in the countries of origin of ethnic communities of immigrant derivation
    (E) assess the impact of the unionization movement on ethnic communities of immigrant derivation

13. Which one of the following most accurately states the function of the third paragraph?

    (A) It explains why the Pico workers brought their cause to the United States.
    (B) It explains how the Pico cause differed from other causes that had previously mobilized the Korean American community.
    (C) It explains why the Pico workers were accorded such broad support.
    (D) It explains how other ethnic groups of immigrant derivation in the United States have profited from the example of the Pico workers.
    (E) It explains why different generations of Korean Americans reacted in different ways to the Pico cause.

Passage #3: June 1998 Questions 14-21

Even in the midst of its resurgence as a vital tradition, many sociologists have viewed the current form of the powwow, a ceremonial gathering of native Americans, as a sign that tribal culture is in decline.
(5) Focusing on the dances and rituals that have recently come to be shared by most tribes, they suggest that an intertribal movement is now in ascension and claim the inevitable outcome of this tendency is the eventual dissolution of tribes and the complete assimilation of
(10) native Americans into Euroamerican society. Proponents of this "Pan-Indian" theory point to the greater frequency of travel and communication between reservations, the greater urbanization of native Americans, and, most recently, their increasing
(15) politicization in response to common grievances as the chief causes of the shift toward intertribalism.

Indeed, the rapid diffusion of dance styles, outfits, and songs from one reservation to another offers compelling evidence that intertribalism has been
(20) increasing. However, these sociologists have failed to note the concurrent revitalization of many traditions unique to individual tribes. Among the Lakota, for instance, the Sun Dance was revived, after a forty-year hiatus, during the 1950s. Similarly, the Black Legging
(25) Society of the Kiowa and the Hethuska Society of the Ponca—both traditional groups within their respective tribes—have gained new popularity. Obviously, a more complex societal shift is taking place than the theory of Pan-Indianism can account for.

(30) An examination of the theory's underpinnings may be critical at this point, especially given that native Americans themselves chafe most against the Pan-Indian classification. Like other assimilationist theories with which it is associated, the Pan-Indian view is
(35) predicated upon an a priori assumption about the nature of cultural contact: that upon contact minority societies immediately begin to succumb in every respect—biologically, linguistically, and culturally—to the majority society. However, there is no evidence
(40) that this is happening to native American groups.

Yet the fact remains that intertribal activities are a major facet of native American culture today. Certain dances at powwows, for instance, are announced as intertribal, others as traditional. Likewise, speeches
(45) given at the beginnings of powwows are often delivered in English, while the prayer that follows is usually spoken in a native language. Cultural borrowing is, of course, old news. What is important to note is the conscious distinction native Americans
(50) make between tribal and intertribal tendencies.

Tribalism, although greatly altered by modern history, remains a potent force among native Americans. It forms a basis for tribal identity, and aligns music and dance with other social and cultural
(55) activities important to individual tribes. Intertribal activities, on the other hand, reinforce native American identity along a broader front, where this identity is directly threatened by outside influences.

14. Which one of the following best summarizes the main idea of the passage?

(A) Despite the fact that sociologists have only recently begun to understand its importance, intertribalism has always been an influential factor in native American culture.
(B) Native Americans are currently struggling with an identity crisis caused primarily by the two competing forces of tribalism and intertribalism.
(C) The recent growth of intertribalism is unlikely to eliminate tribalism because the two forces do not oppose one another but instead reinforce distinct elements of native American identity.
(D) The tendency toward intertribalism, although prevalent within native American culture, has had a minimal effect on the way native Americans interact with the broader community around them.
(E) Despite the recent revival of many native American tribal traditions, the recent trend toward intertribalism is likely to erode cultural differences among the various native American tribes.

15. The author most likely states that "cultural borrowing is, of course, old news" (lines 47-48) primarily to

(A) acknowledge that in itself the existence of intertribal tendencies at powwows is unsurprising
(B) suggest that native Americans' use of English in powwows should be accepted as unavoidable
(C) argue that the deliberate distinction of intertribal and traditional dances is not a recent development
(D) suggest that the recent increase in intertribal activity is the result of native Americans borrowing from non-native American cultures
(E) indicate that the powwow itself could have originated by combining practices drawn from both native and non-native American cultures

16. The author of the passage would most likely agree with which one of the following assertions?

(A) Though some believe the current form of the powwow signals the decline of tribal culture, the powwow contains elements that indicate the continuing strength of tribalism.
(B) The logical outcome of the recent increase in intertribal activity is the eventual disappearance of tribal culture.
(C) Native Americans who participate in both tribal and intertribal activities usually base their identities on intertribal rather than tribal affiliations.
(D) The conclusions of some sociologists about the health of native American cultures show that these sociologists are in fact biased against such cultures.
(E) Until it is balanced by revitalization of tribal customs, intertribalism will continue to weaken the native American sense of identity.

17. The primary function of the third paragraph is to

    (A) search for evidence to corroborate the basic assumption of the theory of Pan-Indianism
    (B) demonstrate the incorrectness of the theory of Pan-Indianism by pointing out that native American groups themselves disagree with the theory
    (C) explain the origin of the theory of Pan-Indianism by showing how it evolved from other assimilationist theories
    (D) examine several assimilationist theories in order to demonstrate that they rest on a common assumption
    (E) criticize the theory of Pan-Indianism by pointing out that it rests upon an assumption for which there is no supporting evidence

18. Which one of the following most accurately describes the author's attitude toward the theory of Pan-Indianism?

    (A) critical of its tendency to attribute political motives to cultural practices
    (B) discomfort at its negative characterization of cultural borrowing by native Americans
    (C) hopeful about its chances for preserving tribal culture
    (D) offended by its claim that assimilation is a desirable consequence of cultural contact
    (E) skeptical that it is a complete explanation of recent changes in native American society

19. With which one of the following statements would the author of the passage be most likely to agree?

    (A) The resurgence of the powwow is a sign that native American customs are beginning to have an important influence on Euroamerican society.
    (B) Although native Americans draw conscious distinctions between tribal and intertribal activities, there is no difference in how the two types of activity actually function within the context of native American society.
    (C) Without intertribal activities, it would be more difficult for native Americans to maintain the cultural differences between native American and Euroamerican society.
    (D) The powwow was recently revived, after an extended hiatus, in order to strengthen native Americans' sense of ethnic identity.
    (E) The degree of urbanization, intertribal communication, and politicization among native Americans has been exaggerated by proponents of the theory of Pan-Indianism.

20. Which one of the following situations most clearly illustrates the phenomenon of intertribalism, as that phenomenon is described in the passage?

    (A) a native American tribe in which a number of powerful societies attempt to prevent the revival of a traditional dance
    (B) a native American tribe whose members attempt to learn the native languages of several other tribes
    (C) a native American tribe whose members attempt to form a political organization in order to redress several grievances important to that tribe
    (D) a native American tribe in which a significant percentage of the members have forsaken their tribal identity and become assimilated into Euroamerican society
    (E) a native American tribe whose members often travel to other parts of the reservation in order to visit friends and relatives

21. In the passage, the author is primarily concerned with doing which one of the following?

    (A) identifying an assumption common to various assimilationist theories and then criticizing these theories by showing this assumption to be false
    (B) arguing that the recent revival of a number of tribal practices shows sociologists are mistaken in believing intertribalism to be a potent force among native American societies
    (C) questioning the belief that native American societies will eventually be assimilated into Euroamerican society by arguing that intertribalism helps strengthen native American identity
    (D) showing how the recent resurgence of tribal activities is a deliberate attempt to counteract the growing influence of intertribalism
    (E) proposing an explanation of why the ascension of intertribalism could result in the eventual dissolution of tribes and complete assimilation of native Americans into Euroamerican society

Passage #4: September 1998 Questions 22-27

In England before 1660, a husband controlled his wife's property. In the late seventeenth and eighteenth centuries, with the shift from land-based to commercial wealth, marriage began to incorporate certain features
(5) of a contract. Historians have traditionally argued that this trend represented a gain for women, one that reflects changing views about democracy and property following the English Restoration in 1660. Susan Staves contests this view; she argues that whatever
(10) gains marriage contracts may briefly have represented for women were undermined by judicial decisions about women's contractual rights.

Sifting through the tangled details of court cases, Staves demonstrates that, despite surface changes, a
(15) rhetoric of equality, and occasional decisions supporting women's financial power, definitions of men's and women's property remained inconsistent generally to women's detriment. For example, dower lands (property inherited by wives after their husbands'
(20) deaths) could not be sold, but "curtesy" property (inherited by husbands from their wives) could be sold. Furthermore, comparatively new concepts that developed in conjunction with the marriage contract, such as jointure, pin money, and separate maintenance,
(25) were compromised by peculiar rules. For instance, if a woman spent her pin money (money paid by the husband according to the marriage contract for the wife's personal items) on possessions other than clothes she could not sell them; in effect they belonged
(30) to her husband. In addition, a wife could sue for pin money only up to a year in arrears—which rendered a suit impractical. Similarly, separate maintenance allowances (stated sums of money for the wife's support if husband and wife agreed to live apart) were
(35) complicated by the fact that if a couple tried to agree in a marriage contract on an amount, they were admitting that a supposedly indissoluble bond could be dissolved, an assumption courts could not recognize. Eighteenth-century historians underplayed these inconsistencies,
(40) calling them "little contrarieties" that would soon vanish. Staves shows, however, that as judges gained power over decisions on marriage contracts, they tended to fall back on pre-1660 assumptions about property.

(45) Staves' work on women's property has general implications for other studies about women in eighteenth-century England. Staves revises her previous claim that separate maintenance allowances proved the weakening of patriarchy; she now finds that
(50) an oversimplification. She also challenges the contention by historians Jeanne and Lawrence Stone that in the late eighteenth century wealthy men married widows less often than before because couples began marrying for love rather than for financial reasons.
(55) Staves does not completely undermine their contention, but she does counter their assumption that widows had more money than never-married women. She points out that jointure property (a widow's lifetime use of an amount of money specified in the marriage contract)
(60) was often lost on remarriage.

22. Which one of the following best expresses the main idea of the passage?

(A) As notions of property and democracy changed in late seventeenth- and eighteenth-century England, marriage settlements began to incorporate contractual features designed to protect women's property rights.
(B) Traditional historians have incorrectly identified the contractual features that were incorporated into marriage contracts in late seventeenth- and eighteenth-century England.
(C) The incorporation of contractual features into marriage settlements in late seventeenth- and eighteenth-century England did not represent a significant gain for women.
(D) An examination of late seventeenth- and eighteenth-century English court cases indicates that most marriage settlements did not incorporate contractual features designed to protect women's property rights.
(E) Before marriage settlements incorporated contractual features protecting women's property rights, women were unable to gain any financial power in England.

23. Which one of the following best describes the function of the last paragraph in the context of the passage as a whole?

(A) It suggests that Staves' recent work has caused significant revision of theories about the rights of women in eighteenth-century England.
(B) It discusses research that may qualify Staves' work on women's property in eighteenth-century England.
(C) It provides further support for Staves' argument by describing more recent research on women's property in eighteenth-century England.
(D) It asserts that Staves' recent work has provided support for two other hypotheses developed by historians of eighteenth-century England.
(E) It suggests the implications Staves' recent research has for other theories about women in eighteenth-century England.

24. The primary purpose of the passage is to
    (A) compare two explanations for the same phenomenon
    (B) summarize research that refutes an argument
    (C) resolve a long-standing controversy
    (D) suggest that a recent hypothesis should be reevaluated
    (E) provide support for a traditional theory

25. According to the passage, Staves' research has which one of the following effects on the Stones' contention about marriage in late eighteenth-century England?
    (A) Staves' research undermines one of the Stones' assumptions but does not effectively invalidate their contention.
    (B) Staves' research refutes the Stones' contention by providing additional data overlooked by the Stones.
    (C) Staves' research shows that the Stones' contention cannot be correct, and that a number of their assumptions are mistaken.
    (D) Staves' research indicates that the Stones' contention is incorrect because it is based on contradictory data.
    (E) Staves' research qualifies the Stones' contention by indicating that it is based on accurate but incomplete data.

26. According to the passage, Staves indicates that which one of the following was true of judicial decisions on contractual rights?
    (A) Judges frequently misunderstood and misapplied laws regarding married women's property.
    (B) Judges were aware of inconsistencies in laws concerning women's contractual rights but claimed that such inconsistencies would soon vanish.
    (C) Judges' decisions about marriage contracts tended to reflect assumptions about property that had been common before 1660.
    (D) Judges had little influence on the development and application of laws concerning married women's property.
    (E) Judges recognized the patriarchal assumptions underlying laws concerning married women's property and tried to interpret the laws in ways that would protect women.

27. The passage suggests that the historians mentioned in line 5 would be most likely to agree with which one of the following statements?
    (A) The shift from land-based to commercial wealth changed views about property but did not significantly benefit married women until the late eighteenth century.
    (B) Despite initial judicial resistance to women's contractual rights, marriage contracts represented a significant gain for married women.
    (C) Although marriage contracts incorporated a series of surface changes and a rhetoric of equality, they did not ultimately benefit married women.
    (D) Changing views about property and democracy in post-Restoration England had an effect on property laws that was beneficial to women.
    (E) Although contractual rights protecting women's property represented a small gain for married women, most laws continued to be more beneficial for men than for women.

Passage #5: December 1998 Questions 8-14

Personal names are generally regarded by European thinkers in two major ways, both of which deny that names have any significant semantic content. In philosophy and linguistics, John Stuart Mill's
(5) formulation that "proper names are meaningless marks set upon . . . persons to distinguish them from one another" retains currency; in anthropology, Claude Lévi-Strauss's characterization of names as being primarily instruments of social classification has been
(10) very influential. Consequently, interpretation of personal names in societies where names have other functions and meanings has been neglected. Among the Hopi of the southwestern United States, names often refer to historical or ritual events in order both to place
(15) individuals within society and to confer an identity upon them. Furthermore, the images used to evoke these events suggest that Hopi names can be seen as a type of poetic composition.

Throughout life, Hopis receive several names in a
(20) sequence of ritual initiations. Birth, entry into one of the ritual societies during childhood, and puberty are among the name-giving occasions. Names are conferred by an adult member of a clan other than the child's clan, and names refer to that name giver's clan,
(25) sometimes combining characteristics of the clan's totem animal with the child's characteristics. Thus, a name might translate to something as simple as "little rabbit," which reflects both the child's size and the representative animal.

(30) More often, though, the name giver has in mind a specific event that is not apparent in a name's literal translation. One Lizard clan member from the village of Oraibi is named Lomayayva, "beautifully ascended." This translation, however, tells nothing
(35) about either the event referred to—who or what ascended—or the name giver's clan. The name giver in this case is from Badger clan. Badger clan is responsible for an annual ceremony featuring a procession in which masked representations of spirits
(40) climb the mesa on which Oraibi sits. Combining the name giver's clan association with the receiver's home village, "beautifully ascended" refers to the splendid colors and movements of the procession up the mesa. The condensed image this name evokes—a typical
(45) feature of Hopi personal names—displays the same quality of Western Apache place names that led one commentator to call them "tiny imagist poems."

Hopi personal names do several things simultaneously. They indicate social relationships—but
(50) only indirectly—and they individuate persons. Equally important, though, is their poetic quality; in a sense they can be understood as oral texts that produce aesthetic delight. This view of Hopi names is thus opposed not only to Mill's claim that personal names
(55) are without inherent meaning but also to Lévi-Strauss's purely functional characterization. Interpreters must understand Hopi clan structures and linguistic practices in order to discern the beauty and significance of Hopi names.

8. Which one of the following statements most accurately summarizes the passage's main point?

(A) Unlike European names, which are used exclusively for identification or exclusively for social classification, Hopi names perform both these functions simultaneously.
(B) Unlike European names, Hopi names tend to neglect the functions of identification and social classification in favor of a concentration on compression and poetic effects.
(C) Lacking knowledge of the intricacies of Hopi linguistic and tribal structures, European thinkers have so far been unable to discern the deeper significance of Hopi names.
(D) Although some Hopi names may seem difficult to interpret, they all conform to a formula whereby a reference to the name giver's clan is combined with a reference to the person named.
(E) While performing the functions ascribed to names by European thinkers, Hopi names also possess a significant aesthetic quality that these thinkers have not adequately recognized.

9. The author most likely refers to Western Apache place names (line 46) in order to

(A) offer an example of how names can contain references not evident in their literal translations
(B) apply a commentator's characterization of Western Apache place names to Hopi personal names
(C) contrast Western Apache naming practices with Hopi naming practices
(D) demonstrate that other names besides Hopi names may have some semantic content
(E) explain how a specific Hopi name refers subtly to a particular Western Apache site

10. Which one of the following statements describes an example of the function accorded to personal names under Lévi-Strauss's view?

(A) Some parents select their children's names from impersonal sources such as books.
(B) Some parents wait to give a child a name in order to choose one that reflects the child's looks or personality.
(C) Some parents name their children in honor of friends or famous people.
(D) Some family members have no parts of their names in common.
(E) Some family names originated as identifications of their bearers' occupations.

11. The primary function of the second paragraph is to

    (A) present reasons why Hopi personal names can be treated as poetic compositions
    (B) support the claim that Hopi personal names make reference to events in the recipient's life
    (C) argue that the fact that Hopis receive many names throughout life refutes European theories about naming
    (D) illustrate ways in which Hopi personal names may have semantic content
    (E) demonstrate that the literal translation of Hopi personal names often obscures their true meaning

12. Based on the passage, with which one of the following statements about Mill's view would the author of the passage be most likely to agree?

    (A) Its characterization of the function of names is too narrow to be universally applicable.
    (B) It would be correct if it recognized the use of names as instruments of social classification.
    (C) Its influence single-handedly led scholars to neglect how names are used outside Europe.
    (D) It is more accurate than Lévi-Strauss's characterization of the purpose of names.
    (E) It is less relevant than Lévi-Strauss's characterization in understanding Hopi naming practices.

13. It can be inferred from the passage that each of the following features of Hopi personal names contributes to their poetic quality EXCEPT:

    (A) their ability to be understood as oral texts
    (B) their use of condensed imagery to evoke events
    (C) their capacity to produce aesthetic delight
    (D) their ability to confer identity upon individuals
    (E) their ability to subtly convey meaning

14. The author's primary purpose in writing the passage is to

    (A) present an anthropological study of Hopi names
    (B) propose a new theory about the origin of names
    (C) describe several competing theories of names
    (D) criticize two influential views of names
    (E) explain the cultural origins of names

Passage #6: October 1999 Questions 8-15

Tribal communities in North America believe that their traditional languages are valuable resources that must be maintained. However, these traditional languages can fall into disuse when some of the effects
(5) of the majority culture on tribal life serve as barriers between a community and its traditional forms of social, economic, or spiritual interaction. In some communities the barrier has been overcome because people have recognized that language loss is serious
(10) and have taken action to prevent it, primarily through community self-teaching.

Before any community can systematically and formally teach a traditional language to its younger members, it must first document the language's
(15) grammar; for example, a group of Northern Utes spent two years conducting a thorough analysis and classification of Northern Ute linguistic structures. The grammatical information is then arranged in sequence from the simpler to the more complex types of usage,
(20) and methods are devised to present the sequence in ways that will be most useful and appropriate to the culture.

Certain obstacles can stand in the way of developing these teaching methods. One is the
(25) difficulty a community may encounter when it attempts to write down elements (particularly the spellings of words) of a language that has been primarily oral for centuries, as is often the case with traditional languages. Sometimes this difficulty can simply be a
(30) matter of the lack of acceptable written equivalents for certain sounds in the traditional language: problems arise because of an insistence that every sound in the language have a unique written equivalent—a desirable but ultimately frustrating condition that no written
(35) language has ever fully satisfied.

Another obstacle is dialect. There may be many language traditions in a particular community; which one is to be written down and taught? The Northern Utes decided not to standardize their language,
(40) agreeing that various phonetic spellings of words would be accepted as long as their meanings were clear. Although this troubled some community members who favored Western notions of standard language writing or whose training in Western-style
(45) linguistics was especially rigid, the lack of standard orthography made sense in the context of the community's needs. Within a year after the adoption of instruction in the Northern Ute language, even elementary school children could write and speak it
(50) effectively.

It has been argued that the attempt to write down traditional languages is misguided and unnecessary; after all, in many cases these languages have been transmitted in their oral form since their origins.
(55) Defenders of the practice counter that they are writing down their languages precisely because of a general decline in oral traditions, but they concede that languages could be preserved in their oral form if a community made every effort to eschew aspects of the
(60) majority culture that make this preservation difficult.

8. Which one of the following most accurately states the main idea of the passage?

    (A) In the face of the pervasive influences of the majority culture, some tribes are having difficulty teaching their traditional languages to younger tribe members.
    (B) If tribes are to continue to hold on to their cultures in the face of majority culture influences, it is necessary for them to first teach their traditional languages to younger tribe members.
    (C) Responding to doubts about the value of preserving oral forms of culture, some tribes, using techniques of Western-style linguistics, have taught their traditional languages to younger tribe members.
    (D) Recognizing the value of their traditional languages, some tribes, despite the difficulties involved, have developed programs to teach their traditional languages to younger tribe members.
    (E) Sidestepping the inherent contradiction of preserving oral forms of culture in writing, some tribes are attempting, eschewing the influences of the majority culture, to teach their traditional languages to younger tribe members.

9. According to the passage, the first step in preparing to formally teach a traditional language is to

    (A) analyze and classify its linguistic structures
    (B) develop a hierarchy of its grammatical information
    (C) determine appropriate methods for its presentation
    (D) search for written equivalents for each of its sounds
    (E) decide whether its syntax and spelling will be standardized

10. Based on the passage, those who hold the view described in lines 51-54 would be most likely to agree with which one of the following statements?

    (A) Even if left exclusively in oral form, traditional languages are likely to survive.
    (B) There has been a decline in communication among tribal members in general.
    (C) Some oral customs do not need to be preserved orally.
    (D) External influences have little effect on tribal customs.
    (E) Tribes must focus on establishing a written tradition.

11. Which one of the following scenarios is LEAST compatible with aspects of traditional-language preservation discussed in the passage?

    (A) A community decides that the best way to maintain its traditional language is to rejuvenate its oral culture.
    (B) A community arranges the grammatical structures of its traditional language sequentially according to the degree of their complexity.
    (C) A community agrees to incorporate words from the majority culture in its traditional language to make it easier to teach.
    (D) A community determines the most appropriate methods for presenting its traditional language to students.
    (E) A community deliberates about which dialect of its traditional language should be taught to students.

12. Which one of the following most accurately describes the organization of the passage?

    (A) A problem is identified, followed by a list of obstacles to its solution; examples of the obstacles are discussed; a solution is proposed; methods of implementing the solution are described; an alternative to the solution is introduced and endorsed.
    (B) A problem is identified, followed by solutions to the problem; methods of implementing the solutions are discussed; obstacles to implementing the solutions are described; an alternative method of implementing one of the solutions is proposed.
    (C) A problem is identified, followed by a solution to the problem; a method of implementing the solution is discussed; obstacles to implementing the solution are described; a challenge to the solution is introduced and countered.
    (D) A problem is identified, followed by examples of the problem; a solution is proposed; a method for implementing the solution is described; examples of successful implementation are discussed; the solution is applied to other similar problems.
    (E) A problem is identified, followed by a proposal for solving the problem; benefits and drawbacks of the proposal are discussed; examples of the benefits and drawbacks are described; a challenge to the proposal is introduced and the proposal is rejected.

13. Based on the passage, the group of Northern Utes mentioned in lines 38-42 would be likely to believe each of the following statements EXCEPT:

    (A) Standardizing traditional languages requires arbitrary choices and is sometimes unnecessary.
    (B) Written languages should reflect one standard dialect rather than several dialects.
    (C) Traditional languages can be taught even if they are not rigorously standardized.
    (D) Variant spellings of words are acceptable in a language if their meanings are clear.
    (E) The extent to which a language should be standardized depends upon a community's needs.

14. Which one of the following most accurately describes the author's attitude toward the goal of having a written language exactly match its oral equivalent?

    (A) conviction that an exact match is all but impossible to achieve
    (B) doubt that an exact match is worthy of consideration even in principle
    (C) faith that an exact match is attainable if certain obstacles are eliminated
    (D) confidence that an exact match can easily be accomplished in most languages
    (E) suspicion that the motives behind the attempts to achieve the goal are not entirely benevolent

15. Based on the passage, which one of the following appears to be a principle guiding the actions of those attempting to preserve their traditional languages?

    (A) In writing down an oral language, one should always be concerned primarily with the degree of correspondence between spoken sounds and written symbols.
    (B) In deciding whether and how to standardize and teach a primarily oral language, one should always keep the needs of the community and the culture foremost.
    (C) In determining whether to preserve a language orally or preserve it in writing, one should always strive to ignore the influences of the majority culture and focus on which method is most effective.
    (D) In considering how to present the grammar of a primarily oral language to students, one should always employ a sequence that tackles more difficult concepts first.
    (E) In adjudicating among variant spellings of words from different language traditions, one should always favor the spelling preferred by the majority of the community.

Passage #7: December 1999 Questions 22-27

While historians once propagated the myth that Africans who were brought to the New World as slaves contributed little of value but their labor, a recent study by Amelia Wallace Vernon helps to dispel this notion
(5) by showing that Africans introduced rice and the methods of cultivating it into what is now the United States in the early eighteenth century. She uncovered, for example, an 1876 document that details that in 1718 starving French settlers instructed the captain of a
(10) slave ship bound for Africa to trade for 400 Africans including some "who know how to cultivate rice." This discovery is especially compelling because the introduction of rice into what is now the United States had previously been attributed to French Acadians,
(15) who did not arrive until the 1760s.

Vernon interviewed elderly African Americans who helped her discover the locations where until about 1920 their forebears had cultivated rice. At the heart of Vernon's research is the question of why, in an
(20) economy dedicated to maximizing cotton production, African Americans grew rice. She proposes two intriguing answers, depending on whether the time is before or after the end of slavery. During the period of slavery, plantation owners also ate rice and therefore
(25) tolerated or demanded its "after-hours" cultivation on patches of land not suited to cotton. In addition, growing the rice gave the slaves some relief from a system of regimented labor under a field supervisor, in that they were left alone to work independently.

(30) After the abolition of slavery, however, rice cultivation is more difficult to explain: African Americans had acquired a preference for eating corn, there was no market for the small amounts of rice they produced, and under the tenant system—in which
(35) farmers surrendered a portion of their crops to the owners of the land they farmed—owners wanted only cotton as payment. The labor required to transform unused land to productive ground would thus seem completely out of proportion to the reward—except
(40) that, according to Vernon, the transforming of the land itself was the point.

Vernon suggests that these African Americans did not transform the land as a means to an end, but rather as an end in itself. In other words, they did not
(45) transform the land in order to grow rice—for the resulting rice was scarcely worth the effort required to clear the land—but instead transformed the land because they viewed land as an extension of self and home and so wished to nurture it and make it their
(50) own. In addition to this cultural explanation, Vernon speculates that rice cultivation might also have been a political act, a next step after the emancipation of the slaves: the symbolic claiming of plantation land that the U.S. government had promised but failed to parcel
(55) off and deed to newly freed African Americans.

22. Which one of the following titles most completely and accurately summarizes the contents of the passage?

(A) "The Introduction of Rice Cultivation into what is now the United States by Africans and Its Continued Practice in the Years During and After Slavery"
(B) "The Origin of Rice Cultivation in what is now the United States and Its Impact on the Economy from 1760 to 1920"
(C) "Widespread Rice Cultivation by African Americans under the Tenant System in the Years After the Abolition of Slavery"
(D) "Cultural and Political Contributions of Africans who were Brought to what is now the United States in the Eighteenth Century"
(E) "African American Tenant Farmers and their Cultivation of Rice in an Economy Committed to the Mass Production of Cotton"

23. Which one of the following most completely and accurately describes the author's attitude toward Vernon's study?

(A) respectful of its author and skeptical toward its theories
(B) admiring of its accomplishments and generally receptive to its theories
(C) appreciative of the effort it required and neutral toward its theories
(D) enthusiastic about its goals but skeptical of its theories
(E) accepting of its author's motives but overtly dismissive of its theories

24. As described in the last paragraph of the passage, rice cultivation after slavery is most analogous to which one of the following?

   (A) A group of neighbors plants flower gardens on common land adjoining their properties in order to beautify their neighborhood and to create more of a natural boundary between properties.
   (B) A group of neighbors plants a vegetable garden for their common use and to compete with the local market's high-priced produce by selling vegetables to other citizens who live outside the neighborhood.
   (C) A group of neighbors initiates an effort to neuter all the domestic animals in their neighborhood out of a sense of civic duty and to forestall the city taking action of its own to remedy the overpopulation.
   (D) A group of neighbors regularly cleans up the litter on a vacant lot in their neighborhood out of a sense of ownership over the lot and to protest the city's neglect of their neighborhood.
   (E) A group of neighbors renovates an abandoned building so they can start a program to watch each other's children out of a sense of communal responsibility and to offset the closing of a day care center in their neighborhood.

25. Which one of the following most completely and accurately describes the organization of the passage?

   (A) A historical phenomenon is presented, several competing theories about the phenomenon are described, and one theory having the most support is settled upon.
   (B) A historical discovery is presented, the method leading to the discovery is provided, and two questions left unanswered by the discovery are identified.
   (C) A historical fact is presented, a question raised by the fact is described, and two answers to the question are given.
   (D) A historical question is raised, possible answers to the question are speculated upon, and two reasons for difficulty in answering the question are given.
   (E) A historical question is raised, a study is described that answers the question, and a number of issues surrounding the study are discussed.

26. The passage cites which one of the following as a reason that rice cultivation in the context of the tenant system was difficult to explain?

   (A) Landowners did not eat rice and thus would not tolerate its cultivation on tenant lands.
   (B) Rice was not considered acceptable payment to landowners for the use of tenant lands.
   (C) Tenant farmers did not have enough time "after hours" to cultivate the rice properly.
   (D) The labor required to cultivate rice was more strenuous than that required for cotton.
   (E) Tenant lands used primarily to grow cotton were not suited to rice.

27. The author's primary purpose in the passage is to

   (A) describe the efforts of a historian to uncover evidence for a puzzling phenomenon
   (B) illustrate the historical background of a puzzling phenomenon
   (C) present a historian's theories about a puzzling phenomenon
   (D) criticize the work of previous historians regarding a puzzling phenomenon
   (E) analyze the effects of a puzzling phenomenon on an economic system

Passage #8: June 2000 Questions 6-12

Thurgood Marshall's litigation of *Brown v. Board of Education* in 1952—the landmark case, decided in 1954, that made segregation illegal in United States public schools—was not his first case before the U.S.
(5) Supreme Court. Some legal scholars claim that the cases he presented to the court in the sixteen years before his successful argument for desegregation of public schools were necessary forerunners of that case: preliminary tests of legal strategies and early erosions
(10) of the foundations of discrimination against African Americans that paved the way for success in *Brown*.

When Marshall joined the legal staff of the National Association for the Advancement of Colored People (NAACP) in 1936, the organization was
(15) divided on how to proceed against the legal doctrine that for forty years had promoted "separate but equal" facilities for African Americans in educational institutions, in public transportation, and various other civic amenities. One approach was to emphasize that
(20) facilities were not in fact equal and to pursue litigation whose practical goal was the improvement both of opportunity for African Americans and of the facilities themselves. A second, more theoretical, approach was to argue that the concept of separate but equal facilities
(25) for the races was by its very nature impossible to fulfill, rendering the doctrine self-contradictory and hence legally unsound. Marshall correctly believed that the latter approach would eventually be the one to bring repeal of the doctrine, but felt it necessary in the
(30) short term to argue several cases using the former approach, in order to demonstrate the numerous ways in which segregation prevented real equality and thus to prepare the courts to recognize the validity of the theoretical argument.
(35) While Marshall enjoyed several successes arguing for the equalization of facilities and opportunities in such areas as voting practices and accommodations for graduate students at public universities, it would be twelve years before he evolved a strategy for arguing
(40) against pervasive discriminatory practices that enabled him to make the leap from individual instances of inequality to the broader social argument needed to later invalidate "separate but equal." In 1948, Marshall litigated *Shelley v. Kraemer*, in which he convinced the
(45) court to outlaw housing discrimination practiced by private parties. Although the court had previously supported such practices implicitly under a doctrine that excused private dealings from the legal requirement for equal protection of citizens under law,
(50) Marshall presented sociological data demonstrating that, in sum and over time, these individual transactions constituted a pattern of insupportable discrimination. Marshall later used this strategy when arguing against individual schools' enrollment
(55) restrictions in *Brown*; scholars argue that his successful use of the strategy in *Shelley* prepared the court to accept such data as convincing evidence for finding "separate but equal" insupportable on its face.

6. Which one of the following titles most accurately describes the contents of the passage?

(A) "Broader Social Patterns: Theoretical Arguments Heard in the Supreme Court, 1936-1952"
(B) "Thurgood Marshall: The Growth of His Career, 1936-1952"
(C) "Toward Change: The Development of Thurgood Marshall's Argument against 'Separate but Equal,' 1936-1952"
(D) "Separate but Not Equal: The Impact of *Brown v. Board of Education* on School Segregation"
(E) "Conflict and Compromise: Early Divisions in the NAACP's Attack on School Segregation"

7. It can most reasonably be inferred from the passage that Marshall's legal strategy for attacking the "separate but equal" doctrine

(A) sought to answer critics within the NAACP
(B) suggested Marshall thought the court would never accept the validity of a theoretical argument
(C) satisfied the requirement that cases first be argued in lower court
(D) presumed that the court could only gradually be convinced to overturn the "separate but equal" doctrine
(E) reflected Marshall's preference to seek practical goals

8. According to the passage, sociological data presented by Marshall in *Shelley v. Kraemer* showed that

(A) numerous examples of individual discriminatory enrollment policies in public schools amounted to a general pattern of discrimination
(B) numerous examples of individual discriminatory transactions by private parties amounted to a general pattern of housing discrimination
(C) the legal requirement for equal treatment of citizens was not applicable to private transactions
(D) the pattern of discrimination in housing transactions was due to inequities in financial resources
(E) the pattern of discrimination in the enrollment policies of public schools was similar to the pattern of insupportable discrimination in housing transactions

9. The passage suggests that the scholars referred to in the passage would be most likely to believe which one of the following statements?

   (A) Without Marshall's argument in *Shelley v. Kraemer*, the court would probably have overturned "separate but equal" for political reasons.
   (B) Without Marshall's argument in *Shelley v. Kraemer*, the court would probably not have ruled in his favor on *Brown v. Board of Education*.
   (C) Without Marshall's argument in *Shelley v. Kraemer*, the court would probably not have excused private dealings from the legal requirement for equal protection of citizens under law.
   (D) Without Marshall's argument in *Shelley v. Kraemer*, the court would probably never have relied on sociological data in any future cases.
   (E) Without Marshall's argument in *Shelley v. Kraemer*, the court would probably have overturned discriminatory housing transactions on other grounds.

10. According to the passage, the more theoretical approach to proceeding against the "separate but equal" doctrine was to

   (A) show that the doctrine often resulted in unequal opportunities for African Americans
   (B) argue that the doctrine was legally unsound because it contradicted itself
   (C) adopt a short-term strategy to prepare for the use of a long-term strategy
   (D) erode its foundations by successfully arguing individual cases
   (E) demonstrate that the separate facilities provided for African Americans were not in fact equitable

11. The function of the third paragraph is to

   (A) provide support for the view presented in the first paragraph
   (B) sharpen the distinction made in the second paragraph
   (C) question the claim made in the first paragraph
   (D) summarize the argument made in the first two paragraphs
   (E) counter the criticism of "separate but equal" made in the second paragraph

12. The primary purpose of the passage is to

   (A) reveal the details of Marshall's career before he litigated *Brown v. Board of Education*
   (B) examine the effects of a particular legal doctrine on the lives of African Americans
   (C) describe the strategy contributing to a successful legal argument
   (D) provide guidance to other litigators who attempt to overturn legal doctrines
   (E) call attention to an unsound legal doctrine by focusing on the strategy of its successful challenger

Passage #9: June 2000 Questions 13-20

Donna Haraway's *Primate Visions* is the most ambitious book on the history of science yet written from a feminist perspective, embracing not only the scientific construction of gender but also the interplay
(5) of race, class, and colonial and postcolonial culture with the "Western" construction of the very concept of nature itself. Primatology is a particularly apt vehicle for such themes because primates seem so much like ourselves that they provide ready material for
(10) scientists' conscious and unconscious projections of their beliefs about nature and culture.

Haraway's most radical departure is to challenge the traditional disjunction between the active knower (scientist/historian) and the passive object
(15) (nature/history). In Haraway's view, the desire to understand nature, whether in order to tame it or to preserve it as a place of wild innocence, is based on a troublingly masculinist and colonialist view of nature as an entity distinct from us and subject to our control.
(20) She argues that it is a view that is no longer politically, ecologically, or even scientifically viable. She proposes an approach that not only recognizes diverse human actors (scientists, government officials, laborers, science fiction writers) as contributing to our
(25) knowledge of nature, but that also recognizes the creatures usually subsumed under nature (such as primates) as active participants in creating that knowledge as well. Finally, she insists that the perspectives afforded by these different agents cannot
(30) be reduced to a single, coherent reality—there are necessarily only multiple, interlinked, partial realities.

This iconoclastic view is reflected in Haraway's unorthodox writing style. Haraway does not weave the many different elements of her work into one unified,
(35) overarching Story of Primatology; they remain distinct voices that will not succumb to a master narrative. This fragmented approach to historiography is familiar enough in historiographical theorizing but has rarely been put into practice by historians of science. It
(40) presents a complex alternative to traditional history, whether strictly narrative or narrative with emphasis on a causal argument.

Haraway is equally innovative in the way she incorporates broad cultural issues into her analysis.
(45) Despite decades of rhetoric from historians of science about the need to unite issues deemed "internal" to science (scientific theory and practice) and those considered "external" to it (social issues, structures, and beliefs), that dichotomy has proven difficult to set
(50) aside. Haraway simply ignores it. The many readers in whom this separation is deeply ingrained may find her discussions of such popular sources as science fiction, movies, and television distracting, and her statements concerning such issues as nuclear war bewildering and
(55) digressive. To accept her approach one must shed a great many assumptions about what properly belongs to the study of science.

13. The passage is primarily concerned with discussing which one of the following?

(A) the roles played by gender and class in Western science in general, and in the field of primatology in particular
(B) two different methods of writing the history of science
(C) the content and style of a proposal to reform the scientific approach to nature
(D) the theoretical bases and the cultural assumptions underlying a recent book on the history of women in science
(E) the effect of theoretical positions on writing styles in books on the history of science

14. Which one of the following best describes the attitude of the author of the passage toward *Primate Visions?*

(A) The book is highly original and exciting, but will be difficult for many readers to accept.
(B) The book is admirable primarily because of the extensive research it reflects.
(C) Although far from ground breaking, the book is elegantly and coherently written.
(D) While commendably imaginative, the book is, in the end, less than convincing.
(E) The book's thesis is promising and provocative but half-heartedly argued.

15. The passage suggests which one of the following about the traditional scientific approach to nature?

(A) Scientists have traditionally preferred to tame nature rather than to preserve it.
(B) Scientists have traditionally sought to counter the masculinist and colonialist aspects of Western culture.
(C) Scientists have traditionally assumed that primates were more active participants in the creation of knowledge than were other forms of natural life.
(D) Scientists have traditionally endeavored to conceal the role of government officials and laborers in the construction of scientific knowledge.
(E) Scientists have traditionally regarded nature as something separate from themselves.

16. The passage suggests that Haraway would most probably agree with which one of the following statements about scientists observing animal behavior in the field?

    (A) Those scientists who have been properly trained in field techniques will all record similar observations about the animals they are studying.
    (B) Primatologists are more likely to record accurate and sensitive observations about the animals they are studying than are other animal behaviorists.
    (C) Scientists studying primate behavior will probably record more accurate and sensitive observations than will scientists studying animals that are less like ourselves.
    (D) Scientists who study primates will probably be more likely than will scientists studying other animals to interpret an animal's behavior in terms of the scientists' own beliefs.
    (E) Scientists who take a passive role in interactions with the animals they study will probably record observations similar to those recorded by scientists taking a more active role.

17. The "iconoclastic view" mentioned in line 32 refers to which one of the following?

    (A) the assertion that there is no way to construct a unified and comprehensive reality out of the different fragments that contribute to the construction of scientific knowledge
    (B) the advocacy of the incorporation of many different sources, both literary and scholarly, into the construction of a unified and overarching Story of Primatology
    (C) the argument that the traditional scientific disjunction between active knower and passive object has had troubling political and ecological repercussions
    (D) the thesis that the projection of scientists' beliefs about nature and culture onto the study of primates has burdened primatology with masculinist and colonialist preconceptions
    (E) the contention that scientists have not succeeded in breaking out of the confines of either traditional narrative history or history organized around a causal argument

18. Which one of the following best exemplifies the type of "traditional history" mentioned in line 40 of the passage?

    (A) a chronological recounting of the life and work of Marie Curie, with special attention paid to the circumstances that led to her discovery of radium
    (B) a television series that dramatizes one scientist's prediction about human life in the twenty-second century
    (C) the transcript of a series of conversations among several scientists of radically opposing philosophies, in which no resolution or conclusion is reached
    (D) a newspaper editorial written by a scientist trying to arouse public support for a certain project by detailing the practical benefits to be gained from it
    (E) detailed mathematical notes recording the precise data gathered from a laboratory experiment

19. According to the author of the passage, which one of the following statements is true of the historiographical method employed by Haraway in *Primate Visions*?

    (A) It is a particularly effective approach in discussions of social issues.
    (B) It is an approach commonly applied in historiography in many disciplines.
    (C) It is generally less effective than traditional approaches.
    (D) It has rarely been used by historians emphasizing causal arguments.
    (E) It has rarely been practiced by historians of science.

20. The author uses the term "rhetoric" in line 45 most probably in order to do which one of the following?

    (A) underscore the importance of clear and effective writing in historiographical works
    (B) highlight the need for historians of science to study modes of language
    (C) emphasize the fact that historians of science have been unable to put innovative ideas into practice
    (D) criticize the excessive concern for form over content in the writings of historians of science
    (E) characterize the writing style and analytical approach employed by Haraway

Passage #10: October 2000 Questions 14-19

In studying the autobiographies of Native Americans, most scholars have focused on as-told-to life histories that were solicited, translated, recorded, and edited by non-Native American collaborators—that
(5) emerged from "bicultural composite authorship." Limiting their studies to such written documents, these scholars have overlooked traditional, preliterate modes of communicating personal history. In addition, they have failed to address the cultural constructs of the
(10) highly diverse Native American peoples, who prior to contact with nonindigenous cultures did not share with Europeans the same assumptions about self, life, and writing that underlie the concept of an autobiography—that indeed constitute the English word's root meaning.
(15) The idea of self was, in a number of pre-contact Native American cultures, markedly inclusive: identity was not merely individual, but also relational to a society, a specific landscape, and the cosmos. Within these cultures, the expression of life experiences tended
(20) to be oriented toward current events: with the participation of fellow tribal members, an individual person would articulate, reenact, or record important experiences as the person lived them, a mode of autobiography seemingly more fragmented than the
(25) European custom of writing down the recollections of a lifetime. Moreover, expression itself was not a matter of writing but of language, which can include speech and signs. Oral autobiography comprised songs, chants, stories, and even the process whereby one repeatedly
(30) took on new names to reflect important events and deeds in one's life. Dance and drama could convey personal history; for example, the advent of a vision to one person might require the enactment of that vision in the form of a tribal pageant.
(35) One can view as autobiographical the elaborate tattoos that symbolized a warrior's valorous deeds, and such artifacts as a decorated shield that communicated the accomplishments and aspirations of its maker, or a robe that was emblazoned with the pictographic history
(40) of the wearer's battles and was sometimes used in reenactments. Also autobiographical, and indicative of high status within the tribe, would have been a tepee painted with symbolic designs to record the achievements and display the dreams or visions of its
(45) owner, who was often assisted in the painting by other tribal members.
A tribe would, then, have contributed to the individual's narrative not merely passively, by its social codes and expectations, but actively by joining
(50) in the expression of that narrative. Such intracultural collaboration may seem alien to the European style of autobiography, yet any autobiography is shaped by its creator's ideas about the audience for which it is intended; in this sense, autobiography is justly called a
(55) simultaneous individual story and cultural narrative. Autobiographical expressions by early Native Americans may additionally have been shaped by the cultural perspectives of the people who transmitted them.

14. Which one of the following most accurately expresses the main conclusion of the passage?

(A) Scholars have tended to overlook the nuances of concepts about identity that existed in some of the early Native American cultures.
(B) As demonstrated by early Native Americans, autobiography can exist in a variety of media other than written documents.
(C) The Native American life histories collected and recorded by non-Native American writers differ from European-style autobiographies in their depictions of an individual's relation to society.
(D) Early Native Americans created autobiographies with forms and underlying assumptions that frequently differ from those of European-style autobiographies.
(E) The autobiographical forms traditionally used by Native Americans are more fragmented than European forms and thus less easily recognizable as personal history.

15. Which one of the following phrases best conveys the author's attitude toward the earlier scholarship on Native American autobiographies that is mentioned in the passage?

(A) "failed to address" (line 9)
(B) "highly diverse" (line 10)
(C) "markedly inclusive" (line 16)
(D) "seemingly more fragmented" (line 24)
(E) "alien to the European style" (line 51)

16. Which one of the following most accurately conveys the meaning of the phrase "bicultural composite authorship" as it is used in line 5 of the passage?

    (A) written by a member of one culture but based on the artifacts and oral traditions of another culture
    (B) written by two people, each of whom belongs to a different culture but contributes in the same way to the finished product
    (C) compiled from the writings of people who come from different cultures and whose identities cannot be determined
    (D) written originally by a member of one culture but edited and revised by a member of another culture
    (E) written by a member of one culture but based on oral communication by a member of another culture

17. Which one of the following most accurately describes the function of the third paragraph within the passage as a whole?

    (A) to refute traditional interpretations of certain artifacts
    (B) to present evidence that undermines a theory
    (C) to provide examples that support an argument
    (D) to contrast several different modes of expression
    (E) to enumerate specific instances in which a phenomenon recurred

18. The author of the passage refers to "self, life, and writing" (lines 12-13) most probably in order to

    (A) identify concepts about which Europeans and Native Americans had contrasting ideas
    (B) define a word that had a different meaning for early Native Americans than it has for contemporary Native Americans
    (C) illustrate how words can undergo a change in meaning after their introduction into the language
    (D) posit a fundamental similarity in the origins of a concept in both European and Native American cultures
    (E) explain how the assumptions that underlie European-style autobiography arose

19. Which one of the following would be most consistent with the ideas about identity that the author attributes to pre-contact Native American cultures?

    (A) A person who is born into one tribe but is brought up by members of another tribe retains a name given at birth.
    (B) A pictograph that represents a specific person incorporates the symbol for a constellation.
    (C) A similar ritual for assuming a new name is used in diverse communities.
    (D) A name given to one member of a community cannot be given to another member of the same community.
    (E) A decorated shield that belonged to an individual cannot be traced to a particular tribe.

CHAPTER TWO: DIVERSITY

Passage #11: December 2000 Questions 8-14

The autobiographical narrative *Incidents in the Life of a Slave Girl, Written by Herself* (1861), by Harriet A. Jacobs, a slave of African descent, not only recounts an individual life but also provides, implicitly and
(5) explicitly, a perspective on the larger United States culture from the viewpoint of one denied access to it. Jacobs, as a woman and a slave, faced the stigmas to which those statuses were subject. Jacobs crafted her narrative, in accordance with the mainstream literary
(10) genre of the sentimental domestic novel, as an embodiment of cherished cultural values such as the desirability of marriage and the sanctity of personal identity, home, and family. She did so because she was writing to the free women of her day–the principal
(15) readers of domestic novels–in the hopes that they would sympathize with and come to understand her unique predicament as a female slave. By applying these conventions of the genre to her situation, Jacobs demonstrates to her readers that family and domesticity
(20) are no less prized by those forced into slavery, thus leading her free readers to perceive those values within a broader social context.
   Some critics have argued that, by conforming to convention, Jacobs shortchanged her own experiences;
(25) one critic, for example, claims that in Jacobs's work the purposes of the domestic novel overshadow those of the typical slave narrative. But the relationship between the two genres is more complex: Jacobs's attempt to frame her story as a domestic novel creates a
(30) tension between the usual portrayal of women in this genre and her actual experience, often calling into question the applicability of the hierarchy of values espoused by the domestic novel to those who are in her situation. Unlike the traditional romantic episodes in
(35) domestic novels in which a man and woman meet, fall in love, encounter various obstacles but eventually marry, Jacobs's protagonist must send her lover, a slave, away in order to protect him from the wrath of her jealous master. In addition, by the end of the
(40) narrative, Jacobs's protagonist achieves her freedom by escaping to the north, but she does not achieve the domestic novel's ideal of a stable home complete with family, as the price she has had to pay for her freedom is separation from most of her family, including one of
(45) her own children. Jacobs points out that slave women view certain events and actions from a perspective different from that of free women, and that they must make difficult choices that free women need not. Her narrative thus becomes an antidomestic novel, for
(50) Jacobs accepts readily the goals of the genre, but demonstrates that its hierarchy of values does not apply when examined from the perspective of a female slave, suggesting thereby that her experience, and that of any female slave, cannot be fully understood without
(55) shedding conventional perspectives.

8. The author of the passage displays which one of the following attitudes toward the position of the critics mentioned in line 23?

   (A) complete rejection
   (B) reluctant rejection
   (C) complete neutrality
   (D) reluctant agreement
   (E) complete agreement

9. According to the passage, Jacobs's narrative departs from the conventions of a typical domestic novel in which one of the following ways?

   (A) Jacobs's protagonist does not ultimately achieve her freedom.
   (B) Jacobs's protagonist does not wish for the same ideals as the protagonists of domestic novels.
   (C) Jacobs's protagonist does not encounter various obstacles in her quest for love.
   (D) Jacobs's protagonist does not ultimately achieve the ideals of home and family.
   (E) Jacobs's protagonist does not experience the stigmas to which women and slaves were subject.

10. It can most reasonably be inferred from the passage that the critics mentioned in line 23 hold which one of the following views?

    (A) The mixture of literary genres in a single narrative often creates a useful tension that adds value to the narrative.
    (B) The mixture of literary genres in a single narrative tends to cause the goals of both genres to be compromised.
    (C) The mixture of literary genres in a single narrative tends to favor the genre having the greater degree of realism.
    (D) The mixture of literary genres in a single narrative tends to favor the genre having the lesser degree of sentimentality.
    (E) The mixture of literary genres in a single narrative can sometimes cause the goals of one of the genres to be compromised.

11. Which one of the following, if true, would most support the position of the critics mentioned in line 23?

    (A) Most readers of Jacobs's narrative when it was first published concluded that it was simply a domestic novel and were thus disinclined to see it as an attempt to provoke thought.
    (B) Many reviewers of Jacobs's narrative included passionate statements in their reviews calling for the immediate abolition of slavery.
    (C) Most scholars believe that Jacobs's narrative would not have been able to communicate its message effectively if it had not adopted the conventions of the domestic novel.
    (D) Jacobs's narrative was modeled not only after domestic novels of the period but after realistic novels whose goal was to point out social injustices.
    (E) Jacobs's goal in crafting her narrative was not only to preach against the injustices of slavery but also to tell a powerful story that would make those injustices vivid to readers.

12. The author describes Jacobs's narrative as an "antidomestic novel" (line 49) for which one of the following reasons?

    (A) Jacobs's protagonist does not lament her separation from her family.
    (B) Jacobs's protagonist is disinclined toward stereotypical domestic aspirations.
    (C) Jacobs's narrative reveals the limitations of the hierarchy of values espoused by the domestic novel genre.
    (D) Jacobs's narrative implicitly suggests that the desire for domestic ideals contributes to the protagonist's plight.
    (E) Jacobs's narrative condemns domestic values as a hindrance to its protagonist's development of personal identity.

13. With which one of the following statements would the author of the passage be most likely to agree?

    (A) Some authors of slave narratives allowed the purposes of the genre to overshadow their own experiences.
    (B) The slave narrative, no less than the domestic novel, constitutes a literary genre.
    (C) Authors who write in a particular genre must obey the conventions of that genre.
    (D) An autobiography, no less than a novel, should tell a powerful story.
    (E) Autobiographies should be evaluated not on their literary merit but on their historical accuracy.

14. Which one of the following principles most likely governs the author's evaluation of Jacobs's narrative?

    (A) Those autobiographical narratives that capture the mood of a particular period are thereby more valuable.
    (B) Those autobiographical narratives that focus on accurately depicting the events in the individual's life are thereby more valuable.
    (C) Those autobiographical narratives that force readers to view certain familiar cultural values in a wider context are thereby more valuable.
    (D) Those autobiographical narratives that are written from a perspective familiar to the majority of their readers are thereby more valuable.
    (E) Those autobiographical narratives that employ the conventions of another literary genre are thereby more valuable.

Passage #12: October 2001 Questions 1-6

Of the more than one thousand people who published memoirs of the French Revolution of 1789, about eighty were women. And of these eighty women memoirists, two thirds were members of the upper
(5) class, a proportion that might be attributed solely to privilege—at the time of the Revolution, only half of all French citizens could read, and only members of the upper class were able to write easily. But there were also political reasons. Most of the memoirs were
(10) published decades after the Revolution, during the restored monarchy that came to power in 1815. Those written by royalists, who opposed the Revolution, were published under the monarchy's aegis; in contrast, republican memoirists, who supported the Revolution,
(15) risked political sanctions against their work.

Because the memoirs were written so long after the events they describe, some historians question their reliability. Certainly, memory is subject to the loss or confusion of facts and, more to the point in these
(20) partisan accounts, to the distortions of a mind intent on preserving its particular picture of the past. But other scholars have shown that close inspection of these documents resolves such doubts on two scores. First, for major public happenings, there are often multiple
(25) accounts, allowing for cross-verification. Second, regarding the truth of personal events known only to the author, more subjective guidelines must be used: Are there internal verifications within a text that suggest the author is describing a plausible sequence of
(30) events, and acting in accord with what is known of the writer's character? Or is the narrative voice so pervaded by self-justifications that it forfeits credibility?

Denis Bertholet, in a study of nineteenth-century
(35) French autobiography, states that the women memoirists of this period defined themselves "in relationship to their sex"—i.e., they conformed to socially prescribed feminine roles of the time, fulfilling obligations as daughters, wives, or mothers.
(40) Nonetheless, instances of social activism by women abounded during the Revolution. On the whole, women's memoirs during this period exhibit a variety of personalities and experiences, and describe how women participated, individually and collectively, in
(45) the events of the Revolution. For example, the imprisoned royalist Madame de La Villirouet details how she managed to liberate not only herself but her co-prisoners through an epistolary campaign, and how she subsequently saved her husband's life by pleading
(50) his case in court. In addition, in both royalist and republican camps, several women defied the ban against women serving as soldiers and bore arms for their causes. Bertholet's study attests to the credibility of these accounts on both factual and subjective
(55) grounds, making the memoirs written by women particularly significant because they embody a clearly feminist mode of discourse and experience that one would not expect to find until the French Feminist movement more than a century later.

1. Which one of the following most completely and accurately states the main idea of the passage?

   (A) Despite the attempts of some historians to discredit them on factual or subjective grounds, women's memoirs of the French Revolution reflect French society's intolerance toward women's involvement in the political sphere.
   (B) Even though studies have yet to draw any definitive conclusions about their factual accuracy, women's memoirs of the French Revolution appear to be at least subjectively reliable accounts of the events of the period.
   (C) Although written years later, women's memoirs of the French Revolution can be regarded as factually and subjectively reliable accounts of the various ways in which women participated in the events of the period.
   (D) Because of the natural tendency of memory to distort facts and of partisanship to bias accounts, it is unlikely that women's memoirs of the French Revolution can be relied upon to convey an accurate portrait of the events of the period.
   (E) Regardless of their reliability, women's memoirs of the French Revolution are nevertheless a valuable resource for scholars attempting to gain insight into the impetus that led to the women's movement in France.

2. Based on the passage, which one of the following can most reasonably be inferred about the majority of the published memoirs of the French Revolution that were written by men?

   (A) They depict women who conformed to socially prescribed roles.
   (B) They depict women who participated in the Revolution.
   (C) They were suppressed by political sanctions.
   (D) They were written by members of the upper class.
   (E) They were written by members of the lower class.

3. The passage's reference to Madame de La Villirouet is most likely intended to

   (A) demonstrate that women's roles during the Revolution were partially determined by their social statuses
   (B) explain why so few women published their accounts of the events of the Revolution
   (C) support the claim that political partisanship inevitably biases recollections
   (D) provide an example of the activism of women described in memoirs of the Revolution
   (E) illustrate that royalist and republican memoirs were focused on differing themes

4. According to the passage, more of the published women's memoirs of the French Revolution were written by royalists than by republicans because

   (A) royalists could publish their accounts without risking persecution
   (B) royalists felt a greater urgency to relate their version of events
   (C) royalists were able to afford the prohibitive expense of publication
   (D) republicans had little desire to leave written accounts of their actions
   (E) republicans typically belonged to professions that left them little time to write

5. Based on the passage, which one of the following views can most reasonably be attributed to the historians mentioned in line 17?

   (A) Royalist memoirs of the French Revolution are more factually reliable than are republican memoirs of the same period.
   (B) Republican memoirs of the French Revolution are less distorted by partisan biases than are royalist memoirs of the same period.
   (C) Many memoirs of the French Revolution published during the restored monarchy likely contain factual inaccuracies.
   (D) Many memoirs of the French Revolution contain accounts of events that are not skewed by the biases of their authors.
   (E) Many memoirs of the French Revolution consist mostly of unverifiable accounts of certain events.

6. Based on the passage, which one of the following most accurately states a criterion that the scholars referred to in line 22 use to judge the credibility of a memoir's depiction of events known only to its author?

   (A) The depiction should appear consistent with the author's personality.
   (B) The depiction should contain demonstrable factual accuracies.
   (C) The depiction should have been verified shortly after being written.
   (D) The depiction should not be part of a partisan account.
   (E) The depiction should preserve a particular picture of the past.

Passage #13: October 2001 Questions 7-14

The paintings of Romare Bearden (1914-1988) represent a double triumph. At the same time that Bearden's work reflects a lifelong commitment to perfecting the innovative painting techniques he
(5) pioneered, it also reveals an artist engaged in a search for ways to explore the varieties of African-American experience.

By presenting scene, character, and atmosphere using a unique layered and fragmented style that
(10) combines elements of painting with elements of collage, Bearden suggested some of the ways in which commonplace subjects could be forced to undergo a metamorphosis when filtered through the techniques available to the resourceful artist. Bearden knew that
(15) regardless of individual painters' personal histories, tastes, or points of view, they must pay their craft the respect of approaching it through an acute awareness of the resources and limitations of the form to which they have dedicated their creative energies.

(20) But how did Bearden, so passionately dedicated to solving the more advanced problems of his painting technique, also succeed so well at portraying the realities of African-American life? During the Great Depression of the 1930s, Bearden painted scenes of
(25) the hardships of the period; the work was powerful, the scenes grim and brooding. Through his depiction of the unemployed in New York's Harlem he was able to move beyond the usual "protest painting" of the period to reveal instances of individual human suffering. His
(30) human figures, placed in abstract yet mysteriously familiar urban settings, managed to express the complex social reality lying beyond the borders of the canvas without compromising their integrity as elements in an artistic composition. Another important
(35) element of Bearden's compositions was his use of muted colors, such as dark blues and purples, to suggest moods of melancholy or despair. While functioning as part of the overall design, these colors also served as symbols of the psychological effects of
(40) debilitating social processes.

During the same period, he also painted happier scenes—depictions of religious ceremony, musical performance, and family life—and instilled them with the same vividness that he applied to his scenes of
(45) suffering. Bearden sought in his work to reveal in all its fullness a world long hidden by the clichés of sociology and rendered cloudy by the simplifications of journalism and documentary photography. Where any number of painters have tried to project the "prose" of
(50) Harlem, Bearden concentrated on releasing its poetry—its family rituals and its ceremonies of affirmation and celebration. His work insists that we truly see the African-American experience in depth, using the fresh light of his creative vision. Through an act of artistic
(55) will, he created strange visual harmonies out of the mosaic of the African-American experience, and in doing so reflected the multiple rhythms, textures, and mysteries of life.

7. Which one of the following best summarizes the main idea of the passage?

(A) Bearden was unique among chroniclers of the Great Depression in that his work depicted not just human suffering but also the happier moments that other artists tended to overlook.
(B) By combining a dedication to the perfection of his craft with a desire to portray African-American life in all its complexity, Bearden was able to produce paintings of unique vision.
(C) Without sacrificing his devotion to depicting the realities of African-American life, Bearden was able to expand the number and kind of painting techniques available to the dedicated artist.
(D) Unlike other artists of the Great Depression, who were interested mainly in sociological observation, Bearden devoted himself to the perfection of his craft.
(E) While Bearden has long been celebrated for his innovative painting techniques, he is less well known but equally notable as a compassionate chronicler of the African American experience.

8. According to the passage, Bearden's innovative painting techniques illustrate

(A) a commitment to calling attention to human suffering
(B) a desire to instruct painters about how to approach problems of form
(C) the ability of art to transform ordinary subject matter
(D) the importance of combining the abstractions of painting with the clarity of photography
(E) the need to emphasize more prosaic elements over poetic elements in a work of art

9. As it is used in the passage, the phrase "protest painting" (line 28) appears to refer to painting that

(A) depicted general scenes of social hardship and group suffering
(B) portrayed solitary figures in abstract surroundings
(C) challenged the traditional techniques employed by painters
(D) emphasized the experiences of African Americans during the Great Depression
(E) used innovative techniques to suggest the effects of social circumstances on individuals

10. Based on the passage, with which one of the following statements would Bearden have been most likely to agree?

    (A) To better highlight the creative technical elements of a painting an artist should choose prosaic and commonplace subjects.
    (B) Technical elements such as color can be effectively used to convey social or political messages.
    (C) A painter's use of technical innovations should be subservient to conveying social and political messages.
    (D) A painter should focus on the positive elements of African-American life and avoid depicting suffering and injustice.
    (E) The techniques of journalism and photography can bring new creative vision to painting and enrich its depiction of African-American life.

11. It can be inferred from the passage that journalistic and photographic records of Depression-era Harlem generally do not

    (A) involve innovative creative techniques
    (B) reveal instances of individual human suffering
    (C) communicate the sociological platitudes of the period
    (D) depict the richness of African-American life
    (E) cloud the picture of everyday life

12. The passage gives information that helps answer all of the following questions EXCEPT:

    (A) What led Bearden to choose painting as his primary means of artistic expression?
    (B) What are some of Bearden's most significant contributions to art?
    (C) What aspects of life during the Great Depression did Bearden depict?
    (D) What specific artistic techniques lent power to Bearden's paintings of individual subjects?
    (E) What did Bearden intend to convey through his use of color?

13. According to the passage, human figures in Bearden's paintings do all of the following EXCEPT:

    (A) serve as particular examples of human hardship
    (B) suggest circumstances outside the explicit subject of the paintings
    (C) function as aspects of an artistic composition
    (D) symbolize emotions or psychological states
    (E) inhabit abstract but recognizable physical settings

14. The passage suggests that the author's attitude toward Bearden's innovative painting techniques is one of

    (A) admiration for how they aided Bearden in communicating his rich vision of African-American life
    (B) appreciation for how they transform complex social realities into simple and direct social critiques
    (C) respect for how they are rooted in the rhythms and textures of African-American experience
    (D) concern that they draw attention away from Bearden's social and political message
    (E) strong conviction that they should be more widely utilized by African-American artists

Passage #14: June 2002 Questions 14-21

Published in 1952, *Invisible Man* featured a protagonist whose activities enabled the novel's author, Ralph Ellison, to explore and to blend themes specifically tied to the history and plight of African
(5) Americans with themes, also explored by many European writers with whose works Ellison was familiar, about the fractured, evanescent quality of individual identity and character. For this thematic blend, Ellison received two related criticisms: that his
(10) allegiance to the concerns of the individual prevented him from directing his art more toward the political action that critics believed was demanded by his era's social and political state of affairs; and that his indulging in European fictional modes lessened his
(15) contribution to the development of a distinctly African American novelistic style.

Ellison found these criticisms to voice a common demand, namely that writers should censor themselves and sacrifice their individuality for supposedly more
(20) important political and cultural purposes. He replied that it demeans a people and its artists to suggest that a particular historical situation requires cultural segregation in the arts. Such a view characterizes all artists as incapable of seeing the world—with all its
(25) subtleties and complications—in unique yet expressive ways, and it makes the narrow assumption that audiences are capable of viewing the world only from their own perspectives.

Models for understanding *Invisible Man* that may
(30) be of more help than those employed by its critics can be found in Ellison's own love for and celebration of jazz. Jazz has never closed itself off from other musical forms, and some jazz musicians have been able to take the European-influenced songs of U.S. theater and
(35) transform them into musical pieces that are unique and personal but also expressive of African American culture. In like manner, Ellison avoided the mere recapitulation of existing literary forms as well as the constraints of artistic isolation by using his work to
(40) explore and express the issues of identity and character that had so interested European writers.

Further, jazz, featuring solos that, however daring, remain rooted in the band's rhythm section, provides a rich model for understanding the relationship of artist
(45) to community and parallels the ways the protagonist's voice in *Invisible Man* is set within a wider communal context. Ellison's explorations in the novel, often in the manner of loving caricature, of the ideas left him by both European and African American predecessors are
(50) a form of homage to them and thus ameliorate the sense of alienation he expresses through the protagonist. And even though *Invisible Man*'s protagonist lives alone in a basement, Ellison proves that an individual whose unique voice is the result of
(55) the transmutation of a cultural inheritance can never be completely cut off from the community.

14. It can be inferred from the passage that the author most clearly holds which one of the following views?

(A) The possibility of successfully blending different cultural forms is demonstrated by jazz's ability to incorporate European influences.
(B) The technique of blending the artistic concerns of two cultures could be an effective tool for social and political action.
(C) Due to the success of *Invisible Man*, Ellison was able to generate a renewed interest in and greater appreciation for jazz.
(D) The protagonist in *Invisible Man* illustrates the difficulty of combining the concerns of African Americans and concerns thought to be European in origin.
(E) Ellison's literary technique, though effective, is unfortunately too esoteric and complex to generate a large audience.

15. Based on the passage, Ellison's critics would most likely have responded favorably to *Invisible Man* if it had

(A) created a positive effect on the social conditions of the time
(B) provided a historical record of the plight of African Americans
(C) contained a tribute to the political contributions of African American predecessors
(D) prompted a necessary and further separation of American literature from European literary style
(E) generated a large audience made up of individuals from many cultural backgrounds

16. The expression "cultural segregation in the arts" (lines 22-23) most clearly refers to

    (A) a general tendency within the arts whereby certain images and themes recur within the works of certain cultures
    (B) an obvious separation within the art community resulting from artists' differing aesthetic principles
    (C) the cultural isolation artists feel when they address issues of individual identity
    (D) the cultural obstacles that affect an audience's appreciation of art
    (E) an expectation placed on an artist to uphold a specific cultural agenda in the creation of art

17. The primary purpose of the third paragraph is to

    (A) summarize the thematic concerns of an artist in relation to other artists within the discipline
    (B) affirm the importance of two artistic disciplines in relation to cultural concerns
    (C) identify the source of the thematic content of one artist's work
    (D) celebrate one artistic discipline by viewing it from the perspective of an artist from another discipline
    (E) introduce a context within which the work of one artist may be more fully illuminated

18. Which one of the following statements about jazz is made in the passage?

    (A) It is not accessible to a wide audience.
    (B) It is the most complex of modern musical forms.
    (C) It embraces other forms of music.
    (D) It avoids political themes.
    (E) It has influenced much of contemporary literature.

19. It can be inferred from the passage that Ellison most clearly holds which one of the following views regarding an audience's relationship to works of art?

    (A) Audiences respond more favorably to art that has no political content.
    (B) Groundless criticism of an artist's work can hinder an audience's reception of the work.
    (C) Audiences have the capacity for empathy required to appreciate unique and expressive art.
    (D) The most conscientious members of any audience are those who are aware of the specific techniques employed by the artist.
    (E) Most audience members are bound by their cultural upbringing to view art from that cultural perspective.

20. The primary purpose of the passage is to

    (A) make a case that a certain novelist is one of the most important novelists of the twentieth century
    (B) demonstrate the value of using jazz as an illustration for further understanding the novels of a certain literary trend
    (C) explain the relevance of a particular work and its protagonist to the political and social issues of the time
    (D) defend the work of a certain novelist against criticism that it should have addressed political and social issues
    (E) distinguish clearly between the value of art for art's sake and art for purposes such as political agendas

21. The passage provides information to answer each of the following questions EXCEPT:

    (A) Did Ellison himself enjoy jazz?
    (B) What themes in *Invisible Man* were influenced by themes prevalent in jazz?
    (C) What was Ellison's response to criticism concerning the thematic blend in *Invisible Man*?
    (D) From what literary tradition did some of the ideas explored in *Invisible Man* come?
    (E) What kind of music did some jazz musicians use in creating their works?

Passage #15: October 2002 Questions 1-8

The myth persists that in 1492 the Western Hemisphere was an untamed wilderness and that it was European settlers who harnessed and transformed its ecosystems. But scholarship shows that forests, in
(5) particular, had been altered to varying degrees well before the arrival of Europeans. Native populations had converted much of the forests to successfully cultivated stands, especially by means of burning. Nevertheless, some researchers have maintained that the extent,
(10) frequency, and impact of such burning was minimal. One geographer claims that climatic change could have accounted for some of the changes in forest composition; another argues that burning by native populations was done only sporadically, to augment the
(15) effects of natural fires.

However, a large body of evidence for the routine practice of burning exists in the geographical record. One group of researchers found, for example, that sedimentary charcoal accumulations in what is now the
(20) northeastern United States are greatest where known native American settlements were greatest. Other evidence shows that, while the characteristics and impact of fires set by native populations varied regionally according to population size, extent of
(25) resource management techniques, and environment, all such fires had markedly different effects on vegetation patterns than did natural fires. Controlled burning created grassy openings such as meadows and glades. Burning also promoted a mosaic quality to North and
(30) South American ecosystems, creating forests in many different stages of ecological development. Much of the mature forestland was characterized by open, herbaceous undergrowth, another result of the clearing brought about by burning.

(35) In North America, controlled burning created conditions favorable to berries and other fire-tolerant and sun-loving foods. Burning also converted mixed stands of trees to homogeneous forest, for example the longleaf, slash pine, and scrub oak forests of the
(40) southeastern U.S. Natural fires do account for some of this vegetation, but regular burning clearly extended and maintained it. Burning also influenced forest composition in the tropics, where natural fires are rare. An example is the pine-dominant forests of Nicaragua,
(45) where warm temperatures and heavy rainfall naturally favor mixed tropical or rain forests. While there are extensive pine forests in Guatemala and Mexico, these primarily grow in cooler, drier, higher elevations, regions where such vegetation is in large part natural
(50) and even prehuman. Today, the Nicaraguan pines occur where there has been clearing followed by regular burning, and the same is likely to have occurred in the past: such forests were present when Europeans arrived and were found only in areas where native
(55) settlements were substantial; when these settlements were abandoned, the land returned to mixed hardwoods. This succession is also evident elsewhere in similar low tropical elevations in the Caribbean and Mexico.

1. Which one of the following most accurately expresses the main idea of the passage?

    (A) Despite extensive evidence that native populations had been burning North and South American forests extensively before 1492, some scholars persist in claiming that such burning was either infrequent or the result of natural causes.

    (B) In opposition to the widespread belief that in 1492 the Western Hemisphere was uncultivated, scholars unanimously agree that native populations were substantially altering North and South American forests well before the arrival of Europeans.

    (C) Although some scholars minimize the scope and importance of the burning of forests engaged in by native populations of North and South America before 1492, evidence of the frequency and impact of such burning is actually quite extensive.

    (D) Where scholars had once believed that North and South American forests remained uncultivated until the arrival of Europeans, there is now general agreement that native populations had been cultivating the forests since well before 1492.

    (E) While scholars have acknowledged that North and South American forests were being burned well before 1492, there is still disagreement over whether such burning was the result of natural causes or of the deliberate actions of native populations.

2. It can be inferred that a forest burned as described in the passage would have been LEAST likely to display

    (A) numerous types of hardwood trees
    (B) extensive herbaceous undergrowth
    (C) a variety of fire-tolerant plants
    (D) various stages of ecological maturity
    (E) grassy openings such as meadows or glades

3. Which one of the following is a type of forest identified by the author as a product of controlled burning in recent times?

    (A) scrub oak forests in the southeastern U.S.
    (B) slash pine forests in the southeastern U.S.
    (C) pine forests in Guatemala at high elevations
    (D) pine forests in Mexico at high elevations
    (E) pine forests in Nicaragua at low elevations

4. Which one of the following is presented by the author as evidence of controlled burning in the tropics before the arrival of Europeans?

    (A) extensive homogeneous forests at high elevation
    (B) extensive homogenous forests at low elevation
    (C) extensive heterogenous forests at high elevation
    (D) extensive heterogenous forests at low elevation
    (E) extensive sedimentary charcoal accumulations at high elevation

5. With which one of the following would the author be most likely to agree?

    (A) The long-term effects of controlled burning could just as easily have been caused by natural fires.
    (B) Herbaceous undergrowth prevents many forests from reaching full maturity.
    (C) European settlers had little impact on the composition of the ecosystems in North and South America.
    (D) Certain species of plants may not have been as widespread in North America without controlled burning.
    (E) Nicaraguan pine forests could have been created either by natural fires or by controlled burning.

6. As evidence for the routine practice of forest burning by native populations before the arrival of Europeans, the author cites all of the following EXCEPT:

    (A) the similar characteristics of fire in different regions
    (B) the simultaneous presence of forests at varying stages of maturity
    (C) the existence of herbaceous undergrowth in certain forests
    (D) the heavy accumulation of charcoal near populous settlements
    (E) the presence of meadows and glades in certain forests

7. The "succession" mentioned in line 57 refers to

    (A) forest clearing followed by controlled burning of forests
    (B) tropical rain forest followed by pine forest
    (C) European settlement followed by abandonment of land
    (D) homogeneous pine forest followed by mixed hardwoods
    (E) pine forests followed by established settlements

8. The primary purpose of the passage is to

    (A) refute certain researchers' views
    (B) support a common belief
    (C) counter certain evidence
    (D) synthesize two viewpoints
    (E) correct the geographical record

Passage #16: December 2002 Questions 1-8

The contemporary Mexican artistic movement known as muralism, a movement of public art that began with images painted on walls in an effort to represent Mexican national culture, is closely linked
(5) ideologically with its main sponsor, the new Mexican government elected in 1920 following the Mexican Revolution. This government promoted an ambitious cultural program, and the young revolutionary state called on artists to display Mexico's richness and
(10) possibility. But the theoretical foundation of the movement was formulated by the artists themselves. The major figures in the muralist movement, David Alfaro Siqueiros, Diego Rivera, and Jose Clemente Orozco, all based their work on a common premise:
(15) that art should incorporate images and familiar ideas as it commented upon the historic period in which it was created. In the process, they assimilated into their work the customs, myths, geography, and history of the local communities that constitute the basis of Mexican
(20) national culture.

But while many muralist works express populist or nationalist ideas, it is a mistake to attempt to reduce Mexican mural painting to formulaic, official government art. It is more than merely the result of the
(25) changes in political and social awareness that the Mexican Revolution represented; it also reflected important innovations in the art world. In creating a wide panorama of Mexico's history on the walls of public buildings throughout the country, muralists
(30) often used a realist style. But awareness of these innovations enabled them to be freer in expression than were more traditional practitioners of this style.

Moreover, while they shared a common interest in rediscovering their Mexican national identity, they
(35) developed their own distinct styles. Rivera, for example, incorporated elements from pre-Columbian sculpture and the Italian Renaissance fresco into his murals and used a strange combination of mechanical shapes to depict the faces and bodies of people.
(40) Orozco, on the other hand, showed a more expressionist approach, with loose brushwork and an openly emotional treatment of form. He relied on a strong diagonal line to give a sense of heightened movement and drama to his work. Siqueiros developed
(45) in a somewhat similar direction as Orozco, but incorporated asymmetric compositions, a high degree of action, and brilliant color.

This stylistic experimentation can be seen as resulting from the demands of a new medium. In
(50) stretching their concepts from small easel paintings with a centralized subject to vast compositions with mural dimensions, muralists learned to think big and to respect the sweeping gesture of the arm—the brush stroke required to achieve the desired bold effect of
(55) mural art. Furthermore, because they were painting murals, they thought in terms of a continuum; their works were designed to be viewable from many different vantage points, to have an equally strong impact in all parts, and to continue to be viewable as
(60) people moved across in front of them.

1. Which one of the following most accurately expresses the main point of the passage?

(A) Muralism developed its political goals in Mexico in service to the revolutionary government, while its aesthetic aspects were borrowed from other countries.
(B) Inspired by political developments in Mexico and trends in modern art, muralist painters devised an innovative style of large-scale painting to reflect Mexican culture.
(C) The stylistic features of muralism represent a consistent working out of the implications of its revolutionary ideology.
(D) Though the Mexican government supported muralism as a means of promoting nationalist ideology, muralists such as Siqueiros, Rivera, and Orozco developed the movement in contradictory, more controversial directions.
(E) Because of its large scale and stylistic innovations, the type of contemporary Mexican art known as muralism is capable of expressing a much wider and more complex view of Mexico's culture and history than previous artistic movements could express.

2. The author mentions Rivera's use of "pre-Columbian sculpture and the Italian Renaissance fresco" (lines 36-37) primarily in order to provide an example of Rivera's

(A) assimilation of elements of Mexican customs and myth
(B) movement beyond single, centralized subjects
(C) experimentation with expressionist techniques
(D) distinctive manner of artistic expression
(E) underlying resistance to change

3. Which one of the following aspects of muralist painting does the author appear to value most highly?

   (A) its revolutionary ideology
   (B) its use of brilliant color
   (C) its tailoring of style to its medium
   (D) its use of elements from everyday life
   (E) its expression of populist ideas

4. Based on the passage, with which one of the following statements about art would the muralists be most likely to agree?

   (A) Art should be evaluated on the basis of its style and form rather than on its content.
   (B) Government sponsorship is essential to the flourishing of art.
   (C) Realism is unsuited to large-scale public art.
   (D) The use of techniques borrowed from other cultures can contribute to the rediscovery of one's national identity.
   (E) Traditional easel painting is an elitist art form.

5. According to the passage, the Mexican government elected in 1920 took which one of the following approaches to art following the Mexican Revolution?

   (A) It encouraged the adoption of modem innovations from abroad.
   (B) It encouraged artists to pursue the realist tradition in art.
   (C) It called on artists to portray Mexico's heritage and future promise.
   (D) It developed the theoretical base of the muralist movement.
   (E) It favored artists who introduced stylistic innovations over those who worked in the realist tradition.

6. Which one of the following, if true, most supports the author's claim about the relationship between muralism and the Mexican Revolution (lines 24-27)?

   (A) The major figures in muralism also created important works in that style that were deliberately not political in content.
   (B) Not all muralist painters were familiar with the innovations being made at that time in the art world.
   (C) The changes taking place at that time in the art world were revivals of earlier movements.
   (D) Officials in the Mexican government were not familiar with the innovations being made at that time in the art world.
   (E) Only those muralist works that reflected nationalist sentiments were permitted to be viewed by the public.

7. Which one of the following does the author explicitly identify as a characteristic of Mexican mural art?

   (A) Its subject matter consisted primarily of current events.
   (B) It could be viewed outdoors only.
   (C) It used the same techniques as are used in easel painting.
   (D) It exhibited remarkable stylistic uniformity.
   (E) It was intended to be viewed from more than one angle.

8. The primary purpose of the second paragraph is to

   (A) describe the unifying features of muralism
   (B) provide support for the argument that the muralists often did not support government causes
   (C) support the claim that muralists always used their work to comment on their own historical period
   (D) illustrate how the muralists appropriated elements of Mexican tradition
   (E) argue that muralism cannot be understood by focusing solely on its political dimension

Passage #17: June 2003 Questions 6-12

In spite of a shared language, Latin American poetry written in Spanish differs from Spanish poetry in many respects. The Spanish of Latin American poets is more open than that of Spanish poets, more exposed
(5) to outside influences—indigenous, English, French, and other languages. While some literary critics maintain that there is as much linguistic unity in Latin American poetry as there is in Spanish poetry, they base this claim on the fact that Castilian Spanish, the
(10) official and literary version of the Spanish language based largely on the dialect originally spoken in the Castile region of Spain, was transplanted to the Americas when it was already a relatively standardized idiom. Although such unity may have characterized
(15) the earliest Latin American poetry, after centuries in the Americas the language of Latin American poetry cannot help but reveal the influences of its unique cultural history.

Latin American poetry is critical or irreverent in its
(20) attitude toward language, where that of Spanish poets is more accepting. For example, the Spanish-language incarnations of modernism and the avant-garde, two literary movements that used language in innovative and challenging ways, originated with Latin American
(25) poets. By contrast, when these movements later reached Spain, Spanish poets greeted them with reluctance. Spanish poets, even those of the modern era, seem to take their language for granted, rarely using it in radical or experimental ways.

(30) The most distinctive note in Latin American poetry is its enthusiastic response to the modern world, while Spanish poetry displays a kind of cultural conservatism—the desire to return to an ideal culture of the distant past. Because no Spanish-language
(35) culture lies in the equally distant (i.e., pre-Columbian) past of the Americas, but has instead been invented by Latin Americans day by day, Latin American poetry has no such long-standing past to romanticize. Instead, Latin American poetry often displays a curiosity about
(40) the literature of other cultures, an interest in exploring poetic structures beyond those typical of Spanish poetry. For example, the first Spanish-language haiku—a Japanese poetic form—were written by Jose Juan Tablada, a Mexican. Another of the Latin
(45) American poets' responses to this absence is the search for a world before recorded history-not only that of Spain or the Americas, but in some cases of the planet; the Chilean poet Pablo Neruda's work, for example, is noteworthy for its development of an ahistorical
(50) mythology for the creation of the earth. For Latin American poets there is no such thing as the pristine cultural past affirmed in the poetry of Spain: there is only the fluid interaction of all world cultures, or else the extensive time before cultures began.

6. The discussion in the second paragraph is intended primarily to

(A) argue that Latin American poets originated modernism and the avant-garde
(B) explain how Spanish poetry and Latin American poetry differ in their attitudes toward the Spanish language
(C) demonstrate why Latin American poetry is not well received in Spain
(D) show that the Castilian Spanish employed in Spanish poetry has remained relatively unchanged by the advent of modernism and the avant-garde
(E) illustrate the extent to which Spanish poetry romanticizes Spanish-language culture

7. Given the information in the passage, which one of the following is most analogous to the evolution of Latin American poetry?

(A) A family moves its restaurant to a new town and incorporates local ingredients into its traditional recipes.
(B) A family moves its business to a new town after the business fails in its original location.
(C) A family with a two-hundred-year-old house labors industriously in order to restore the house to its original appearance.
(D) A family does research into its ancestry in order to construct its family tree.
(E) A family eagerly anticipates its annual vacation but never takes photographs or purchases souvenirs to preserve its memories.

8. The passage's claims about Spanish poetry would be most weakened if new evidence indicating which one of the following were discovered?

(A) Spanish linguistic constructs had greater influence on Latin American poets than had previously been thought.
(B) Castilian Spanish was still evolving linguistically at the time of the inception of Latin American poetry.
(C) Spanish poets originated an influential literary movement that used language in radical ways.
(D) Castilian Spanish was influenced during its evolution by other Spanish dialects.
(E) Spanish poets rejected the English and French incarnations of modernism.

9. The passage affirms each of the following EXCEPT:

    (A) The first haiku in the Spanish language were written by a Latin American poet.
    (B) Spanish poetry is rarely innovative or experimental in its use of language.
    (C) Spanish poetry rarely incorporates poetic traditions from other cultures.
    (D) Latin American poetry tends to take the Spanish language for granted.
    (E) Latin American poetry incorporates aspects of various other languages.

10. Which one of the following can most reasonably be inferred from the passage about Latin American poetry's use of poetic structures from other world cultures?

    (A) The use of poetic structures from other world cultures is an attempt by Latin American poets to create a cultural past.
    (B) The use of poetic structures from other world cultures by Latin American poets is a response to their lack of a long-standing Spanish-language cultural past in the Americas.
    (C) The use of poetic structures from other world cultures has led Latin American poets to reconsider their lack of a long-standing Spanish-language cultural past in the Americas.
    (D) Latin American poets who write about a world before recorded history do not use poetic structures from other world cultures.
    (E) Latin American poetry does not borrow poetic structures from other world cultures whose literature exhibits cultural conservatism.

11. Based on the passage, the author most likely holds which one of the following views toward Spanish poetry's relationship to the Spanish cultural past?

    (A) This relationship has inspired Spanish poets to examine their cultural past with a critical eye.
    (B) This relationship forces Spanish poets to write about subjects with which they feel little natural affinity.
    (C) This relationship is itself the central theme of much Spanish poetry.
    (D) This relationship infuses Spanish poetry with a romanticism that is reluctant to embrace the modern era.
    (E) This relationship results in poems that are of little interest to contemporary Spanish readers.

12. Which one of the following inferences is most supported by the passage?

    (A) A tradition of cultural conservatism has allowed the Spanish language to evolve into a stable, reliable form of expression.
    (B) It was only recently that Latin American poetry began to incorporate elements of other languages.
    (C) The cultural conservatism of Spanish poetry is exemplified by the uncritical attitude of Spanish poets toward the Spanish language.
    (D) Latin American poets' interest in other world cultures is illustrated by their use of Japanese words and phrases.
    (E) Spanish poetry is receptive to the influence of some Spanish-language poets outside of Spain.

Passage #1: December 2002 Questions 9-16

Fairy tales address themselves to two communities, each with its own interests and each in periodic conflict with the other: parents and children. Nearly every study of fairy tales has taken the perspective of the
(5) parent, constructing the meaning of the tales by using the reading strategies of an adult bent on identifying universally valid tenets of moral instruction for children.

For example, the plot of "Hansel and Gretel" is set
(10) in motion by hard-hearted parents who abandon their children in the woods, but for psychologist Bruno Bettelheim the tale is really about children who learn to give up their unhealthy dependency on their parents. According to Bettelheim, this story—in which the
(15) children ultimately overpower a witch who has taken them prisoner for the crime of attempting to eat the witch's gingerbread house—forces its young audience to recognize the dangers of unrestrained greed. As dependent children, Bettelheim argues, Hansel and
(20) Gretel had been a burden to their parents, but on their return home with the witch's jewels, they become the family's support. Thus, says Bettelheim, does the story train its young listeners to become "mature children."

There are two ways of interpreting a story: one is a
(25) "superficial" reading that focuses on the tale's manifest content, and the other is a "deeper" reading that looks for latent meanings. Many adults who read fairy tales are drawn to this second kind of interpretation in order to avoid facing the unpleasant truths that can emerge
(30) from the tales when adults—even parents—are portrayed as capable of acting out of selfish motives themselves. What makes fairy tales attractive to Bettelheim and other psychologists is that they can be used as scenarios that position the child as a
(35) transgressor whose deserved punishment provides a lesson for unruly children. Stories that run counter to such orthodoxies about child-rearing are, to a large extent, suppressed by Bettelheim or "rewritten" through reinterpretation. Once we examine his
(40) interpretations closely, we see that his readings produce meanings that are very different from those constructed by readers with different cultural assumptions and expectations, who, unlike Bettelheim, do not find inflexible tenets of moral instruction in the
(45) tales.

Bettelheim interprets all fairy tales as driven by children's fantasies of desire and revenge, and in doing so suppresses the true nature of parental behavior ranging from abuse to indulgence. Fortunately, these
(50) characterizations of selfish children and innocent adults have been discredited to some extent by recent psychoanalytic literature. The need to deny adult evil has been a pervasive feature of our society, leading us to position children not only as the sole agents of evil
(55) but also as the objects of unending moral instruction, hence the idea that a literature targeted for them must stand in the service of pragmatic instrumentality rather than foster an unproductive form of playful pleasure.

9. Which one of the following most accurately states the main idea of the passage?

    (A) While originally written for children, fairy tales also contain a deeper significance for adults that psychologists such as Bettelheim have shown to be their true meaning.
    (B) The "superficial" reading of a fairy tale, which deals only with the tale's content, is actually more enlightening for children than the "deeper" reading preferred by psychologists such as Bettelheim.
    (C) Because the content of fairy tales has historically run counter to prevailing orthodoxies about child-rearing, psychologists such as Bettelheim sometimes reinterpret them to suit their own pedagogical needs.
    (D) The pervasive need to deny adult evil has led psychologists such as Bettelheim to erroneously view fairy tales solely as instruments of moral instruction for children.
    (E) Although dismissed as unproductive by psychologists such as Bettelheim, fairy tales offer children imaginative experiences that help them grow into morally responsible adults.

10. Based on the passage, which one of the following elements of "Hansel and Gretel" would most likely be de-emphasized in Bettelheim's interpretation of the tale?

    (A) Hansel and Gretel are abandoned by their hard hearted parents.
    (B) Hansel and Gretel are imprisoned by the witch.
    (C) Hansel and Gretel overpower the witch.
    (D) Hansel and Gretel take the witch's jewels.
    (E) Hansel and Gretel bring the witch's jewels home to their parents.

11. Which one of the following is the most accurate description of the author's attitude toward Bettelheim's view of fairy tales?

    (A) concern that the view will undermine the ability of fairy tales to provide moral instruction
    (B) scorn toward the view's supposition that moral tenets can be universally valid
    (C) disapproval of the view's depiction of children as selfish and adults as innocent
    (D) anger toward the view's claim that children often improve as a result of deserved punishment
    (E) disappointment with the view's emphasis on the manifest content of a tale

12. The author of the passage would be most likely to agree with which one of the following statements?

    (A) Children who never attempt to look for the deeper meanings in fairy tales will miss out on one of the principal pleasures of reading such tales.
    (B) It is better if children discover fairy tales on their own than for an adult to suggest that they read the tales.
    (C) A child who is unruly will behave better after reading a fairy tale if the tale is suggested to them by another child.
    (D) Most children are too young to comprehend the deeper meanings contained in fairy tales.
    (E) Children should be allowed to enjoy literature that has no instructive purpose.

13. Which one of the following principles most likely underlies the author's characterization of literary interpretation?

    (A) Only those trained in literary interpretation can detect the latent meanings in stories.
    (B) Only adults are psychologically mature enough to find the latent meanings in stories.
    (C) Only one of the various meanings readers may find in a story is truly correct.
    (D) The meanings we see in stories are influenced by the assumptions and expectations we bring to the story.
    (E) The latent meanings a story contains are deliberately placed there by the author.

14. According to the author, recent psychoanalytic literature suggests that

    (A) the moral instruction children receive from fairy tales is detrimental to their emotional development
    (B) fewer adults are guilty of improper child-rearing than had once been thought
    (C) the need to deny adult evil is a pervasive feature of all modem societies
    (D) the plots of many fairy tales are similar to children's revenge fantasies
    (E) the idea that children are typically selfish and adults innocent is of questionable validity

15. It can be inferred from the passage that Bettelheim believes that children are

    (A) uninterested in inflexible tenets of moral instruction
    (B) unfairly subjected to the moral beliefs of their parents
    (C) often aware of inappropriate parental behavior
    (D) capable of shedding undesirable personal qualities
    (E) basically playful and carefree

16. Which one of the following statements is least compatible with Bettelheim's views, as those views are described in the passage?

    (A) The imaginations of children do not draw clear distinctions between inanimate objects and living things.
    (B) Children must learn that their own needs and feelings are to be valued, even when these differ from those of their parents.
    (C) As their minds mature, children tend to experience the world in terms of the dynamics of the family into which they were born.
    (D) The more secure that children feel within the world, the less they need to hold onto infantile notions.
    (E) Children's ability to distinguish between stories and reality is not fully developed until puberty.

Passage #1: December 1996 Questions 22-27

Most studies of recent Southeast Asian immigrants to the United States have focused on their adjustment to life in their adopted country and on the effects of leaving their homelands. James
(5) Tollefson's *Alien Winds* examines the resettlement process from a different perspective by investigating the educational programs offered in immigrant processing centers. Based on interviews, transcripts from classes, essays by immigrants, personal visits
(10) to a teacher-training unit, and official government documents, Tollefson relies on an impressive amount and variety of documentation in making his arguments about processing centers' educational programs.
(15) Tollefson's main contention is that the emphasis placed on immediate employment and on teaching the values, attitudes, and behaviors that the training personnel think will help the immigrants adjust more easily to life in the United States is often
(20) counterproductive and demoralizing. Because of concerns that the immigrants be self-supporting as soon as possible, they are trained almost exclusively for low-level jobs that do not require English proficiency. In this respect, Tollefson claims, the
(25) processing centers suit the needs of employers more than they suit the long-term needs of the immigrant community. Tollefson also detects a fundamental flaw in the attempts by program educators to instill in the immigrants the traditionally Western
(30) principles of self-sufficiency and individual success. These efforts often have the effect of undermining the immigrants' sense of community and, in doing so, sometimes isolate them from the moral support and even from business opportunities afforded by
(35) the immigrant community. The programs also encourage the immigrants to shed their cultural traditions and ethnic identity and adopt the lifestyles, beliefs, and characteristics of their adopted country if they wish to enter fully into the
(40) national life.
Tollefson notes that the ideological nature of these educational programs has roots in the turn-of-the-century educational programs designed to assimilate European immigrants into United
(45) States society. Tollefson provides a concise history of the assimilationist movement in immigrant education, in which European immigrants were encouraged to leave behind the ways of the Old World and to adopt instead the principles and
(50) practices of the New World.
Tollefson ably shows that the issues demanding real attention in the educational programs for Southeast Asian immigrants are not merely employment rates and government funding, but also
(55) the assumptions underpinning the educational values in the programs. He recommends many improvements for the programs, including giving the immigrants a stronger voice in determining their needs and how to meet them, redesigning the
(60) curricula, and emphasizing long-term language education and job training over immediate employment and the avoiding of public assistance. Unfortunately, though, Tollefson does not offer enough concrete solutions as to how these reforms
(65) could be carried out, despite his own descriptions of the complicated bureaucratic nature of the programs.

22. Which one of the following statements best expresses the main idea of the passage?

(A) Tollefson's focus on the economic and cultural factors involved in adjusting to a new country offers a significant departure from most studies of Southeast Asian immigration.
(B) In his analysis of educational programs for Southeast Asian immigrants, Tollefson fails to acknowledge many of the positive effects the programs have had on immigrants' lives.
(C) Tollefson convincingly blames the philosophy underlying immigrant educational programs for some of the adjustment problems afflicting Southeast Asian immigrants.
(D) Tollefson's most significant contribution is his analysis of how Southeast Asian immigrants overcome the obstacles they encounter in immigrant educational programs.
(E) Tollefson traces a gradual yet significant change in the attitudes held by processing center educators toward Southeast Asian immigrants.

23. With which one of the following statements concerning the educational programs of the immigration centers would Tollefson most probably agree?

    (A) Although the programs offer adequate job training, they offer inadequate English training.
    (B) Some of the programs' attempts to improve the earning power of the immigrants cut them off from potential sources of income.
    (C) Inclusion of the history of immigration in the United States in the programs' curricula facilitates adjustment for the immigrants.
    (D) Immigrants would benefit if instructors in the programs were better prepared to teach the curricula developed in the teacher-training courses.
    (E) The programs' curricula should be redesigned to include greater emphasis on the shared values, beliefs, and practices in the United States.

24. Which one of the following best describes the opinion of the author of the passage with respect to Tollefson's work?

    (A) thorough but misguided
    (B) innovative but incomplete
    (C) novel but contradictory
    (D) illuminating but unappreciated
    (E) well documented but unoriginal

25. The passage suggests that which one of the following is an assumption underlying the educational approach in immigrant processing centers?

    (A) There is a set of values and behaviors that, if adopted by immigrants, facilitate adjustment to United States society.
    (B) When recent immigrants are self-supporting rather than supported by public assistance, they tend to gain English proficiency more quickly.
    (C) Immediate employment tends to undermine the immigrants' sense of community with each other.
    (D) Long-term success for immigrants is best achieved by encouraging the immigrants to maintain a strong sense of community.
    (E) The principles of self-sufficiency and individual success are central to Southeast Asian culture and ethnicity.

26. Which one of the following best describes the function of the first paragraph of the passage?

    (A) It provides the scholarly context for Tollefson's study and a description of his methodology.
    (B) It compares Tollefson's study to other works and presents the main argument of his study.
    (C) It compares the types of documents Tollefson uses to those used in other studies.
    (D) It presents the accepted theory on Tollefson's topic and the method by which Tollefson challenges it.
    (E) It argues for the analytical and technical superiority of Tollefson's study over other works on the topic.

27. The author of the passage refers to Tollefson's descriptions of the bureaucratic nature of the immigrant educational programs in the fourth paragraph most probably in order to

    (A) criticize Tollefson's decision to combine a description of the bureaucracies with suggestions for improvement
    (B) emphasize the author's disappointment in Tollefson's overly general recommendations for improvements to the programs
    (C) point out the irony of Tollefson concluding his study with suggestions for drastic changes in the programs
    (D) support a contention that Tollefson's recommendations for improvements do not focus on the real sources of the programs' problems
    (E) suggest a parallel between the complexity of the bureaucracies and the complexity of Tollefson's arguments

Passage #2: October 1997 Questions 19-26

Recently the focus of historical studies of different ethnic groups in the United States has shifted from the transformation of ethnic identity to its preservation. Whereas earlier historians argued
(5) that the ethnic identity of various immigrant groups to the United States blended to form an American national character, the new scholarship has focused on the transplantation of ethnic cultures to the United States. Fugita and O'Brien's *Japanese*
(10) *American Ethnicity* provides an example of this recent trend; it also exemplifies a problem that is common to such scholarship.

In comparing the first three generations of Japanese Americans (the Issei, Nisei, and Sansei),
(15) Fugita and O'Brien conclude that assimilation to United States culture increased among Japanese Americans over three generations, but that a sense of ethnic community endured. Although the persistence of community is stressed by the authors,
(20) their emphasis in the book could just as easily have been on the high degree of assimilation of the Japanese American population in the late twentieth century, which Fugita and O'Brien believe is demonstrated by the high levels of education,
(25) income, and occupational mobility achieved by Japanese Americans. In addition, their data reveal that the character of the ethnic community itself changed: the integration of Sanseis into new professional communities and nonethnic voluntary
(30) associations meant at the very least that ethnic ties had to accommodate multiple and layered identities. Fugita and O'Brien themselves acknowledge that there has been a "weakening of Japanese American ethnic community life."

(35) Because of the social changes weakening the bonds of community, Fugita and O'Brien maintain that the community cohesion of Japanese Americans is notable not for its initial intensity but because "there remains a degree of involvement in the
(40) ethnic community surpassing that found in most other ethnic groups at similar points in their ethnic group life cycle." This comparative difference is important to Fugita and O'Brien, and they hypothesize that the Japanese American community
(45) persisted in the face of assimilation because of a particularly strong preexisting sense of "peoplehood." They argue that this sense of peoplehood extended beyond local and family ties.

Fugita and O'Brien's hypothesis illustrates a
(50) common problem in studies that investigate the history of ethnic community. Like historians who have studied European ethnic cultures in the United States, Fugita and O'Brien have explained persistence of ethnic community by citing a
(55) preexisting sense of national consciousness that is independent of how a group adapts to United States culture. However, it is difficult to prove, as Fugita and O'Brien have attempted to do, that a sense of peoplehood is a distinct phenomenon. Historians
(60) should instead attempt to identify directly the factors that sustain community cohesion in generations that have adapted to United States culture and been exposed to the pluralism of American life.

19. Which one of the following best summarizes the main point of the author of the passage?

(A) Fugita and O'Brien's study provides a comparison of the degree of involvement in ethnic community of different groups in the United States.
(B) Fugita and O'Brien's study describes the assimilation of three generations of Japanese Americans to United States culture.
(C) Fugita and O'Brien's study illustrates both a recent trend in historical studies of ethnic groups and a problem typical of that trend.
(D) Historical studies of ethnic preservation among Japanese Americans have done much to define the interpretive framework for studies of other ethnic groups.
(E) Historical studies are more concerned with the recent development of ethnic communities in the United States than with the process of adaptation to United States culture.

20. According to the passage, Fugita and O'Brien's data indicate which one of the following about the Japanese American ethnic community?

(A) Community bonds have weakened primarily as a result of occupational mobility by Japanese Americans.
(B) The community is notable because it has accommodated multiple and layered identities without losing its traditional intensity.
(C) Community cohesion is similar in intensity to the community cohesion of other ethnic groups that have been in the United States for the same period of time.
(D) Community involvement weakened during the second generation, but strengthened as the third generation regained an interest in cultural traditions.
(E) The nature of the community has been altered by Japanese American participation in new professional communities and nonethnic voluntary associations.

21. Which one of the following provides an example of a research study that has a conclusion most analogous to that argued for by the historians mentioned in line 4?

    (A) a study showing how musical forms brought from other countries have persisted in the United States
    (B) a study showing the organization and function of ethnic associations in the United States
    (C) a study showing how architectural styles brought from other countries have merged to form an American style
    (D) a study showing how cultural traditions have been preserved for generations in American ethnic neighborhoods
    (E) a study showing how different religious practices brought from other countries have been sustained in the United States

22. According to the passage, which one of the following is true about the focus of historical studies on ethnic groups in the United States?

    (A) Current studies are similar to earlier studies in claiming that a sense of peoplehood helps preserve ethnic community.
    (B) Current studies have clearly identified factors that sustain ethnic community in generations that have been exposed to the pluralism of American life.
    (C) Current studies examine the cultural practices that make up the American national character.
    (D) Earlier studies focused on how ethnic identities became transformed in the United States.
    (E) Earlier studies focused on the factors that led people to immigrate to the United States.

23. The author of the passage quotes Fugita and O'Brien in lines 39-42 most probably in order to

    (A) point out a weakness in their hypothesis about the strength of community ties among Japanese Americans
    (B) show how they support their claim about the notability of community cohesion for Japanese Americans
    (C) indicate how they demonstrate the high degree of adaptation of Japanese Americans to United States culture
    (D) suggest that they have inaccurately compared Japanese Americans to other ethnic groups in the United States
    (E) emphasize their contention that the Japanese American sense of peoplehood extended beyond local and family ties

24. The passage suggests that the author would be most likely to describe the hypothesis mentioned in line 49 as

    (A) highly persuasive
    (B) original but poorly developed
    (C) difficult to substantiate
    (D) illogical and uninteresting
    (E) too similar to earlier theories

25. The passage suggests which one of the following about the historians mentioned in line 51?

    (A) They have been unable to provide satisfactory explanations for the persistence of European ethnic communities in the United States.
    (B) They have suggested that European cultural practices have survived although the community ties of European ethnic groups have weakened.
    (C) They have hypothesized that European ethnic communities are based on family ties rather than on a sense of national consciousness.
    (D) They have argued that European cultural traditions have been transformed in the United States because of the pluralism of American life.
    (E) They have claimed that the community ties of European Americans are still as strong as they were when the immigrants first arrived.

26. As their views are discussed in the passage, Fugita and O'Brien would be most likely to agree with which one of the following?

    (A) The community cohesion of an ethnic group is not affected by the length of time it has been in the United States.
    (B) An ethnic group in the United States can have a high degree of adaptation to United States culture and still sustain strong community ties.
    (C) The strength of an ethnic community in the United States is primarily dependent on the strength of local and family ties.
    (D) High levels of education and occupational mobility necessarily erode the community cohesion of an ethnic group in the United States.
    (E) It has become increasingly difficult for ethnic groups to sustain any sense of ethnic identity in the pluralism of United States life.

Passage #3: September 1998 Questions 6-13

James Porter (1905-1970) was the first scholar to identify the African influence on visual art in the Americas, and much of what is known about the cultural legacy that African-American artists inherited
(5) from their African forebears has come to us by way of his work. Porter, a painter and art historian, began by studying African-American crafts of the eighteenth and nineteenth centuries. This research revealed that many of the household items created by African-American
(10) men and women—walking sticks, jugs, and textiles—displayed characteristics that linked them iconographically to artifacts of West Africa. Porter then went on to establish clearly the range of the cultural territory inherited by later African-American
(15) artists.

An example of this aspect of Porter's research occurs in his essay "Robert S. Duncanson, Midwestern Romantic-Realist." The work of Duncanson, a nineteenth-century painter of the Hudson River school,
(20) like that of his predecessor in the movement, Joshua Johnston, was commonly thought to have been created by a Euro-American artist. Porter proved definitively that both Duncanson and Johnston were of African ancestry. Porter published this finding and thousands of
(25) others in a comprehensive volume tracing the history of African-American art. At the time of its first printing in 1943, only two other books devoted exclusively to the accomplishments of African-American artists existed. Both of these books were written by Alain
(30) LeRoy Locke, a professor at the university where Porter also taught. While these earlier studies by Locke are interesting for being the first to survey the field, neither addressed the critical issue of African precursors; Porter's book addressed this issue,
(35) painstakingly integrating the history of African-American art into the larger history of art in the Americas without separating it from those qualities that gave it its unique ties to African artisanship. Porter may have been especially attuned to these ties because
(40) of his conscious effort to maintain them in his own paintings, many of which combine the style of the genre portrait with evidence of an extensive knowledge of the cultural history of various African peoples.

In his later years, Porter wrote additional chapters
(45) for later editions of his book, constantly revising and correcting his findings, some of which had been based of necessity on fragmentary evidence. Among his later achievements were his definitive reckoning of the birth year of the painter Patrick Reason, long a point of
(50) scholarly uncertainty, and his identification of an unmarked grave in San Francisco as that of the sculptor Edmonia Lewis. At his death, Porter left extensive notes for an unfinished project aimed at exploring the influence of African art on the art of the Western world
(55) generally, a body of research whose riches scholars still have not exhausted.

6. Which one of the following most accurately states the main idea of the passage?

(A) Because the connections between African-American art and other art in the Americas had been established by earlier scholars, Porter's work focused on showing African-American art's connections to African artisanship.
(B) In addition to showing the connections between African-American art and African artisanship, Porter's most important achievement was illustrating the links between African-American art and other art in the Americas.
(C) Despite the fact that his last book remains unfinished, Porter's work was the first to devote its attention exclusively to the accomplishments of African-American artists.
(D) Although showing the connections between African-American art and African artisanship, Porter's work concentrated primarily on placing African-American art in the context of Western art in general.
(E) While not the first body of scholarship to treat the subject of African-American art, Porter's work was the first to show the connections between African-American art and African artisanship.

7. The discussion of Locke's books is intended primarily to

(A) argue that Porter's book depended upon Locke's pioneering scholarship
(B) highlight an important way in which Porter's work differed from previous work in his field
(C) suggest an explanation for why Porter's book was little known outside academic circles
(D) support the claim that Porter was not the first to notice African influences in African-American art
(E) argue that Locke's example was a major influence on Porter's decision to publish his findings

8. The passage states which one of the following about the 1943 edition of Porter's book on African-American art?

(A) It received little scholarly attention at first.
(B) It was revised and improved upon in later editions.
(C) It took issue with several of Locke's conclusions.
(D) It is considered the definitive version of Porter's work.
(E) It explored the influence of African art on Western art in general.

9. Given the information in the passage, Porter's identification of the ancestry of Duncanson and Johnston provides conclusive evidence for which one of the following statements?

   (A) Some of the characteristics defining the Hudson River school are iconographically linked to West African artisanship.
   (B) Some of the works of Duncanson and Johnston are not in the style of the Hudson River school.
   (C) Some of the work of Euro-American painters displays similarities to African-American crafts of the eighteenth and nineteenth centuries.
   (D) Some of the works of the Hudson River school were done by African-American painters.
   (E) Some of the works of Duncanson and Johnston were influenced by West African artifacts.

10. Which one of the following can most reasonably be inferred from the passage about the study that Porter left unfinished at his death?

    (A) If completed, it would have contradicted some of the conclusions contained in his earlier book.
    (B) If completed, it would have amended some of the conclusions contained in his earlier book.
    (C) If completed, it would have brought up to date the comprehensive history of African-American art begun in his earlier book.
    (D) If completed, it would have expanded upon the project of his earlier book by broadening the scope of inquiry found in the earlier book.
    (E) If completed, it would have supported some of the theories put forth by Porter's contemporaries since the publication of his earlier book.

11. Which one of the following hypothetical observations is most closely analogous to the discoveries Porter made about African-American crafts of the eighteenth and nineteenth centuries?

    (A) Contemporary Haitian social customs have a unique character dependent on but different from both their African and French origins.
    (B) Popular music in the United States, some of which is based on African musical traditions, often influences music being composed on the African continent.
    (C) Many novels written in Canada by Chinese immigrants exhibit narrative themes very similar to those found in Chinese folktales.
    (D) Extensive Indian immigration to England has made traditional Indian foods nearly as popular there as the traditional English foods that had been popular there before Indian immigration.
    (E) Some Mexican muralists of the early twentieth century consciously imitated the art of native peoples as a response to the Spanish influences that had predominated in Mexican art.

12. The passage most strongly supports which one of the following inferences about Porter's own paintings?

    (A) They often contained figures or images derived from the work of African artisans.
    (B) They fueled his interest in pursuing a career in art history.
    (C) They were used in Porter's book to show the extent of African influence on African-American art.
    (D) They were a deliberate attempt to prove his theories about art history.
    (E) They were done after all of his academic work had been completed.

13. Based on the passage, which one of the following, if true, would have been most relevant to the project Porter was working on at the time of his death?

    (A) African-American crafts of the eighteenth and nineteenth centuries have certain resemblances to European folk crafts of earlier periods.
    (B) The paintings of some twentieth-century European artists prefigured certain stylistic developments in North African graphic art.
    (C) The designs of many of the quilts made by African-American women in the nineteenth century reflect designs of European trade goods.
    (D) After the movement of large numbers of African Americans to cities, the African influences in the work of many African-American painters increased.
    (E) Several portraits by certain twentieth-century European painters were modeled after examples of Central African ceremonial masks.

Passage #4: October 2000 Questions 8-13

Many educators in Canada and the United States advocate multicultural education as a means of achieving multicultural understanding. There are, however, a variety of proposals as to what multicultural
(5) education should consist of. The most modest of these proposals holds that schools and colleges should promote multicultural understanding by teaching about other cultures, teaching which proceeds from within the context of the majority culture. Students should
(10) learn about other cultures, proponents claim, but examination of these cultures should operate with the methods, perspectives, and values of the majority culture. These values are typically those of liberalism: democracy, tolerance, and equality of persons.
(15) Critics of this first proposal have argued that genuine understanding of other cultures is impossible if the study of other cultures is refracted through the distorting lens of the majority culture's perspective. Not all cultures share liberal values. Their value
(20) systems have arisen in often radically different social and historical circumstances, and thus, these critics argue, cannot be understood and adequately appreciated if one insists on approaching them solely from within the majority culture's perspective.
(25) In response to this objection, a second version of multicultural education has developed that differs from the first in holding that multicultural education ought to adopt a neutral stance with respect to the value differences among cultures. The values of one culture
(30) should not be standards by which others are judged; each culture should be taken on its own terms. However, the methods of examination, study, and explanation of cultures in this second version of multicultural education are still identifiably Western.
(35) They are the methods of anthropology, social psychology, political science, and sociology. They are, that is, methods which derive from the Western scientific perspective and heritage.
Critics of this second form of multicultural
(40) education argue as follows: The Western scientific heritage is founded upon an epistemological system that prizes the objective over the subjective, the logical over the intuitive, and the empirically verifiable over the mystical. The methods of social-scientific
(45) examination of cultures are thus already value laden; the choice to examine and understand other cultures by these methods involves a commitment to certain values such as objectivity. Thus, the second version of multicultural education is not essentially different from
(50) the first. Scientific discourse has a privileged place in Western cultures, but the discourses of myth, tradition, religion, and mystical insight are often the dominant forms of thought and language of non-Western cultures. To insist on trying to understand nonscientific
(55) cultures by the methods of Western science is not only distorting, but is also an expression of an attempt to maintain a Eurocentric cultural chauvinism: the chauvinism of science. According to this objection, it is only by adopting the (often nonscientific) perspectives
(60) and methods of the cultures studied that real understanding can be achieved.

8. Which one of the following most accurately states the main point of the passage?

(A) Proponents of two proposals for promoting multicultural understanding disagree about both the goal of multicultural education and the means for achieving this goal.
(B) Proponents of two proposals for promoting multicultural understanding claim that education should be founded upon an epistemological system that recognizes the importance of the subjective, the intuitive, and the mystical.
(C) Proponents of two proposals for promoting multicultural understanding claim that it is not enough to refrain from judging non-Western cultures if the methods used to study these cultures are themselves Western.
(D) Critics of two proposals for promoting multicultural understanding disagree about the extent to which a culture's values are a product of its social and historical circumstances.
(E) Critics of two proposals for promoting multicultural understanding claim these proposals are not value neutral and are therefore unable to yield a genuine understanding of cultures with a different value system.

9. Critics who raise the objection discussed in the second paragraph would be most likely to agree with which one of the following?

(A) The social and historical circumstances that give rise to a culture's values cannot be understood by members of a culture with different values.
(B) The historical and social circumstances of a culture can play an important role in the development of that culture's values.
(C) It is impossible for one culture to successfully study another culture unless it does so from more than one cultural perspective.
(D) Genuine understanding of another culture is impossible unless that culture shares the same cultural values.
(E) The values of liberalism cannot be adequately understood if we approach them solely through the methods of Western science.

10. Which one of the following most accurately describes the organization of the passage as a whole?

    (A) Difficulties in achieving a goal are contrasted with the benefits of obtaining that goal.
    (B) A goal is argued to be unrealizable by raising objections to the means proposed to achieve it.
    (C) Two means for achieving a goal are presented along with an objection to each.
    (D) Difficulties in achieving a goal are used to defend several radical revisions to that goal.
    (E) The desirability of a goal is used to defend against a number of objections to its feasibility.

11. The version of multicultural education discussed in the first paragraph is described as "modest" (line 5) most likely because it

    (A) relies on the least amount of speculation about non-Western cultures
    (B) calls for the least amount of change in the educational system
    (C) involves the least amount of Eurocentric cultural chauvinism
    (D) is the least distorting since it employs several cultural perspectives
    (E) deviates least from a neutral stance with respect to differences in values

12. Given the information in the passage, which one of the following would most likely be considered objectionable by proponents of the version of multicultural education discussed in the third paragraph?

    (A) a study of the differences between the moral codes of several Western and non-Western societies
    (B) a study of a given culture's literature to determine the kinds of personal characteristics the culture admires
    (C) a study that employs the methods of Western science to investigate a nonscientific culture
    (D) a study that uses the literary theories of one society to criticize the literature of a society that has different values
    (E) a study that uses the methods of anthropology and sociology to criticize the values of Western culture

13. Which one of the following, if true, would provide the strongest objection to the criticism in the passage of the second version of multicultural education?

    (A) It is impossible to adopt the perspectives and methods of a culture unless one is a member of that culture.
    (B) Many non-Western societies have value systems that are very similar to one another.
    (C) Some non-Western societies use their own value system when studying cultures that have different values.
    (D) Students in Western societies cannot understand their culture's achievements unless such achievements are treated as the subject of Western scientific investigations.
    (E) Genuine understanding of another culture is necessary for adequately appreciating that culture.

LAW

Law Passages

Passage #1: December 1996 Questions 9-16 66
Passage #2: June 1997 Questions 9-16 68
Passage #3: October 1997 Questions 6-13 70
Passage #4: June 1998 Questions 1-7 72
Passage #5: December 1998 Questions 1-7 74
Passage #6: June 1999 Questions 1-5 76
Passage #7: October 1999 Questions 22-27 78
Passage #8: December 1999 Questions 15-21 80
Passage #9: October 2000 Questions 1-7 82
Passage #10: December 2000 Questions 23-28 84
Passage #11: October 2001 Questions 21-26 86
Passage #12: June 2002 Questions 1-7 88
Passage #13: October 2002 Questions 9-14 90
Passage #14: June 2003 Questions 20-27 92

Regulation Passages

Passage #1: December 2001 Questions 21-26 94
Passage #2: December 2002 Questions 24-28 96

Passage #1: December 1996 Questions 9-16

What is "law"? By what processes do judges arrive at opinions, those documents that justify their belief that the "law" dictates a conclusion one way or the other? These are among the oldest
(5) questions in jurisprudence, debate about which has traditionally been dominated by representatives of two schools of thought: proponents of natural law, who see law as intertwined with a moral order independent of society's rules and mores, and legal
(10) positivists, who see law solely as embodying the commands of a society's ruling authority.

Since the early 1970s, these familiar questions have received some new and surprising answers in the legal academy. This novelty is in part a
(15) consequence of the increasing influence there of academic disciplines and intellectual traditions previously unconnected with the study of law. Perhaps the most influential have been the answers given by the Law and Economics school. According
(20) to these legal economists, law consists and ought to consist of those rules that maximize a society's material wealth and that abet the efficient operation of markets designed to generate wealth. More controversial have been the various answers
(25) provided by members of the Critical Legal Studies movement, according to whom law is one among several cultural mechanisms by which holders of power seek to legitimate their domination. Drawing on related arguments developed in anthropology,
(30) sociology, and history, the critical legal scholars contend that law is an expression of power, but not, as held by the positivists, the power of the legitimate sovereign government. Rather, it is an expression of the power of elites who may have
(35) no legitimate authority, but who are intent on preserving the privileges of their race, class, or gender.

In the mid-1970s, James Boyd White began to articulate yet another interdisciplinary response to
(40) the traditional questions, and in so doing spawned what is now known as the Law and Literature movement. White has insisted that law, particularly as it is interpreted in judicial opinions, should be understood as an essentially literary activity.
(45) Judicial opinions should be read and evaluated not primarily as political acts or as attempts to maximize society's wealth through efficient rules, but rather as artistic performances. And like all such performances, White argues, each judicial opinion
(50) attempts in its own way to promote a particular political or ethical value.

In the recent *Justice as Translation*, White argues that opinion-writing should be regarded as an act of "translation," and judges as "translators." As
(55) such, judges find themselves mediating between the authoritative legal text and the pressing legal problem that demands resolution. A judge must essentially "re-constitute" that text by fashioning a new one, which is faithful to the old text but also
(60) responsive to and informed by the conditions, constraints, and aspirations of the world in which the new legal problem has arisen.

9. Which one of the following best states the main idea of the passage?

(A) Within the last few decades, a number of novel approaches to jurisprudence have defined the nature of the law in diverse ways.
(B) Within the last few decades, changes in society and in the number and type of cases brought to court have necessitated new methods of interpreting the law.
(C) Of the many interdisciplinary approaches to jurisprudence that have surfaced in the last two decades, the Law and Literature movement is the most intellectually coherent.
(D) The Law and Literature movement, first articulated by James Boyd White in the mid-1970s, represents a synthesis of the many theories of jurisprudence inspired by the social sciences.
(E) Such traditional legal scholars as legal positivists and natural lawyers are increasingly on the defensive against attacks from younger, more progressive theorists.

10. According to the passage, judicial opinions have been described as each of the following EXCEPT:

(A) political statements
(B) arcane statements
(C) economic statements
(D) artistic performances
(E) acts of translation

11. Which one of the following statements is most compatible with the principles of the Critical Legal Studies movement as that movement is described in the passage?

    (A) Laws governing the succession of power at the death of a head of state represent a synthesis of legal precedents, specific situations, and the values of lawmakers.
    (B) Laws allowing income tax deductions for charitable contributions, though ostensibly passed by lawmakers, were devised by and are perpetuated by the rich.
    (C) Laws governing the tariffs placed on imported goods must favor the continuation of mutually beneficial trade arrangements, even at the expense of long-standing legal precedent.
    (D) Laws governing the treatment of the disadvantaged and powerless members of a given society are an accurate indication of that society's moral state.
    (E) Laws controlling the electoral processes of a representative democracy have been devised by lawmakers to ensure the continuation of that governmental system.

12. Which one of the following does the passage mention as a similarity between the Critical Legal Studies movement and the Law and Literature movement?

    (A) Both offer explanations of how elites maintain their hold on power.
    (B) Both are logical extensions of either natural law or legal positivism.
    (C) Both see economic and political primacy as the basis of all legitimate power.
    (D) Both rely on disciplines not traditionally connected with the study of law.
    (E) Both see the practice of opinion-writing as a mediating activity.

13. Which one of the following can be inferred from the passage about the academic study of jurisprudence before the 1970s?

    (A) It was concerned primarily with codifying and maintaining the privileges of elites.
    (B) It rejected theories that interpreted law as an expression of a group's power.
    (C) It seldom focused on how and by what authority judges arrived at opinions.
    (D) It was concerned primarily with the study of law as an economic and moral agent.
    (E) It was not concerned with such disciplines as anthropology and sociology.

14. Proponents of the Law and Literature movement would most likely agree with which one of the following statements concerning the relationship between the law and judges' written opinions?

    (A) The once-stable relationship between law and opinion-writing has been undermined by new and radical theoretical developments.
    (B) Only the most politically conservative of judges continue to base their opinions on natural law or on legal positivism.
    (C) The occurrence of different legal situations requires a judge to adopt diverse theoretical approaches to opinion-writing.
    (D) Different judges will not necessarily write the same sorts of opinions when confronted with the same legal situation.
    (E) Judges who subscribe to divergent theories of jurisprudence will necessarily render divergent opinions.

15. Which one of the following phrases best describes the meaning of "re-constitute" as that word is used in line 58 of the passage?

    (A) categorize and rephrase
    (B) investigate and summarize
    (C) interpret and refashion
    (D) paraphrase and announce
    (E) negotiate and synthesize

16. The primary purpose of the passage is to

    (A) identify differing approaches
    (B) discount a novel trend
    (C) advocate traditional methods
    (D) correct misinterpretations
    (E) reconcile seeming inconsistencies

Passage #2: June 1997 Questions 9-16

In recent years, a growing belief that the way society decides what to treat as true is controlled through largely unrecognized discursive practices has led legal reformers to examine the complex
(5) interconnections between narrative and law. In many legal systems, legal judgments are based on competing stories about events. Without having witnessed these events, judges and juries must validate some stories as true and reject others as false. This procedure is rooted
(10) in objectivism, a philosophical approach that has supported most Western legal and intellectual systems for centuries. Objectivism holds that there is a single neutral description of each event that is unskewed by any particular point of view and that has a privileged
(15) position over all other accounts. The law's quest for truth, therefore, consists of locating this objective description, the one that tells what really happened, as opposed to what those involved thought happened. The serious flaw in objectivism is that there is no such thing
(20) as the neutral, objective observer. As psychologists have demonstrated, all observers bring to a situation a set of expectations, values, and beliefs that determine what the observers are able to see and hear. Two individuals listening to the same story will hear
(25) different things, because they emphasize those aspects that accord with their learned experiences and ignore those aspects that are dissonate with their view of the world. Hence there is never any escape in life or in law from selective perception, or from subjective
(30) judgments based on prior experiences, values, and beliefs.
    The societal harm caused by the assumption of objectivist principles in traditional legal discourse is that, historically, the stories judged to be objectively
(35) true are those told by people who are trained in legal discourse, while the stories of those who are not fluent in the language of the law are rejected as false.
    Legal scholars such as Patricia Williams, Derrick Bell, and Mari Matsuda have sought empowerment for
(40) the latter group of people through the construction of alternative legal narratives. Objectivist legal discourse systematically disallows the language of emotion and experience by focusing on cognition in its narrowest sense. These legal reformers propose replacing such
(45) abstract discourse with powerful personal stories. They argue that the absorbing, nonthreatening structure and tone of personal stories may convince legal insiders for the first time to listen to those not fluent in legal language. The compelling force of personal narrative
(50) can create a sense of empathy between legal insiders and people traditionally excluded from legal discourse and, hence, from power. Such alternative narratives can shatter the complacency of the legal establishment and disturb its tranquility. Thus, the engaging power of
(55) narrative might play a crucial, positive role in the process of legal reconstruction by overcoming differences in background and training and forming a new collectivity based on emotional empathy.

9. Which one of the following best states the main idea of the passage?

(A) Some legal scholars have sought to empower people historically excluded from traditional legal discourse by instructing them in the forms of discourse favored by legal insiders.
(B) Some legal scholars have begun to realize the social harm caused by the adversarial atmosphere that has pervaded many legal systems for centuries.
(C) Some legal scholars have proposed alleviating the harm caused by the prominence of objectivist principles within legal discourse by replacing that discourse with alternative forms of legal narrative.
(D) Some legal scholars have contended that those who feel excluded from objectivist legal systems would be empowered by the construction of a new legal language that better reflected objectivist principles.
(E) Some legal scholars have argued that the basic flaw inherent in objectivist theory can be remedied by recognizing that it is not possible to obtain a single neutral description of a particular event.

10. According to the passage, which one of the following is true about the intellectual systems mentioned in line 11?

(A) They have long assumed the possibility of a neutral depiction of events.
(B) They have generally remained unskewed by particular points of view.
(C) Their discursive practices have yet to be analyzed by legal scholars.
(D) They accord a privileged position to the language of emotion and experience.
(E) The accuracy of their basic tenets has been confirmed by psychologists.

11. Which one of the following best describes the sense of "cognition" referred to in line 43 of the passage?

(A) logical thinking uninfluenced by passion
(B) the interpretation of visual cues
(C) human thought that encompasses all emotion and experience
(D) the reasoning actually employed by judges to arrive at legal judgments
(E) sudden insights inspired by the power of personal stories

12. It can be inferred from the passage that Williams, Bell, and Matsuda believe which one of the following to be a central component of legal reform?

    (A) incorporating into the law the latest developments in the fields of psychology and philosophy
    (B) eradicating from legal judgments discourse with a particular point of view
    (C) granting all participants in legal proceedings equal access to training in the forms and manipulation of legal discourse
    (D) making the law more responsive to the discursive practices of a wider variety of people
    (E) instilling an appreciation of legal history and methodology in all the participants in a legal proceeding

13. Which one of the following most accurately describes the author's attitude toward proposals to introduce personal stories into legal discourse?

    (A) strongly opposed
    (B) somewhat skeptical
    (C) ambivalent
    (D) strongly supportive
    (E) unreservedly optimistic

14. The passage suggests that Williams, Bell, and Matsuda would most likely agree with which one of the following statements regarding personal stories?

    (A) Personal stories are more likely to adhere to the principles of objectivism than are other forms of discourse.
    (B) Personal stories are more likely to deemphasize differences in background and training than are traditional forms of legal discourse.
    (C) Personal stories are more likely to restore tranquility to the legal establishment than are more adversarial forms of discourse.
    (D) Personal stories are more likely to lead to the accurate reconstruction of facts than are traditional forms of legal narrative.
    (E) Personal stories are more likely to be influenced by a person's expectations, values, and beliefs than are other forms of discourse.

15. Which one of the following statements about legal discourse in legal systems based on objectivism can be inferred from the passage?

    (A) In most Western societies, the legal establishment controls access to training in legal discourse.
    (B) Expertise in legal discourse affords power in most Western societies.
    (C) Legal discourse has become progressively more abstract for some centuries.
    (D) Legal discourse has traditionally denied the existence of neutral, objective observers.
    (E) Traditional legal discourse seeks to reconcile dissonant world views.

16. Those who reject objectivism would regard "the law's quest for truth" (lines 15-16) as most similar to which one of the following?

    (A) a hunt for an imaginary animal
    (B) the search for a valuable mineral among worthless stones
    (C) the painstaking assembly of a jigsaw puzzle
    (D) comparing an apple with an orange
    (E) the scientific analysis of a chemical compound

Passage #3: October 1997 Questions 6-13

Medievalists usually distinguish medieval public law from private law: the former was concerned with government and military affairs and the latter with the family, social status, and land transactions.
(5) Examination of medieval women's lives shows this distinction to be overly simplistic. Although medieval women were legally excluded from roles thus categorized as public, such as soldier, justice, jury member, or professional administrative official,
(10) women's control of land—usually considered a private or domestic phenomenon—had important political implications in the feudal system of thirteenth-century England. Since land equaled wealth and wealth equaled power, certain women
(15) exercised influence by controlling land. Unlike unmarried women (who were legally subject to their guardians) or married women (who had no legal identity separate from their husbands), women who were widows had autonomy with respect to
(20) acquiring or disposing of certain property, suing in court, incurring liability for their own debts, and making wills.

Although feudal lands were normally transferred through primogeniture (the eldest son inheriting all),
(25) when no sons survived, the surviving daughters inherited equal shares under what was known as partible inheritance. In addition to controlling any such land inherited from her parents and any bridal dowry—property a woman brought to the marriage
(30) from her own family—a widow was entitled to use of one-third of her late husband's lands. Called "dower" in England, this grant had greater legal importance under common law than did the bridal dowry; no marriage was legal unless the groom
(35) endowed the bride with this property at the wedding ceremony. In 1215 Magna Carta guaranteed a widow's right to claim her dower without paying a fine; this document also strengthened widows' ability to control land by prohibiting forced
(40) remarriage. After 1272 women could also benefit from jointure: the groom could agree to hold part or all of his lands jointly with the bride, so that if one spouse died, the other received these lands.

Since many widows had inheritances as well as
(45) dowers, widows were frequently the financial heads of the family; even though legal theory assumed the maintenance of the principle of primogeniture, the amount of land the widow controlled could exceed that of her son or of other male heirs. Anyone who
(50) held feudal land exercised authority over the people attached to the land—knights, rental tenants, and peasants—and had to hire estate administrators, oversee accounts, receive rents, protect tenants from outside encroachment, punish tenants for not paying
(55) rents, appoint priests to local parishes, and act as guardians of tenants' children and executors of their wills. Many married women fulfilled these duties as deputies for husbands away at court or at war, but widows could act on their own behalf. Widows'
(60) legal independence is suggested by their frequent appearance in thirteenth-century English legal records. Moreover, the scope of their sway is indicated by the fact that some controlled not merely single estates, but multiple counties.

6. Which one of the following best expresses the main idea of the passage?

(A) The traditional view of medieval women as legally excluded from many public offices fails to consider thirteenth-century women in England who were exempted from such restrictions because of their wealth and social status.

(B) The economic independence of women in thirteenth-century England was primarily determined not by their marital status, but by their status as heirs to their parents' estates.

(C) The laws and customs of the feudal system in thirteenth-century England enabled some women to exercise a certain amount of power despite their legal exclusion from most public roles.

(D) During the thirteenth century in England, widows gained greater autonomy and legal rights to their property than they had had in previous centuries.

(E) Widows in thirteenth-century England were able to acquire and dispose of lands through a number of different legal processes.

7. With which one of the following statements about the views held by the medievalists mentioned in line 1-2 would the author of the passage most probably agree?

    (A) The medieval role of landowner was less affected by thirteenth-century changes in law than these medievalists customarily have recognized.
    (B) The realm of law labeled public by these medievalists ultimately had greater political implications than that labeled private.
    (C) The amount of wealth controlled by medieval women was greater than these medievalists have recorded.
    (D) The distinction made by these medievalists between private law and public law fails to consider some of the actual legal cases of the period.
    (E) The distinction made by these medievalists between private and public law fails to address the political importance of control over land in the medieval era.

8. Which one of the following most accurately expresses the meaning of the word "sway" as it is used in line 62 of the passage?

    (A) vacillation
    (B) dominion
    (C) predisposition
    (D) inclination
    (E) mediation

9. Which one of the following most accurately describes the function of the second paragraph of the passage?

    (A) providing examples of specific historical events as support for the conclusion drawn in the third paragraph
    (B) narrating a sequence of events whose outcome is discussed in the third paragraph
    (C) explaining how circumstances described in the first paragraph could have occurred
    (D) describing the effects of an event mentioned in the first paragraph
    (E) evaluating the arguments of a group mentioned in the first paragraph

10. According to information in the passage, a widow in early thirteenth-century England could control more land than did her eldest son if

    (A) the widow had been granted the customary amount of dower land and the eldest son inherited the rest of the land
    (B) the widow had three daughters in addition to her eldest son
    (C) the principle of primogeniture had been applied in transferring the lands owned by the widow's late husband
    (D) none of the lands held by the widow's late husband had been placed in jointure
    (E) the combined amount of land the widow had acquired from her own family and from dower was greater than the amount inherited by her son

11. Which one of the following is mentioned in the passage as a reason why a married woman might have fulfilled certain duties associated with holding feudal land in thirteenth-century England?

    (A) the legal statutes set forth by Magna Carta
    (B) the rights a woman held over her inheritance during her marriage
    (C) the customary division of duties between husbands and wives
    (D) the absence of the woman's husband
    (E) the terms specified by the woman's jointure agreement

12. The phrase "in England" (line 32) does which one of the following?

    (A) It suggests that women in other countries also received grants of their husbands' lands.
    (B) It identifies a particular code of law affecting women who were surviving daughters.
    (C) It demonstrates that dower had greater legal importance in one European country than in others.
    (D) It emphasizes that women in one European country had more means of controlling property than did women in other European countries.
    (E) It traces a legal term back to the time at which it entered the language.

13. The primary purpose of the passage is to

    (A) explain a legal controversy of the past in light of modern theory
    (B) evaluate the economic and legal status of a particular historical group
    (C) resolve a scholarly debate about legal history
    (D) trace the historical origins of a modern economic situation
    (E) provide new evidence about a historical event

Passage #4: June 1998 Questions 1-7

Most office workers assume that the messages they send to each other via electronic mail are as private as a telephone call or a face-to-face meeting. That assumption is wrong. Although it is illegal in many
(5) areas for an employer to eavesdrop on private conversations or telephone calls—even if they take place on a company-owned telephone—there are no clear rules governing electronic mail. In fact, the question of how private electronic mail transmissions
(10) should be has emerged as one of the more complicated legal issues of the electronic age.

People's opinions about the degree of privacy that electronic mail should have vary depending on whose electronic mail system is being used and who is reading
(15) the messages. Does a government office, for example, have the right to destroy electronic messages created in the course of running the government, thereby denying public access to such documents? Some hold that government offices should issue guidelines that allow
(20) their staff to delete such electronic records, and defend this practice by claiming that the messages thus deleted already exist in paper versions whose destruction is forbidden. Opponents of such practices argue that the paper versions often omit such information as who
(25) received the messages and when they received them, information commonly carried on electronic mail systems. Government officials, opponents maintain, are civil servants; the public should thus have the right to review any documents created during the conducting of
(30) government business.

Questions about electronic mail privacy have also arisen in the private sector. Recently, two employees of an automotive company were discovered to have been communicating disparaging information about their
(35) supervisor via electronic mail. The supervisor, who had been monitoring the communication, threatened to fire the employees. When the employees filed a grievance complaining that their privacy had been violated, they were let go. Later, their court case for unlawful
(40) termination was dismissed; the company's lawyers successfully argued that because the company owned the computer system, its supervisors had the right to read anything created on it.

In some areas, laws prohibit outside interception of
(45) electronic mail by a third party without proper authorization such as a search warrant. However, these laws do not cover "inside" interception such as occurred at the automotive company. In the past, courts have ruled that interoffice communications may be
(50) considered private only if employees have a "reasonable expectation" of privacy when they send the messages. The fact is that no absolute guarantee of privacy exists in any computer system. The only solution may be for users to scramble their own
(55) messages with encryption codes; unfortunately, such complex codes are likely to undermine the principal virtue of electronic mail: its convenience.

1. Which one of the following statements most accurately summarizes the main point of the passage?

   (A) Until the legal questions surrounding the privacy of electronic mail in both the public and private sectors have been resolved, office workers will need to scramble their electronic mail messages with encryption codes.
   (B) The legal questions surrounding the privacy of electronic mail in the workplace can best be resolved by treating such communications as if they were as private as telephone conversations or face-to-face meetings.
   (C) Any attempt to resolve the legal questions surrounding the privacy of electronic mail in the workplace must take into account the essential difference between public-sector and private-sector business.
   (D) At present, in both the public and private sectors, there seem to be no clear general answers to the legal questions surrounding the privacy of electronic mail in the workplace.
   (E) The legal questions surrounding the privacy of electronic mail in the workplace can best be resolved by allowing supervisors in public-sector but not private-sector offices to monitor their employees' communications.

2. According to the passage, which one of the following best expresses the reason some people use to oppose the deletion of electronic mail records at government offices?

   (A) Such deletion reveals the extent of government's unhealthy obsession with secrecy.
   (B) Such deletion runs counter to the notion of government's accountability to its constituency.
   (C) Such deletion clearly violates the legal requirement that government offices keep duplicate copies of all their transactions.
   (D) Such deletion violates the government's own guidelines against destruction of electronic records.
   (E) Such deletion harms relations between government employees and their supervisors.

3. Which one of the following most accurately states the organization of the passage?

   (A) A problem is introduced, followed by specific examples illustrating the problem; a possible solution is suggested, followed by an acknowledgment of its shortcomings.
   (B) A problem is introduced, followed by explications of two possible solutions to the problem; the first solution is preferred to the second, and reasons are given for why it is the better alternative.
   (C) A problem is introduced, followed by analysis of the historical circumstances that helped bring the problem about; a possible solution is offered and rejected as being only a partial remedy.
   (D) A problem is introduced, followed by enumeration of various questions that need to be answered before a solution can be found; one possible solution is proposed and argued for.
   (E) A problem is introduced, followed by descriptions of two contrasting approaches to thinking about the problem; the second approach is preferred to the first, and reasons are given for why it is more likely to yield a successful solution.

4. Based on the passage, the author's attitude toward interception of electronic mail can most accurately be described as

   (A) outright disapproval of the practice
   (B) support for employers who engage in it
   (C) support for employees who lose their jobs because of it
   (D) intellectual interest in its legal issues
   (E) cynicism about the motives behind the practice

5. It can be inferred from the passage that the author would most likely hold which one of the following opinions about an encryption system that could encode and decode electronic mail messages with a single keystroke?

   (A) It would be an unreasonable burden on a company's ability to monitor electronic mail created by its employees.
   (B) It would significantly reduce the difficulty of attempting to safeguard the privacy of electronic mail.
   (C) It would create substantial legal complications for companies trying to prevent employees from revealing trade secrets to competitors.
   (D) It would guarantee only a minimal level of employee privacy, and so would not be worth the cost involved in installing such a system.
   (E) It would require a change in the legal definition of "reasonable expectation of privacy" as it applies to employer-employee relations.

6. Given the information in the passage, which one of the following hypothetical events is LEAST likely to occur?

   (A) A court rules that a government office's practice of deleting its electronic mail is not in the public's best interests.
   (B) A private-sector employer is found liable for wiretapping an office telephone conversation in which two employees exchanged disparaging information about their supervisor.
   (C) A court upholds the right of a government office to destroy both paper and electronic versions of its in-house documents.
   (D) A court upholds a private-sector employer's right to monitor messages sent between employees over the company's in-house electronic mail system.
   (E) A court rules in favor of a private-sector employee whose supervisor stated that in-house electronic mail would not be monitored but later fired the employee for communicating disparaging information via electronic mail.

7. The author's primary purpose in writing the passage is to

   (A) demonstrate that the individual right to privacy has been eroded by advances in computer technology
   (B) compare the legal status of electronic mail in the public and private sectors
   (C) draw an extended analogy between the privacy of electronic mail and the privacy of telephone conversations or face-to-face meetings
   (D) illustrate the complexities of the privacy issues surrounding electronic mail in the workplace
   (E) explain why the courts have not been able to rule definitively on the issue of the privacy of electronic mail

CHAPTER THREE: LAW

Passage #5: December 1998 Questions 1-7

The expansion of mass media has led to an explosion in news coverage of criminal activities to the point where it has become virtually impossible to find citizens who are unaware of the details of crimes
(5) committed in their communities. Since it is generally believed that people who know the facts of a case are more likely than those who do not to hold an opinion about the case, and that it is more desirable to empanel jurors who do not need to set aside personal prejudices
(10) in order to render a verdict, empaneling impartial juries has proven to be a daunting task in North American courts, particularly in trials involving issues or people of public interest.

Judges rely on several techniques to minimize
(15) partiality in the courtroom, including moving trials to new venues and giving specific instructions to juries. While many judges are convinced that these techniques work, many critics have concluded that they are ineffective. Change of venue, the critics argue, cannot
(20) shield potential jurors from pretrial publicity in widely reported cases. Nor, they claim, can judges' instructions to juries to ignore information learned outside the courtroom be relied upon; one critic characterizes such instruction as requiring of jurors
(25) "mental contortions which are beyond anyone's power to execute."

The remedy for partiality most favored by judges is *voir dire*, the questioning of potential jurors to determine whether they can be impartial. But critics
(30) charge that this method, too, is unreliable for a number of reasons. Some potential jurors, they argue, do not speak out during *voir dire* (French for "to speak the truth") because they are afraid to admit their prejudices, while others confess untruthfully to having
(35) prejudices as a way of avoiding jury duty. Moreover, some potential jurors underestimate their own knowledge, claiming ignorance of a case when they have read about it in newspapers or discussed it with friends. Finally, the critics argue, judges sometimes
(40) phrase questions in ways that indicate a desired response, and potential jurors simply answer accordingly.

These criticisms have been taken seriously enough by some countries that rely on juries, such as Canada
(45) and Great Britain, that they have abandoned *voir dire* except in unusual circumstances. But merely eliminating existing judicial remedies like *voir dire* does not really provide a solution to the problem of impartiality. It merely recognizes that the mass media
(50) have made total ignorance of criminal cases among jurors a virtual impossibility. But if a jury is to be truly impartial, it must be composed of informed citizens representative of the community's collective experience; today, this experience includes exposure to
(55) mass media. Impartiality does not reside in the mind of any one juror; it instead results from a process of deliberation among the many members of a panel of informed, curious, and even opinionated people.

1. Which one of the following most accurately expresses the main point of the passage?

    (A) Due to the expansion of mass media, traditional methods for ensuring the impartiality of jurors are flawed and must be eliminated so that other methods can be implemented.
    (B) Criticisms of traditional methods for ensuring the impartiality of jurors have led some countries to abandon these methods entirely.
    (C) Of the three traditional methods for ensuring the impartiality of jurors, *voir dire* is the most popular among judges but is also the most flawed.
    (D) *Voir dire* is ineffective at ensuring impartiality due to the latitude it offers potential jurors to misrepresent their knowledge of the cases they are called to hear.
    (E) Due to the expansion of mass media, solving the problem of minimizing partiality in the courtroom requires a redefinition of what constitutes an impartial jury.

2. One critic characterizes judges' instructions as requiring "mental contortions" (line 25) most likely because of a belief that jurors cannot be expected to

    (A) deliberate only on what they learn in a trial and not on what they knew beforehand
    (B) distinguish between pretrial speculation and the actual facts of a case
    (C) hear about a case before trial without forming an opinion about it
    (D) identify accurately the degree of prior knowledge they may possess about a case
    (E) protect themselves from widely disseminated pretrial publicity

3. The primary purpose of the third paragraph is to

   (A) propose a new method of ensuring impartiality
   (B) describe criticisms of one traditional method of ensuring impartiality
   (C) argue against several traditional methods of ensuring impartiality
   (D) explain why judges are wary of certain methods of ensuring impartiality
   (E) criticize the views of those who believe judges to be incapable of ensuring impartiality

4. With which one of the following statements would the author be most likely to agree?

   (A) Flaws in *voir dire* procedures make it unlikely that juries capable of rendering impartial decisions can be selected.
   (B) Knowledge of a case before it goes to trial offers individual jurors the best chance of rendering impartial decisions.
   (C) Jurors who bring prior opinions about a case to their deliberations need not decrease the chance of the jury's rendering an impartial decision.
   (D) Only juries consisting of people who bring no prior knowledge of a case to their deliberations are capable of rendering truly impartial decisions.
   (E) People who know the facts of a case are more opinionated about it than those who do not.

5. The passage suggests that a potential benefit of mass-media coverage on court cases is that it will

   (A) determine which facts are appropriate for juries to hear
   (B) improve the ability of jurors to minimize their biases
   (C) strengthen the process by which juries come to decisions
   (D) change the methods judges use to question potential jurors
   (E) increase potential jurors' awareness of their degree of bias

6. Which one of the following principles is most in keeping with the passage's argument?

   (A) Jurors should put aside their personal experiences when deliberating a case and base their decision only on the available information.
   (B) Jurors should rely on their overall experience when deliberating a case even when the case was subject to mass-media exposure before trial.
   (C) Jurors should make every effort when deliberating a case to ignore information about the case that they may have learned from the mass media.
   (D) Jurors should be selected to hear a case based on their degree of exposure to mass-media coverage of the case before trial.
   (E) Jurors should be selected to hear a case based on their capacity to refrain from reading or viewing mass-media coverage of the case while the trial is in progress.

7. Of the following, the author's primary purpose in writing the passage most likely is to

   (A) search for compromise between proponents and critics of *voir dire*
   (B) call attention to the effects of mass media on court proceedings
   (C) encourage judges to find new ways to ensure impartial jurors
   (D) debate critics who find fault with current *voir dire* procedures
   (E) argue for a change in how courts address the problem of impartiality

Passage #6: June 1999 Questions 1-5

Some Native American tribes have had difficulty establishing their land claims because the United States government did not recognize their status as tribes; therefore during the 1970s some Native Americans
(5) attempted to obtain such recognition through the medium of U.S. courts. In presenting these suits, Native Americans had to operate within a particular sphere of U.S. government procedure, that of its legal system, and their arguments were necessarily
(10) interpreted by the courts in terms the law could understand: e.g., through application of precedent or review of evidence. This process brought to light some of the differing perceptions and definitions that can exist between cultures whose systems of discourse are
(15) sometimes at variance.

In one instance, the entire legal dispute turned on whether the suing community—a group of Mashpee Wampanoag in the town of Mashpee, Massachusetts—constituted a tribe. The area had long been occupied by
(20) the Mashpee, who continued to have control over land use after the town's incorporation. But in the 1960s, after an influx of non-Mashpee people shifted the balance of political power in the town, the new residents were able to buy Mashpee-controlled land
(25) from the town and develop it for commercial or private use. The Mashpee's 1976 suit claimed that these lands were taken in violation of a statute prohibiting transfers of land from any tribe of Native Americans without federal approval. The town argued that the Mashpee
(30) were not a tribe in the sense intended by the statute and so were outside its protection. As a result, the Mashpee were required to demonstrate their status as a tribe according to a definition contained in an earlier ruling: a body of Native Americans "governing themselves
(35) under one leadership and inhabiting a particular territory."

The town claimed that the Mashpee were not self-governing and that they had no defined territory: the Mashpee could legally be self-governing, the town
(40) argued, only if they could show written documentation of such a system, and could legally inhabit territory only if they had precisely delineated its boundaries and possessed a deed to it. The Mashpee marshaled oral testimony against these claims, arguing that what the
(45) town perceived as a lack of evidence was simply information that an oral culture such as the Mashpee's would not have recorded in writing. In this instance, the disjunction between U.S. legal discourse and Mashpee culture—exemplified in the court's inability
(50) to "understand" the Mashpee's oral testimony as documentary evidence—rendered the suit unsuccessful. Similar claims have recently met with greater success, however, as U.S. courts have begun to acknowledge that the failure to accommodate differences in
(55) discourse between cultures can sometimes stand in the way of guaranteeing the fairness of legal decisions.

1. Which one of the following most completely and accurately expresses the main point of the passage?

    (A) Land claim suits such as the Mashpee's establish that such suits must be bolstered by written documentation if they are to succeed in U.S. courts.
    (B) Land claim suits such as the Mashpee's underscore the need for U.S. courts to modify their definition of "tribe."
    (C) Land claim suits such as the Mashpee's illustrate the complications that can result when cultures with different systems of discourse attempt to resolve disputes.
    (D) Land claim suits such as the Mashpee's point out discrepancies between what U.S. courts claim they will recognize as evidence and what forms of evidence they actually accept.
    (E) Land claim suits such as the Mashpee's bring to light the problems faced by Native American tribes attempting to establish their claims within a legal system governed by the application of precedent.

2. According to the passage, the Mashpee's lawsuit was based on their objection to

    (A) the increase in the non-Mashpee population of the town during the 1960s
    (B) the repeal of a statute forbidding land transfers without U.S. government approval
    (C) the loss of Mashpee control over land use immediately after the town's incorporation
    (D) the town's refusal to recognize the Mashpee's deed to the land in dispute
    (E) the sale of Mashpee-controlled land to non-Mashpee residents without U.S. government approval

3. The author's attitude toward the court's decision in the Mashpee's lawsuit is most clearly revealed by the author's use of which one of the following phrases?

   (A) "operate within a particular sphere" (lines 7-8)
   (B) "continued to have control" (line 20)
   (C) "required to demonstrate" (line 32)
   (D) "precisely delineated its boundaries" (line 42)
   (E) "failure to accommodate" (line 54)

4. Based on the passage, which one of the following can most reasonably be said to have occurred in the years since the Mashpee's lawsuit?

   (A) The Mashpee have now regained control over the land they inhabit.
   (B) Native American tribes have won all of their land claim suits in U.S. courts.
   (C) U.S. courts no longer abide by the statute requiring federal approval of certain land transfers.
   (D) U.S. courts have become more likely to accept oral testimony as evidence in land claim suits.
   (E) U.S. courts have changed their definition of what legally constitutes a tribe.

5. The passage is primarily concerned with

   (A) evaluating various approaches to solving a problem
   (B) illuminating a general problem by discussing a specific example
   (C) reconciling the differences in how two opposing sides approach a problem
   (D) critiquing an earlier solution to a problem in light of new information
   (E) reinterpreting an earlier analysis and proposing a new solution to the problem

Passage #7: October 1999 Questions 22-27

Until about 1970, anyone who wanted to write a comprehensive history of medieval English law as it actually affected women would have found a dearth of published books or articles concerned with specific
(5) legal topics relating to women and derived from extensive research in actual court records. This is a serious deficiency, since court records are of vital importance in discovering how the law actually affected women, as opposed to how the law was
(10) intended to affect them or thought to affect them. These latter questions can be answered by consulting such sources as treatises, commentaries, and statutes; such texts were what most scholars of the nineteenth and early twentieth centuries concentrated on whenever
(15) they did write about medieval law. But these sources are of little help in determining, for example, how often women's special statutory privileges were thwarted by intimidation or harassment, or how often women managed to evade special statutory limitations. And,
(20) quite apart from provisions designed to apply only, or especially, to women, they cannot tell us how general law affected the female half of the population—how women defendants and plaintiffs were treated in the courts in practice when they tried to exercise the rights
(25) they shared with men. Only quantitative studies of large numbers of cases would allow even a guess at the answers to these questions, and this scholarly work has been attempted by few.

One can easily imagine why. Most medieval
(30) English court records are written in Latin or Anglo-Norman French and have never been published. The sheer volume of material to be sifted is daunting: there are over 27,500 parchment pages in the common plea rolls of the thirteenth century alone, every page nearly
(35) three feet long, and written often front and back in highly stylized court hand. But the difficulty of the sources, while it might appear to explain why the relevant scholarship has not been undertaken, seems actually to have deterred few: the fact is that few
(40) historians have wanted to write anything approaching women's legal history in the first place. Most modern legal historians who have written on one aspect or another of special laws pertaining to women have begun with an interest in a legal idea or event or
(45) institution, not with a concern for how it affected women. Very few legal historians have started with an interest in women's history that they might have elected to pursue through various areas of general law. And the result of all this is that the current state of our
(50) scholarly knowledge relating to law and the medieval Englishwoman is still fragmentary at best, though the situation is slowly improving.

22. It can be inferred from the passage that the author believes which one of the following to be true of the sources consulted by nineteenth-century historians of medieval law?

(A) They are adequate to the research needs of a modern legal historian wishing to investigate medieval law.
(B) They are to be preferred to medieval legal sources, which are cumbersome and difficult to use.
(C) They lack fundamental relevance to the history of modern legal institutions and ideas.
(D) They provide relatively little information relevant to the issues with which writers of women's legal history ought most to concern themselves.
(E) They are valuable primarily because of the answers they can provide to some of the questions that have most interested writers of women's legal history.

23. Which one of the following best describes the organization of the first paragraph of the passage?

(A) The preparations necessary for the production of a particular kind of study are discussed, and reasons are given for why such preparations have not been undertaken until recently.
(B) A problem is described, a taxonomy of various kinds of questions relevant to its solution is proposed, and an evaluation regarding which of those questions would be most useful to answer is made.
(C) An example suggesting the nature of present conditions in a discipline is given, past conditions in that discipline are described, and a prediction is made regarding the future of the discipline.
(D) A deficiency is described, the specific nature of the deficiency is discussed, and a particular kind of remedy is asserted to be the sole possible means of correcting that deficiency.
(E) The resources necessary to the carrying out of a task are described, the inherent limitations of those resources are suggested by means of a list of questions, and a suggestion is made for overcoming these limitations.

24. According to the passage, quantitative studies of the kind referred to in line 25 can aid in determining

 (A) what were the stated intentions of those who wrote medieval statutes
 (B) what were the unconscious or hidden motives of medieval lawmakers with regard to women
 (C) what was the impact of medieval legal thought concerning women on the development of important modern legal ideas and institutions
 (D) how medieval women's lives were really affected by medieval laws
 (E) how best to categorize the masses of medieval documents relating to women

25. According to the passage, the sources consulted by legal scholars of the nineteenth and early twentieth centuries provided adequate information concerning which one of the following topics?

 (A) the intent of medieval English laws regarding women and the opinions of commentators concerning how those laws affected women
 (B) the overall effectiveness of English law in the medieval period and some aspects of the special statutes that applied to women only
 (C) the degree of probability that a woman defendant or plaintiff would win a legal case in medieval England
 (D) the degree to which the male relatives of medieval Englishwomen could succeed in preventing those women from exercising their legal rights
 (E) which of the legal rights theoretically shared by men and women were, in practice, guaranteed only to men

26. As used in lines 37-38, the phrase "the relevant scholarship" can best be understood as referring to which one of the following kinds of scholarly work?

 (A) linguistic studies of Anglo-Norman French and Latin undertaken in order to prepare for further study of medieval legal history
 (B) the editing and publication of medieval court records undertaken in order to facilitate the work of legal and other historians
 (C) quantitative studies of large numbers of medieval court cases undertaken in order to discover the actual effects of law on medieval women's lives
 (D) comparative studies of medieval statutes, treatises, and commentaries undertaken in order to discover the views and intentions of medieval legislators
 (E) reviews of the existing scholarly literature concerning women and medieval law undertaken as groundwork for the writing of a comprehensive history of medieval law as it applied to women

27. It can be inferred from the passage that, in the author's view, which one of the following factors is most responsible for the current deficiencies in our knowledge of women's legal history?

 (A) most modern legal historians' relative lack of interest in pursuing the subject
 (B) the linguistic and practical difficulties inherent in pursuing research relevant to such knowledge
 (C) a tendency on the part of most modern legal historians to rely too heavily on sources such as commentaries and treatises
 (D) the mistaken view that the field of women's legal history should be defined as the study of laws that apply only, or especially, to women
 (E) the relative scarcity of studies providing a comprehensive overview of women's legal history

Passage #8: December 1999 Questions 15-21

Philosopher Denise Meyerson views the Critical Legal Studies (CLS) movement as seeking to debunk orthodox legal theory by exposing its contradictions. However, Meyerson argues that CLS proponents tend
(5) to see contradictions where none exist, and that CLS overrates the threat that conflict poses to orthodox legal theory.

According to Meyerson, CLS proponents hold that the existence of conflicting values in the law implies
(10) the absence of any uniquely right solution to legal cases. CLS argues that these conflicting values generate equally plausible but opposing answers to any given legal question, and, consequently, that the choice between the conflicting answers must necessarily be
(15) arbitrary or irrational. Meyerson denies that the existence of conflicting values makes a case irresolvable, and asserts that at least some such cases can be resolved by ranking the conflicting values. For example, a lawyer's obligation to preserve a client's
(20) confidences may entail harming other parties, thus violating moral principle. This conflict can be resolved if it can be shown that in certain cases the professional obligation overrides ordinary moral obligations.

In addition, says Meyerson, even when the two
(25) solutions are equally compelling, it does not follow that the choice between them must be irrational. On the contrary, a solution that is not rationally required need not be unreasonable. Meyerson concurs with another critic that instead of concentrating on the choice
(30) between two compelling alternatives, we should rather reflect on the difference between both of these answers on the one hand, and some utterly unreasonable answer on the other—such as deciding a property dispute on the basis of which claimant is louder. The
(35) acknowledgment that conflicting values can exist, then, does not have the far-reaching implications imputed by CLS; even if some answer to a problem is not the only answer, opting for it can still be reasonable.

Last, Meyerson takes issue with the CLS charge
(40) that legal formalism, the belief that there is a quasi-deductive method capable of giving solutions to problems of legal choice, requires objectivism, the belief that the legal process has moral authority. Meyerson claims that showing the law to be
(45) unambiguous does not demonstrate its legitimacy: consider a game in which participants compete to steal the item of highest value from a shop; while a person may easily identify the winner in terms of the rules, it does not follow that the person endorses the rules of
(50) the game. A CLS scholar might object that legal cases are unlike games, in that one cannot merely apply the rules without appealing to, and therefore endorsing, external considerations of purpose, policy, and value. But Meyerson replies that such considerations may be
(55) viewed as part of, not separate from, the rules of the game.

15. Which one of the following best expresses the main idea of the passage?

(A) The arguments of the Critical Legal Studies movement are under attack not only by legal theorists, but also by thinkers in related areas such as philosophy.
(B) In critiquing the Critical Legal Studies movement, Meyerson charges that the positions articulated by the movement's proponents overlook the complexity of actual legal dilemmas.
(C) Meyerson objects to the propositions of the Critical Legal Studies movement because she views them as being self-contradictory.
(D) Meyerson poses several objections to the tenets of the Critical Legal Studies movement, but her most important argument involves constructing a hierarchy of conflicting values.
(E) Meyerson seeks to counter the claims that are made by proponents of the Critical Legal Studies movement in their effort to challenge conventional legal theory.

16. The primary purpose of the reference to a game in the last paragraph is to

(A) provide an example of how a principle has previously been applied
(B) demonstrate a point by means of an analogy
(C) emphasize the relative unimportance of an activity
(D) contrast two situations by exaggerating their differences
(E) dismiss an idea by portraying it as reprehensible

17. The author's primary purpose in the passage is to

    (A) evaluate divergent legal doctrines
    (B) explain how a controversy arose
    (C) advocate a new interpretation of legal tradition
    (D) describe a challenge to a school of thought
    (E) refute claims made by various scholars

18. It can be inferred from the passage that Meyerson would be most likely to agree with which one of the following statements about "external considerations" (line 53)?

    (A) How one determines the extent to which these considerations are relevant depends on one's degree of belief in the legal process.
    (B) The extent to which these considerations are part of the legal process depends on the extent to which the policies and values can be endorsed.
    (C) When these considerations have more moral authority than the law, the former should outweigh the latter.
    (D) If one uses these considerations in determining a legal solution, one is assuming that the policies and values are desirable.
    (E) Whether these considerations are separate from or integral to the legal process is a matter of debate.

19. The phrase "far-reaching implications" (line 36) refers to the idea that

    (A) any choice made between conflicting solutions to a legal question will be arbitrary
    (B) every legal question will involve the consideration of a set of values
    (C) two or more alternative solutions to a legal question may carry equal moral weight
    (D) no legal question will have a single correct answer
    (E) the most relevant criterion for judging solutions is the degree of rationality they possess

20. Which one of the following most accurately describes the organization of the final paragraph in the passage?

    (A) A criticism is identified and its plausibility is investigated.
    (B) The different arguments made by two opponents of a certain viewpoint are advanced.
    (C) The arguments for and against a certain position are outlined, then a new position is offered to reconcile them.
    (D) A belief is presented and its worth is debated on the basis of its practical consequences.
    (E) Two different solutions are imagined in order to summarize a controversy.

21. It can be inferred from the passage that proponents of the Critical Legal Studies movement would be most likely to hold which one of the following views about the law?

    (A) It incorporates moral principles in order to yield definitive solutions to legal problems.
    (B) It does not necessarily imply approval of any policies or values.
    (C) It is insufficient in itself to determine the answer to a legal question.
    (D) It is comparable to the application of rules in a game.
    (E) It can be used to determine the best choice between conflicting values.

Passage #9: October 2000 Questions 1-7

Is it necessary for defense lawyers to believe that the clients they defend are innocent of the charges against them? Some legal scholars hold that lawyers' sole obligation is to provide the best defense they are
(5) capable of, claiming that in democratic societies all people accused of crimes are entitled to the best possible legal representation. They argue that lawyers have no right to judge defendants because it is the job of the courts to determine guilt or innocence and the
(10) job of the lawyer to represent the defendant before the court. They believe that the lawyer's responsibility is to state those facts that will assist each client's case, construct sound arguments based on these facts, and identify flaws in the arguments of opposing counsel.
(15) According to these scholars, the lawyer's role is not to express or act on personal opinions but to act as an advocate, saying only what defendants would say if they possessed the proper training or resources with which to represent themselves.
(20) But such a position overlooks the fact that the defense lawyer's obligation is twofold: to the defendant, certainly, but no less so to the court and, by extension, to society. For this reason, lawyers, great as their obligation to defendants is, should not, as officers
(25) of the court, present to the court assertions that they know to be false. But by the same principle, lawyers who are convinced that their clients are guilty should not undertake to demonstrate their innocence. Guilty defendants should not be entitled to false or insincere
(30) representation. When lawyers know with certainty that a defendant is guilty, it is their duty not to deny this. Rather, they should appraise the case as much as possible in their client's favor, after giving due consideration to the facts on the other side, and then
(35) present any extenuating circumstances and argue for whatever degree of leniency in sentencing they sincerely believe is warranted. In cases where it is uncertain whether the client is guilty but the lawyer sincerely believes the client may well be innocent, the
(40) lawyer should of course try to prove that the client is innocent.

The lawyer's obligation to the court and to society also ultimately benefits the defendant, because the "best defense" can only truly be provided by an
(45) advocate who, after a careful analysis of the facts, is convinced of the merits of the case. The fact that every client is entitled to a defense does not mean that defense lawyers should take every case they are offered. Lawyers should not be mere mouthpieces for a
(50) defendant but instead advocates for the rights of the defendant given the facts of the case.

1. Which one of the following most accurately expresses the main idea of the passage?

    (A) Some legal scholars defend a morally questionable view that defense lawyers' sole obligation to their clients is to provide the best defense, while it is the court's job to determine guilt or innocence.
    (B) Defense lawyers should put aside personal judgments about their clients' guilt when determining how best to proceed when representing a client.
    (C) In a democracy, all persons accused of crimes have a right to an attorney who will state the facts, construct sound arguments, and identify flaws in the arguments of opposing counsel.
    (D) Lawyers should be mindful of their duty to society as well as to their clients and base the decision as to whether, and how, to defend a client on the facts of the case.
    (E) Defense attorneys are obligated to defend clients who request their professional services, especially when the attorney is absolutely convinced of the client's innocence.

2. Which one of the following most accurately describes the author's attitude toward the twofold obligation introduced in lines 20-23?

    (A) confident that it enables defense lawyers to balance their competing responsibilities to the court and to society
    (B) certain that it prevents defense lawyers from representing clients whom they know to be guilty
    (C) satisfied that it helps defense lawyers to uncover the relevant facts of a case
    (D) pleased that it does not interfere with common defense strategies used by defense lawyers
    (E) convinced that it does not represent a conflict of interest for defense lawyers

3. Which one of the following sentences would most logically begin a paragraph immediately following the end of the passage?

   (A) In keeping with this role, defense lawyers should base their cases upon the foundations of honesty, substantive accuracy, and selectivity.
   (B) Therefore, the practice of law remains morally dubious, in that misrepresentation may achieve acquittal for an attorney's client.
   (C) Consequently, the defendant's right to legal representation varies from case to case, depending on the severity of the alleged crime and the defense lawyer's personal interpretation of the case.
   (D) Thus, the lawyers' obligations are threefold—to be faithful to the dictates of the court, society, and themselves by proving their professional worth in securing acquittal for the clients whom they represent.
   (E) Therefore, judges or other officials of the court should interrogate defense attorneys regarding any prior knowledge they may have of their clients' innocence or guilt.

4. According to the passage, the legal scholars mentioned in lines 15-19 believe that it is a defense lawyer's role to be

   (A) a source of legal information that can help a jury to reach decisions that are fair and equitable
   (B) a thorough investigator of all relevant evidence
   (C) a diligent representative of the client's position
   (D) a facilitator and expediter of the cause of justice
   (E) an energetic advocate of the client's right to legal representation

5. The relationship of the information contained in the two sentences at lines 28-31 to that in the sentence at lines 7-11 can most accurately be described as

   (A) no significant relationship because they represent two unrelated factual statements
   (B) the author's opinion opposing another opinion reported by the author in the earlier lines
   (C) a hypothetical situation supporting a statement reported by the author in the earlier lines
   (D) agreement in general with the earlier position but disagreement over the particulars
   (E) essentially equivalent assertions arising from different perspectives

6. It can be inferred from the passage that the author holds that a defense attorney who argues in court that a client is innocent

   (A) should sincerely believe that the client may be innocent
   (B) would be right to do so even if the attorney knows that the client is actually guilty
   (C) is assuming the role of mouthpiece for the client
   (D) has favored the obligation to the client over that to society
   (E) has typically not researched the facts of the case thoroughly

7. The primary purpose of the passage is to

   (A) show that ethical dilemmas in the legal profession can complicate the defense lawyer's role
   (B) argue that the defense lawyer's duty to the court and society complements effective legal representation for the client
   (C) explain why the actual guilt or innocence of a defendant is not an important issue to many defense attorneys
   (D) discuss some of the issues that a defense lawyer must resolve prior to accepting a case
   (E) reveal how the practice of law strengthens the values and principles of democratic societies

Passage #10: December 2000 Questions 23-28

By the time Bentham turned his interest to the subject, late in the eighteenth century, most components of modern evidence law had been assembled. Among common-law doctrines regarding
(5) evidence there were, however, principles that today are regarded as bizarre; thus, a well-established (but now abandoned) rule forbade the parties to a case from testifying. Well into the nineteenth century, even defendants in criminal cases were denied the right to
(10) testify to facts that would prove their innocence.

Although extreme in its irrationality, this proscription was in other respects quite typical of the law of evidence. Much of that law consisted of rules excluding relevant evidence, usually on some rational
(15) grounds. Hearsay evidence was generally excluded because absent persons could not be cross-examined. Yet such evidence was mechanically excluded even where out-of-court statements were both relevant and reliable, but the absent persons could not appear in
(20) court (for example, because they were dead).

The morass of evidentiary technicalities often made it unlikely that the truth would emerge in a judicial contest, no matter how expensive and protracted. Reform was frustrated both by the vested interests of
(25) lawyers and by the profession's reverence for tradition and precedent. Bentham's prescription was revolutionary: virtually all evidence tending to prove or disprove the issue in dispute should be admissible. Narrow exceptions were envisioned: instances in
(30) which the trouble or expense of presenting or considering proof outweighed its value, confessions to a Catholic priest, and a few other instances.

One difficulty with Bentham's nonexclusion principle is that some kinds of evidence are inherently
(35) unreliable or misleading. Such was the argument underlying the exclusions of interested-party testimony and hearsay evidence. Bentham argued that the character of evidence should be weighed by the jury: the alternative was to prefer ignorance to knowledge.
(40) Yet some evidence, although relevant, is actually more likely to produce a false jury verdict than a true one. To use a modern example, evidence of a defendant's past bank robberies is excluded, since the prejudicial character of the evidence substantially outweighs its
(45) value in helping the jury decide correctly. Further, in granting exclusions such as sacramental confessions, Bentham conceded that competing social interests or values might override the desire for relevant evidence. But then, why not protect conversations between social
(50) workers and their clients, or parents and children?

Despite concerns such as these, the approach underlying modern evidence law began to prevail soon after Bentham's death: relevant evidence should be admitted unless there are clear grounds of policy for
(55) excluding it. This clear-grounds proviso allows more exclusions than Bentham would have liked, but the main thrust of the current outlook is Bentham's own nonexclusion principle, demoted from a rule to a presumption.

23. Which one of the following is the main idea of the passage?

(A) Bentham questioned the expediency of modern rules of legal evidence.
(B) Bentham's proposed reform of rules of evidence was imperfect but beneficial.
(C) Bentham's nonexclusion principle should be reexamined in the light of subsequent developments.
(D) Rules of legal evidence inevitably entail imperfect mediations of conflicting values and constraints.
(E) Despite their impairment of judicial efficiency, rules of legal evidence are resistant to change.

24. The author's attitude toward eighteenth-century lawyers can best be described as

(A) sympathetic
(B) critical
(C) respectful
(D) scornful
(E) ambivalent

25. The author mentions "conversations between social workers and their clients" (lines 49-50) most probably in order to

(A) suggest a situation in which application of the nonexclusion principle may be questionable
(B) cite an example of objections that were raised to Bentham's proposed reform
(C) illustrate the conflict between competing social interests
(D) demonstrate the difference between social interests and social values
(E) emphasize that Bentham's exceptions to the nonexclusion principle covered a wide range of situations

26. Which one of the following statements concerning the history of the law of evidence is supported by information in the passage?

    (A) Common-law rules of evidence have been replaced by modern principles.
    (B) Modern evidence law is less rigid than was eighteenth-century evidence law.
    (C) Some current laws regarding evidence do not derive from common-law doctrines.
    (D) The late eighteenth century marked the beginning of evidence law.
    (E) Prior to the eighteenth century, rules of evidence were not based on common law.

27. The passage is primarily concerned with which one of the following?

    (A) suggesting the advantages and limitations of a legal reform
    (B) summarizing certain deficiencies of an outmoded legal system
    (C) justifying the apparent inadequacies of current evidence law
    (D) detailing objections to the nonexclusion principle
    (E) advocating reexamination of a proposal that has been dismissed by the legal profession

28. According to the fourth paragraph of the passage, what specifically does Bentham characterize as preference of ignorance to knowledge?

    (A) uncritical acceptance of legal conventions
    (B) failure to weigh the advantages of legal reform
    (C) exclusion of sacramental confessions
    (D) refusal to allow the jury to hear and assess relevant testimony
    (E) rejection of exceptions to Bentham's nonexclusion principle

Passage #11: October 2001 Questions 21-26

Ronald Dworkin argues that judges are in danger of uncritically embracing an erroneous theory known as legal positivism because they think the only alternative is a theory that they (and Dworkin) see as clearly
(5) unacceptable—natural law. The latter theory holds that judges ought to interpret the law by consulting their own moral convictions, even if this means ignoring the letter of the law and the legal precedents for its interpretation. Dworkin regards this as an
(10) impermissible form of judicial activism that arrogates to judges powers properly reserved for legislators.

Legal positivism, the more popular of the two theories, holds that law and morality are wholly distinct. The meaning of the law rests on social
(15) convention in the same way as does the meaning of a word. Dworkin's view is that legal positivists regard disagreement among jurists as legitimate only if it arises over what the underlying convention is, and it is to be resolved by registering a consensus, not by
(20) deciding what is morally right. In the same way, disagreement about the meaning of a word is settled by determining how people actually use it, and not by deciding what it ought to mean. Where there is no consensus, there is no legal fact of the matter. The
(25) judge's interpretive role is limited to discerning this consensus, or the absence thereof.

According to Dworkin, this account is incompatible with the actual practice of judges and lawyers, who act as if there is a fact of the matter even
(30) in cases where there is no consensus. The theory he proposes seeks to validate this practice without falling into what Dworkin correctly sees as the error of natural law theory. It represents a kind of middle ground between the latter and legal positivism. Dworkin
(35) stresses the fact that there is an internal logic to a society's laws and the general principles they typically embody. An interpretation that conforms to these principles may be correct even if it is not supported by a consensus. Since these general principles may
(40) involve such moral concepts as justice and fairness, judges may be called upon to consult their own moral intuitions in arriving at an interpretation. But this is not to say that judges are free to impose their own morality at will, without regard to the internal logic of the laws.

(45) The positivist's mistake, as Dworkin points out, is assuming that the meaning of the law can only consist in what people think it means, whether these people be the original authors of the law or a majority of the interpreter's peers. Once we realize, as Dworkin does,
(50) that the law has an internal logic of its own that constrains interpretation, we open up the possibility of improving upon the interpretations not only of our contemporaries but of the original authors.

21. Which one of the following most accurately expresses the main point of the passage?

(A) Dworkin regards natural law theory as a middle ground between legal positivism and judicial activism.
(B) Dworkin holds that judicial interpretations should not be based solely on identifying a consensus or solely on moral intuition, but should be consistent with the reasoning that underlies the law.
(C) Dworkin argues that the internal logic of the law should generally guide judges except in instances where consensus is registered or judges have strong moral intuitions.
(D) Dworkin's theory of legal interpretation is based on borrowing equally from natural law theory and legal positivism.
(E) Dworkin validates judges' dependence on moral intuition, reason, and the intent of the authors of a law, but only in cases where a social consensus is not present.

22. What is the main purpose of the second paragraph?

(A) to explain why legal positivism is so popular
(B) to evaluate the theory of legal positivism
(C) to discuss how judicial consensus is determined
(D) to identify the basic tenets of legal positivism
(E) to argue in favor of the theory of legal positivism

23. Which one of the following most accurately characterizes the author's attitude toward Dworkin's theory?

(A) confident endorsement of its central assertions
(B) caution about its potential for justifying some forms of judicial activism
(C) modest expectation that some of its claims will be found to be unwarranted
(D) quiet conviction that its importance derives only from its originality
(E) enthusiasm that it will replace legal positivism as the most popular theory of legal interpretation

24. According to the passage, which one of the following is a goal of Dworkin's theory of legal interpretation?

   (A) to evaluate previous legal interpretations by judges influenced by legal positivism
   (B) to dispute the notion that social consensus plays any role in legal interpretation
   (C) to provide a theoretical argument against the use of moral intuition in legal interpretation
   (D) to argue that legal decisions must be based on the principles of the original authors of the laws
   (E) to validate theoretically the method commonly used by judges in practice

25. The passage suggests that Dworkin would be most likely to agree with which one of the following statements?

   (A) Judges and lawyers too often act as though there is a fact of the matter in legal cases.
   (B) Judges should not use their moral intuition when it conflicts with the intentions of those legislators who authored the law being interpreted.
   (C) Legal positivism is a more popular theory than natural law theory because legal positivism simplifies the judge's role.
   (D) If there is consensus about how to interpret a law, then jurists should not examine the internal logic of the law being interpreted.
   (E) Legal positivists misunderstand the role of moral intuition in legal interpretation.

26. It can be inferred that legal positivists, as described in the passage, agree with which one of the following statements?

   (A) Judges sometimes ought to be allowed to use personal moral convictions as a basis for a legal interpretation.
   (B) Disagreements about the meaning of a law are never legitimate.
   (C) The ultimate standard of interpretation is the logic of the law itself, not moral intuition.
   (D) The meaning of a law derives from jurists' interpretations of that law.
   (E) There is no legal fact of the matter when jurists have differing moral convictions about an issue.

Passage #12: June 2002 Questions 1-7

The jury trial is one of the handful of democratic institutions that allow individual citizens, rather than the government, to make important societal decisions. A crucial component of the jury trial, at least in serious
(5) criminal cases, is the rule that verdicts be unanimous among the jurors (usually twelve in number). Under this requirement, dissenting jurors must either be convinced of the rightness of the prevailing opinion, or, conversely, persuade the other jurors to change their
(10) minds. In either instance, the unanimity requirement compels the jury to deliberate fully and truly before reaching its verdict. Critics of the unanimity requirement, however, see it as a costly relic that extends the deliberation process and sometimes, in a
(15) hung (i.e., deadlocked) jury, brings it to a halt at the hands of a single, recalcitrant juror, forcing the judge to order a retrial. Some of these critics recommend reducing verdict requirements to something less than unanimity, so that one or even two dissenting jurors
(20) will not be able to force a retrial.

But the material costs of hung juries do not warrant losing the benefit to society of the unanimous verdict. Statistically, jury trials are relatively rare; the vast majority of defendants do not have the option of a jury
(25) trial or elect to have a trial without a jury—or they plead guilty to the original or a reduced charge. And the incidence of hung juries is only a small fraction of the already small fraction of cases that receive a jury trial. Furthermore, that juries occasionally deadlock
(30) does not demonstrate a flaw in the criminal justice system, but rather suggests that jurors are conscientiously doing the job they have been asked to do. Hung juries usually occur when the case is very close—that is, when neither side has presented
(35) completely convincing evidence—and although the unanimity requirement may sometimes lead to inconclusive outcomes, a hung jury is certainly preferable to an unjust verdict.

Requiring unanimity provides a better chance that a
(40) trial, and thus a verdict, will be fair. Innocent people are already occasionally convicted—perhaps in some cases because jurors presume that anyone who has been brought to trial is probably guilty—and eliminating the unanimity requirement would only
(45) increase the opportunity for such mistakes. Furthermore, if a juror's dissenting opinion can easily be dismissed, an important and necessary part of the deliberation process will be lost, for effective deliberation requires that each juror's opinion be given
(50) a fair hearing. Only then can the verdict reached by the jury be said to represent all of its members, and if even one juror has doubts that are dismissed out of hand, society's confidence that a proper verdict has been reached would be undermined.

1. Which one of the following most accurately states the main point of the passage?

(A) Because trials requiring juries are relatively rare, the usefulness of the unanimity requirement does not need to be reexamined.
(B) The unanimity requirement should be maintained because most hung juries are caused by irresponsible jurors rather than by any flaws in the requirement.
(C) The problem of hung juries is not a result of flaws in the justice system but of the less than convincing evidence presented in some cases.
(D) The unanimity requirement should be maintained, but it is only effective if jurors conscientiously do the job they have been asked to do.
(E) Because its material costs are outweighed by what it contributes to the fairness of jury trials, the unanimity requirement should not be rescinded.

2. Which one of the following most accurately describes the author's attitude toward the unanimity requirement?

   (A) cursory appreciation
   (B) neutral interest
   (C) cautious endorsement
   (D) firm support
   (E) unreasoned reverence

3. Which one of the following principles can most clearly be said to underlie the author's arguments in the third paragraph?

   (A) The risk of unjust verdicts is serious enough to warrant strong measures to avoid it.
   (B) Fairness in jury trials is crucial and so judges must be extremely thorough in order to ensure it.
   (C) Careful adherence to the unanimity requirement will eventually eliminate unjust verdicts.
   (D) Safeguards must be in place because not all citizens called to jury duty perform their role responsibly.
   (E) The jury system is inherently flawed and therefore unfairness cannot be eliminated but only reduced.

4. Which one of the following sentences could most logically be added to the end of the last paragraph of the passage?

   (A) It is not surprising, then, that the arguments presented by the critics of the unanimity requirement grow out of a separate tradition from that embodied in the unanimity requirement.
   (B) Similarly, if there is a public debate concerning the unanimity requirement, public faith in the requirement will be strengthened.
   (C) The opinion of each juror is as essential to the pursuit of justice as the universal vote is to the functioning of a true democracy.
   (D) Unfortunately, because some lawmakers have characterized hung juries as intolerable, the integrity of the entire legal system has been undermined.
   (E) But even without the unanimity requirement, fair trials and fair verdicts will occur more frequently as the methods of prosecutors and defense attorneys become more scientific.

5. Which one of the following could replace the term "recalcitrant" (line 16) without a substantial change in the meaning of the critics' claim?

   (A) obstinate
   (B) suspicious
   (C) careful
   (D) conscientious
   (E) naive

6. The author explicitly claims that which one of the following would be a result of allowing a juror's dissenting opinion to be dismissed?

   (A) Only verdicts in very close cases would be affected.
   (B) The responsibility felt by jurors to be respectful to one another would be lessened.
   (C) Society's confidence in the fairness of the verdicts would be undermined.
   (D) The problem of hung juries would not be solved but would surface less frequently.
   (E) An important flaw thus would be removed from the criminal justice system.

7. It can be inferred from the passage that the author would be most likely to agree with which one of the following?

   (A) Hung juries most often result from an error in judgment on the part of one juror.
   (B) Aside from the material costs of hung juries, the criminal justice system has few flaws.
   (C) The fact that jury trials are so rare renders any flaws in the jury system insignificant.
   (D) Hung juries are acceptable and usually indicate that the criminal justice system is functioning properly.
   (E) Hung juries most often occur when one juror's opinion does not receive a fair hearing.

Passage #13: October 2002 Questions 9-14

Intellectual authority is defined as the authority of arguments that prevail by virtue of good reasoning and do not depend on coercion or convention. A contrasting notion, institutional authority, refers to the power of
(5) social institutions to enforce acceptance of arguments that may or may not possess intellectual authority. The authority wielded by legal systems is especially interesting because such systems are institutions that nonetheless aspire to a purely intellectual authority.
(10) One judge goes so far as to claim that courts are merely passive vehicles for applying the intellectual authority of the law and possess no coercive powers of their own.
   In contrast, some critics maintain that whatever
(15) authority judicial pronouncements have is exclusively institutional. Some of these critics go further, claiming that intellectual authority does not really exist—i.e., it reduces to institutional authority. But it can be countered that these claims break down when a
(20) sufficiently broad historical perspective is taken: Not all arguments accepted by institutions withstand the test of time, and some well-reasoned arguments never receive institutional imprimatur. The reasonable argument that goes unrecognized in its own time
(25) because it challenges institutional beliefs is common in intellectual history; intellectual authority and institutional consensus are not the same thing.
   But, the critics might respond, intellectual authority is only recognized as such because of institutional
(30) consensus. For example, if a musicologist were to claim that an alleged musical genius who, after several decades, had not gained respect and recognition for his or her compositions is probably not a genius, the critics might say that basing a judgment on a unit of time—
(35) "several decades"—is an institutional rather than an intellectual construct. What, the critics might ask, makes a particular number of decades reasonable evidence by which to judge genius? The answer, of course, is nothing, except for the fact that such
(40) institutional procedures have proved useful to musicologists in making such distinctions in the past.
   The analogous legal concept is the doctrine of precedent, i.e., a judge's merely deciding a case a certain way becoming a basis for deciding later cases
(45) the same way—a pure example of institutional authority. But the critics miss the crucial distinction that when a judicial decision is badly reasoned, or simply no longer applies in the face of evolving social standards or practices, the notion of intellectual
(50) authority is introduced: judges reconsider, revise, or in some cases throw out the decision. The conflict between intellectual and institutional authority in legal systems is thus played out in the reconsideration of decisions, leading one to draw the conclusion that legal
(55) systems contain a significant degree of intellectual authority even if the thrust of their power is predominantly institutional.

9. Which one of the following most accurately states the main idea of the passage?

(A) Although some argue that the authority of legal systems is purely intellectual, these systems possess a degree of institutional authority due to their ability to enforce acceptance of badly reasoned or socially inappropriate judicial decisions.
(B) Although some argue that the authority of legal systems is purely institutional, these systems are more correctly seen as vehicles for applying the intellectual authority of the law while possessing no coercive power of their own.
(C) Although some argue that the authority of legal systems is purely intellectual, these systems in fact wield institutional authority by virtue of the fact that intellectual authority reduces to institutional authority.
(D) Although some argue that the authority of legal system is purely institutional, these systems possess a degree of intellectual authority due to their ability to reconsider badly reasoned or socially inappropriate judicial decisions.
(E) Although some argue that the authority of legal systems is purely intellectual, these systems in fact wield exclusively institutional authority in that they possess the power to enforce acceptance of badly reasoned or socially inappropriate judicial decisions.

10. That some arguments "never receive institutional imprimatur" (lines 22-23) most likely means that these arguments

(A) fail to gain institutional consensus
(B) fail to challenge institutional beliefs
(C) fail to conform to the example of precedent
(D) fail to convince by virtue of good reasoning
(E) fail to gain acceptance except by coercion

11. Which one of the following, if true, most challenges the author's contention that legal systems contain a significant degree of intellectual authority?

    (A) Judges often act under time constraints and occasionally render a badly reasoned or socially inappropriate decision.
    (B) In some legal systems, the percentage of judicial decisions that contain faulty reasoning is far higher than it is in other legal systems.
    (C) Many socially inappropriate legal decisions are thrown out by judges only after citizens begin to voice opposition to them.
    (D) In some legal systems, the percentage of judicial decisions that are reconsidered and revised is far higher than it is in other legal systems.
    (E) Judges are rarely willing to rectify the examples of faulty reasoning they discover when reviewing previous legal decisions.

12. Given the information in the passage, the author is LEAST likely to believe which one of the following?

    (A) Institutional authority may depend on coercion; intellectual authority never does.
    (B) Intellectual authority may accept well-reasoned arguments; institutional authority never does.
    (C) Institutional authority may depend on convention; intellectual authority never does.
    (D) Intellectual authority sometimes challenges institutional beliefs; institutional authority never does.
    (E) Intellectual authority sometimes conflicts with precedent; institutional authority never does.

13. The author discusses the example from musicology primarily in order to

    (A) distinguish the notion of institutional authority from that of intellectual authority
    (B) give an example of an argument possessing intellectual authority that did not prevail in its own time
    (C) identify an example in which the ascription of musical genius did not withstand the test of time
    (D) illustrate the claim that assessing intellectual authority requires an appeal to institutional authority
    (E) demonstrate that the authority wielded by the arbiters of musical genius is entirely institutional

14. Based on the passage, the author would be most likely to hold which one of the following views about the doctrine of precedent?

    (A) It is the only tool judges should use if they wish to achieve a purely intellectual authority.
    (B) It is a useful tool in theory but in practice it invariably conflicts with the demands of intellectual authority.
    (C) It is a useful tool but lacks intellectual authority unless it is combined with the reconsidering of decisions.
    (D) It is often an unreliable tool because it prevents judges from reconsidering the intellectual authority of past decisions.
    (E) It is an unreliable tool that should be abandoned because it lacks intellectual authority.

Passage #14: June 2003 Questions 20-27

Leading questions—questions worded in such a way as to suggest a particular answer—can yield unreliable testimony either by design, as when a lawyer tries to trick a witness into affirming a particular
(5) version of the evidence of a case, or by accident, when a questioner unintentionally prejudices the witness's response. For this reason, a judge can disallow such questions in the courtroom interrogation of witnesses. But their exclusion from the courtroom by no means
(10) eliminates the remote effects of earlier leading questions on eyewitness testimony. Alarmingly, the beliefs about an event that a witness brings to the courtroom may often be adulterated by the effects of leading questions that were introduced intentionally
(15) or unintentionally by lawyers, police investigators, reporters, or others with whom the witness has already interacted.

Recent studies have confirmed the ability of leading questions to alter the details of our memories
(20) and have led to a better understanding of how this process occurs and, perhaps, of the conditions that make for greater risks that an eyewitness's memories have been tainted by leading questions. These studies suggest that not all details of our experiences become
(25) clearly or stably stored in memory-only those to which we give adequate attention. Moreover, experimental evidence indicates that if subtly introduced new data involving remembered events do not actively conflict with our stored memory data, we
(30) tend to process such new data similarly whether they correspond to details as we remember them, or to gaps in those details. In the former case, we often retain the new data as a reinforcement of the corresponding aspect of the memory, and in the latter case, we often
(35) retain them as a construction to fill the corresponding gap. An eyewitness who is asked, prior to courtroom testimony, "How fast was the car going when it passed the stop sign?" may respond to the query about speed without addressing the question of the stop sign. But
(40) the "stop sign" datum has now been introduced, and when later recalled, perhaps during courtroom testimony, it may be processed as belonging to the original memory even if the witness actually saw no stop sign.

(45) The farther removed from the event, the greater the chance of a vague or incomplete recollection and the greater the likelihood of newly suggested information blending with original memories. Since we can be more easily misled with respect to fainter and more
(50) uncertain memories, tangential details are more apt to become constructed out of subsequently introduced information than are more central details. But what is tangential to a witness's original experience of an event may nevertheless be crucial to the courtroom issues
(55) that the witness's memories are supposed to resolve. For example, a perpetrator's shirt color or hairstyle might be tangential to one's shocked observance of an armed robbery, but later those factors might be crucial to establishing the identity of the perpetrator.

20. Which one of the following most accurately expresses the main point of the passage?
   (A) The unreliability of memories about incidental aspects of observed events makes eyewitness testimony especially questionable in cases in which the witness was not directly involved.
   (B) Because of the nature of human memory storage and retrieval, the courtroom testimony of eyewitnesses may contain crucial inaccuracies due to leading questions asked prior to the courtroom appearance.
   (C) Researchers are surprised to find that courtroom testimony is often dependent on suggestion to fill gaps left by insufficient attention to detail at the time that the incident in question occurred.
   (D) Although judges can disallow leading questions from the courtroom, it is virtually impossible to prevent them from being used elsewhere, to the detriment of many cases.
   (E) Stricter regulation should be placed on lawyers whose leading questions can corrupt witnesses' testimony by introducing inaccurate data prior to the witnesses' appearance in the courtroom.

21. It can be reasonably inferred from the passage that which one of the following, if it were effectively implemented, would most increase the justice system's ability to prevent leading questions from causing mistaken court decisions?
   (A) a policy ensuring that witnesses have extra time to answer questions concerning details that are tangential to their original experiences of events
   (B) thorough revision of the criteria for determining which kinds of interrogation may be disallowed in courtroom testimony under the category of "leading questions"
   (C) increased attention to the nuances of all witnesses' responses to courtroom questions, even those that are not leading questions
   (D) extensive interviewing of witnesses by all lawyers for both sides of a case prior to those witnesses' courtroom appearance
   (E) availability of accurate transcripts of all interrogations of witnesses that occurred prior to those witnesses' appearance in court

22. Which one of the following is mentioned in the passage as a way in which new data suggested to a witness by a leading question are sometimes processed?
   (A) They are integrated with current memories as support for those memories.
   (B) They are stored tentatively as conjectural data that fade with time.
   (C) They stay more vivid in memory than do previously stored memory data.
   (D) They are reinterpreted so as to be compatible with the details already stored in memory.
   (E) They are retained in memory even when they conflict with previously stored memory data.

92   POWERSCORE LSAT READING COMPREHENSION: PASSAGE TYPE TRAINING II

23. In discussing the tangential details of events, the passage contrasts their original significance to witnesses with their possible significance in the courtroom (lines 52-59). That contrast is most closely analogous to which one of the following?

    (A) For purposes of flavor and preservation, salt and vinegar are important additions to cucumbers during the process of pickling, but these purposes could be attained by adding other ingredients instead.
    (B) For the purpose of adding a mild stimulant effect, caffeine is included in some types of carbonated drinks, but for the purposes of appealing to health-conscious consumers, some types of carbonated drinks are advertised as being caffeine-free.
    (C) For purposes of flavor and tenderness, the skins of apples and some other fruits are removed during preparation for drying, but grape skins are an essential part of raisins, and thus grape skins are not removed.
    (D) For purposes of flavor and appearance, wheat germ is not needed in flour and is usually removed during milling, but for purposes of nutrition, the germ is an important part of the grain.
    (E) For purposes of texture and appearance, some fat may be removed from meat when it is ground into sausage, but the removal of fat is also important for purposes of health.

24. Which one of the following questions is most directly answered by information in the passage?

    (A) In witnessing what types of crimes are people especially likely to pay close attention to circumstantial details?
    (B) Which aspects of courtroom interrogation cause witnesses to be especially reluctant to testify in extensive detail?
    (C) Can the stress of having to testify in a courtroom situation affect the accuracy of memory storage and retrieval?
    (D) Do different people tend to possess different capacities for remembering details accurately?
    (E) When is it more likely that a detail of an observed event will be accurately remembered?

25. The second paragraph consists primarily of material that

    (A) corroborates and adds detail to a claim made in the first paragraph
    (B) provides examples illustrating the applications of a theory discussed in the first paragraph
    (C) forms an argument in support of a proposal that is made in the final paragraph
    (D) anticipates and provides grounds for the rejection of a theory alluded to by the author in the final paragraph
    (E) explains how newly obtained data favor one of two traditional theories mentioned elsewhere in the second paragraph

26. It can be most reasonably inferred from the passage that the author holds that the recent studies discussed in the passage

    (A) have produced some unexpected findings regarding the extent of human reliance on external verification of memory details
    (B) shed new light on a longstanding procedural controversy in the law
    (C) may be of theoretical interest despite their tentative nature and inconclusive findings
    (D) provide insights into the origins of several disparate types of logically fallacious reasoning
    (E) should be of more than abstract academic interest to the legal profession

27. Which one of the following can be most reasonably inferred from the information in the passage?

    (A) The tendency of leading questions to cause unreliable courtroom testimony has no correlation with the extent to which witnesses are emotionally affected by the events that they have observed.
    (B) Leading questions asked in the process of a courtroom examination of a witness are more likely to cause inaccurate testimony than are leading questions asked outside the courtroom.
    (C) The memory processes by which newly introduced data tend to reinforce accurately remembered details of events are not relevant to explaining the effects of leading questions.
    (D) The risk of testimony being inaccurate due to certain other factors tends to increase as an eyewitness's susceptibility to giving inaccurate testimony due to the effects of leading questions increases.
    (E) The traditional grounds on which leading questions can be excluded from courtroom interrogation of witnesses have been called into question by the findings of recent studies.

Passage #1: December 2001 Questions 21-26

With the elimination of the apartheid system, South Africa now confronts the transition to a rights-based legal system in a constitutional democracy. Among lawyers and judges, exhilaration over the legal tools
(5) soon to be available is tempered by uncertainty about how to use them. The changes in the legal system are significant, not just for human rights lawyers, but for all lawyers—as they will have to learn a less rule-bound and more interpretative way of looking at the
(10) law. That is to say, in the past, the parliament was the supreme maker and arbiter of laws; when judges made rulings with which the parliament disagreed, the parliament simply passed new laws to counteract their rulings. Under the new system, however, a
(15) constitutional court will hear arguments on all constitutional matters, including questions of whether the laws passed by the parliament are valid in light of the individual liberties set out in the constitution's bill of rights. This shift will lead to extraordinary changes,
(20) for South Africa has never before had a legal system based on individual rights—one in which citizens can challenge any law or administrative decision on the basis of their constitutional rights.
  South African lawyers are concerned about the
(25) difficulty of fostering a rights-based culture in a multiracial society containing a wide range of political and personal beliefs simply by including a bill of rights in the constitution and establishing the means for its defense. Because the bill of rights has been drawn in
(30) very general terms, the lack of precedents will make the task of determining its precise meaning a bewildering one. With this in mind, the new constitution acknowledges the need to look to other countries for guidance. But some scholars warn that
(35) judges, in their rush to fill the constitutional void, may misuse foreign law—they may blindly follow the interpretations given bills of rights in other countries, not taking into account the circumstances in those countries that led to certain decisions. Nonetheless,
(40) these scholars are hopeful that, with patience and judicious decisions, South Africa can use international experience in developing a body of precedent that will address the particular needs of its citizens.
  South Africa must also contend with the image of
(45) the law held by many of its citizens. Because the law in South Africa has long been a tool of racial oppression, many of its citizens have come to view obeying the law as implicitly sanctioning an illegitimate, brutal government. Among these South Africans the political
(50) climate has thus been one of opposition, and many see it as their duty to cheat the government as much as possible, whether by not paying taxes or by disobeying parking laws. If a rights-based culture is to succeed, the government will need to show its citizens that the legal
(55) system is no longer a tool of oppression but instead a way to bring about change and help further the cause of justice.

21. Which one of the following most completely and accurately states the main point of the passage?

 (A) Following the elimination of the apartheid system in South Africa, lawyers, judges, and citizens will need to abandon their posture of opposition to law and design a new and fairer legal system.
 (B) If the new legal system in South Africa is to succeed, lawyers, judges, and citizens must learn to challenge parliamentary decisions based on their individual rights as set out in the new constitution.
 (C) Whereas in the past the parliament was both the initiator and arbiter of laws in South Africa, under the new constitution these powers will be assumed by a constitutional court.
 (D) Despite the lack of relevant legal precedents and the public's antagonistic relation to the law, South Africa is moving from a legal system where the parliament is the final authority to one where the rights of citizens are protected by a constitution.
 (E) While South Africa's judges will have to look initially to other countries to provide interpretations for its new bill of rights, eventually it must develop a body of precedent sensitive to the needs of its own citizens.

22. Which one of the following most accurately describes the author's primary purpose in lines 10-19?

 (A) to describe the role of the parliament under South Africa's new constitution
 (B) to argue for returning final legal authority to the parliament
 (C) to contrast the character of legal practice under the apartheid system with that to be implemented under the new constitution
 (D) to criticize the creation of a court with final authority on constitutional matters
 (E) to explain why a bill of rights was included in the new constitution

23. The passage suggests that the author's attitude toward the possibility of success for a rights-based legal system in South Africa is most likely one of

 (A) deep skepticism
 (B) open pessimism
 (C) total indifference
 (D) guarded optimism
 (E) complete confidence

24. According to the passage, under the apartheid system the rulings of judges were sometimes counteracted by

   (A) decisions rendered in constitutional court
   (B) challenges from concerned citizens
   (C) new laws passed in the parliament
   (D) provisions in the constitution's bill of rights
   (E) other judges with a more rule-bound approach to the law

25. Which one of the following most accurately describes the organization of the last paragraph of the passage?

   (A) A solution to a problem is identified, several methods of implementing the solution are discussed, and one of the methods is argued for.
   (B) The background to a problem is presented, past methods of solving the problem are criticized, and a new solution is proposed.
   (C) An analysis of a problem is presented, possible solutions to the problem are given, and one of the possible solutions is argued for.
   (D) Reasons are given why a problem has existed, the current state of affairs is described, and the problem is shown to exist no longer.
   (E) A problem is identified, specific manifestations of the problem are given, and an essential element in its solution is presented.

26. Based on the passage, the scholars mentioned in the second paragraph would be most likely to agree with which one of the following statements?

   (A) Reliance of judges on the interpretations given bills of rights in other countries must be tempered by the recognition that such interpretations may be based on circumstances not necessarily applicable to South Africa.
   (B) Basing interpretations of the South African bill of rights on interpretations given bills of rights in other countries will reinforce the climate of mistrust for authority in South Africa.
   (C) The lack of precedents in South African law for interpreting a bill of rights will likely make it impossible to interpret correctly the bill of rights in the South African constitution.
   (D) Reliance by judges on the interpretations given bills of rights in other countries offers an unacceptable means of attempting to interpret the South African constitution in a way that will meet the particular needs of South African citizens.
   (E) Because bills of rights in other countries are written in much less general terms than the South African bill of rights, interpretations of them are unlikely to prove helpful in interpreting the South African bill of rights.

Passage #2: December 2002 Questions 24-28

The following passage was written in the mid-1990s.

Users of the Internet—the worldwide network of interconnected computer systems—envision it as a way for people to have free access to information via their personal computers. Most Internet communication
(5) consists of sending electronic mail or exchanging ideas on electronic bulletin boards; however, a growing number of transmissions are of copyrighted works—books, photographs, videos and films, and sound recordings. In Canada, as elsewhere, the goals of
(10) Internet users have begun to conflict with reality as copyright holders look for ways to protect their material from unauthorized and uncompensated distribution.

Copyright experts say that Canadian copyright law,
(15) which was revised in 1987 to cover works such as choreography and photography, has not kept pace with technology—specifically with digitalization, the conversion of data into a series of digits that are transmitted as electronic signals over computer
(20) networks. Digitalization makes it possible to create an unlimited number of copies of a book, recording, or movie and distribute them to millions of people around the world. Current law prohibits unauthorized parties from reproducing a work or any substantial part of it in
(25) any material form (e.g., photocopies of books or pirated audiotapes), but because digitalization merely transforms the work into electronic signals in a computer's memory, it is not clear whether digitalization constitutes a material reproduction—and
(30) so unauthorized digitalization is not yet technically a crime.

Some experts propose simply adding unauthorized digitalization to the list of activities proscribed under current law, to make it clear that copyright holders own
(35) electronic reproduction rights just as they own rights to other types of reproduction. But criminalizing digitalization raises a host of questions. For example, given that digitalization allows the multiple recipients of a transmission to re-create copies of a work, would
(40) only the act of digitalization itself be criminal, or should each copy made from the transmission be considered a separate instance of piracy—even though those who made the copies never had access to the original? In addition, laws against digitalization might
(45) be virtually unenforceable given that an estimated 20 million people around the world have access to the Internet, and that copying and distributing material is a relatively simple process. Furthermore, even an expanded law might not cover the majority of
(50) transmissions, given the vast numbers of users who are academics and the fact that current copyright law allows generous exemptions for those engaged in private study or research. But even if the law is revised to contain a more sophisticated treatment of
(55) digitalization, most experts think it will be hard to resolve the clash between the Internet community, which is accustomed to treating information as raw material available for everyone to use, and the publishing community, which is accustomed to treating
(60) it as a commodity owned by its creator.

24. Which one of the following most accurately expresses the main point of the passage?

(A) Despite the widely recognized need to revise Canadian copyright law to protect works from unauthorized reproduction and distribution over the Internet, users of the Internet have mounted many legal challenges to the criminalizing of digitalization.
(B) Although the necessity of revising Canadian copyright law to protect works from unauthorized reproduction and distribution over the Internet is widely recognized, effective criminalizing of digitalization is likely to prove highly complicated.
(C) While the unauthorized reproduction and distribution of copyrighted works over the Internet is not yet a crime, legal experts believe it is only a matter of time before Canadian copyright law is amended to prohibit unauthorized digitalization.
(D) Despite the fact that current Canadian copyright law does not cover digitalization, the unauthorized reproduction and distribution of copyrighted works over the Internet clearly ought to be considered a crime.
(E) Although legal experts in Canada disagree about the most effective way to punish the unauthorized reproduction and distribution of copyrighted works over the Internet, they nonetheless agree that such digitalization should clearly be a punishable crime.

25. Given the author's argument, which one of the following additions to current Canadian copyright law would most likely be an agreeable compromise to both the Internet community and the publishing community?

(A) Digitalization of copyrighted works is permitted to Internet users who pay a small fee to copyright holders.
(B) Digitalization of copyrighted works is prohibited to Internet users who are not academics.
(C) Digitalization of copyrighted works is permitted to all Internet users without restriction.
(D) Digitalization of copyrighted works is prohibited to all Internet users without exception.
(E) Digitalization of copyrighted works is permitted to Internet users engaged in research.

26. The discussion in the second paragraph is intended primarily to explain which one of the following?

    (A) how copyright infringement of protected works is punished under current Canadian copyright law
    (B) why current Canadian copyright law is not easily applicable to digitalization
    (C) how the Internet has caused copyright holders to look for new forms of legal protection
    (D) why copyright experts propose protecting copyrighted works from unauthorized digitalization
    (E) how unauthorized reproductions of copyrighted works are transmitted over the Internet

27. The passage supports each of the following inferences EXCEPT:

    (A) It is unlikely that every instance of digitalization could be detected under a copyright law revised to criminalize digitalization.
    (B) Criminalizing unauthorized digitalization appears to be consistent with the publishing community's treatment of information as an owned commodity.
    (C) When copyright law is revised to cover digitalization, the revised law will include a prohibition on making copies from an unauthorized digitalization of a copyrighted work.
    (D) The number of instances of unauthorized digitalization would likely rise if digitalization technology were made even easier to use.
    (E) Under current law, many academics are allowed to make copies of copyrighted works as long as they are used only for private research.

28. Which one of the following views can most reasonably be attributed to the experts cited in line 32?

    (A) Unauthorized digitalization of a copyrighted work should be considered a crime except when it is done for purposes of private study or research.
    (B) Unauthorized digitalization of a copyrighted work should be considered a crime even when it is done for purposes of private study or research.
    (C) Making a copy of a copyrighted work from an unauthorized digitalization of the work should not be considered a crime.
    (D) Making a copy of a copyrighted work from an unauthorized digitalization of the work should be punished, but not as severely as making the original digitalization.
    (E) Making a copy of a copyrighted work from an unauthorized digitalization of the work should be punished just as severely as making the original digitalization.

LAW-REGULATION

SOCIAL SCIENCE

Social Science Passages

Passage #1: June 1997 Questions 22-26 100
Passage #2: December 1997 Questions 1-6 102
Passage #3: December 1997 Questions 14-20 104
Passage #4: June 1998 Questions 22-26 106
Passage #5: December 1998 Questions 22-26 108
Passage #6: June 2000 Questions 1-5 110
Passage #7: June 2002 Questions 22-26 112
Passage #8: October 2002 Questions 15-20 114

Passage #1: June 1997 Questions 22-26

What it means to "explain" something in science often comes down to the application of mathematics. Some thinkers hold that mathematics is a kind of language—a systematic contrivance of
(5) signs, the criteria for the authority of which are internal coherence, elegance, and depth. The application of such a highly artificial system to the physical world, they claim, results in the creation of a kind of statement about the world. Accordingly,
(10) what matters in the sciences is finding a mathematical concept that attempts, as other language does, to accurately describe the functioning of some aspect of the world.

At the center of the issue of scientific
(15) knowledge can thus be found questions about the relationship between language and what it refers to. A discussion about the role played by language in the pursuit of knowledge has been going on among linguists for several decades. The debate centers
(20) around whether language corresponds in some essential way to objects and behaviors, making knowledge a solid and reliable commodity; or, on the other hand, whether the relationship between language and things is purely a matter of agreed-
(25) upon conventions, making knowledge tenuous, relative, and inexact.

Lately the latter theory has been gaining wider acceptance. According to linguists who support this theory, the way language is used varies depending
(30) upon changes in accepted practices and theories among those who work in a particular discipline. These linguists argue that, in the pursuit of knowledge, a statement is true only when there are no promising alternatives that might lead one to
(35) question it. Certainly this characterization would seem to be applicable to the sciences. In science, a mathematical statement may be taken to account for every aspect of a phenomenon it is applied to, but, some would argue, there is nothing inherent in
(40) mathematical language that guarantees such a correspondence. Under this view, acceptance of a mathematical statement by the scientific community—by virtue of the statement's predictive power or methodological efficiency—transforms
(45) what is basically an analogy or metaphor into an explanation of the physical process in question, to be held as true until another, more compelling analogy takes its place.

In pursuing the implications of this theory,
(50) linguists have reached the point at which they must ask: If words or sentences do not correspond in an essential way to life or to our ideas about life, then just what are they capable of telling us about the world? In science and mathematics, then, it would
(55) seem equally necessary to ask: If models of electrolytes or $E = mc^2$, say, do not correspond essentially to the physical world, then just what functions do they perform in the acquisition of scientific knowledge? But this question has yet to
(60) be significantly addressed in the sciences.

22. Which one of the following statements most accurately expresses the passage's main point?

(A) Although scientists must rely on both language and mathematics in their pursuit of scientific knowledge, each is an imperfect tool for perceiving and interpreting aspects of the physical world.
(B) The acquisition of scientific knowledge depends on an agreement among scientists to accept some mathematical statements as more precise than others while acknowledging that all mathematics is inexact.
(C) If science is truly to progress, scientists must temporarily abandon the pursuit of new knowledge in favor of a systematic analysis of how the knowledge they already possess came to be accepted as true.
(D) In order to better understand the acquisition of scientific knowledge, scientists must investigate mathematical statements' relationship to the world just as linguists study language's relationship to the world.
(E) Without the debates among linguists that preceded them, it is unlikely that scientists would ever have begun to explore the essential role played by mathematics in the acquisition of scientific knowledge.

23. Which one of the following statements, if true, lends the most support to the view that language has an essential correspondence to the things it describes?

    (A) The categories of physical objects employed by one language correspond remarkably to the categories employed by another language that developed independently of the first.
    (B) The categories of physical objects employed by one language correspond remarkably to the categories employed by another language that derives from the first.
    (C) The categories of physical objects employed by speakers of a language correspond remarkably to the categories employed by other speakers of the same language.
    (D) The sentence structures of languages in scientifically sophisticated societies vary little from language to language.
    (E) Native speakers of many languages believe that the categories of physical objects employed by their language correspond to natural categories of objects in the world.

24. According to the passage, mathematics can be considered a language because it

    (A) conveys meaning in the same way that metaphors do
    (B) constitutes a systematic collection of signs
    (C) corresponds exactly to aspects of physical phenomena
    (D) confers explanatory power on scientific theories
    (E) relies on previously agreed-upon conventions

25. The primary purpose of the third paragraph is to

    (A) offer support for the view of linguists who believe that language has an essential correspondence to things
    (B) elaborate the position of linguists who believe that truth is merely a matter of convention
    (C) illustrate the differences between the essentialist and conventionalist positions in the linguists' debate
    (D) demonstrate the similarity of the linguists' debate to a current debate among scientists about the nature of explanation
    (E) explain the theory that mathematical statements are a kind of language

26. Based on the passage, linguists who subscribe to the theory described in lines 23-26 would hold that the statement "The ball is red" is true because

    (A) speakers of English have accepted that "The ball is red" applies to the particular physical relationship being described
    (B) speakers of English do not accept that synonyms for "ball" and "red" express these concepts as elegantly
    (C) "The ball is red" corresponds essentially to every aspect of the particular physical relationship being described
    (D) "ball" and "red" actually refer to an entity and a property respectively
    (E) "ball" and "red" are mathematical concepts that attempt to accurately describe some particular physical relationship in the world

Passage #2: December 1997 Questions 1-6

To many developers of technologies that affect public health or the environment, "risk communication" means persuading the public that the potential risks of such technologies are small and
(5) should be ignored. Those who communicate risks in this way seem to believe that lay people do not understand the actual nature of technological risk, and they can cite studies asserting that, although people apparently ignore mundane hazards that pose
(10) significant danger, they get upset about exotic hazards that pose little chance of death or injury. Because some risk communicators take this persuasive stance, many lay people see "risk communication" as a euphemism for brainwashing done by experts.
(15) Since, however, the goal of risk communication should be to enable people to make informed decisions about technological risks, a clear understanding about how the public perceives risk is needed. Lay people's definitions of "risk" are more likely to reflect
(20) subjective ethical concerns than are experts' definitions. Lay people, for example, tend to perceive a small risk to children as more significant than a larger risk to consenting adults who benefit from the risk-creating technology. However, if asked to rank hazards
(25) by the number of annual fatalities, without reference to ethical judgments, lay people provide quite reasonable estimates, demonstrating that they have substantial knowledge about many risks. Although some studies claim to demonstrate that lay people have inappropriate
(30) concerns about exotic hazards, these studies often use questionable methods, such as asking lay people to rank risks that are hard to compare. In contrast, a recent study showed that when lay people were given the necessary facts and time, they understood the specific
(35) risks of electromagnetic fields produced by high-voltage power transmission well enough to make informed decisions.

Risk communication should therefore be based on the principle that people process new information in
(40) the context of their existing beliefs. If people know nothing about a topic, they will find messages about that topic incomprehensible. If they have erroneous beliefs, they are likely to misconstrue the messages. Thus, communicators need to know the nature and
(45) extent of recipients' knowledge and beliefs in order to design messages that will not be dismissed or misinterpreted. This need was demonstrated in a research project concerning the public's level of knowledge about risks posed by the presence of radon
(50) in the home. Researchers used open-ended interviews and questionnaires to determine what information should be included in their brochure on radon. Subjects who read the researchers' brochure performed significantly better in understanding radon risks than
(55) did a control group who read a brochure that was written using a different approach by a government agency. Thus, careful preparation can help risk communicators to produce balanced material that tells people what they need to know to make decisions
(60) about technological risks.

1. Which one of the following best expresses the main point of the passage?

    (A) Risk communicators are effectively addressing the proliferation of complex technologies that have increasing impact on public health and safety.
    (B) Risk communicators should assess lay people's understanding of technologies in order to be able to give them the information they need to make reasonable decisions.
    (C) Experts who want to communicate to the public about the possible risks of complex technologies must simplify their message to ensure that it is understandable.
    (D) Risk communication can be perceived as the task of persuading lay people to accept the impact of a particular technology on their lives.
    (E) Lay people can be unduly influenced by subjective concerns when making decisions about technological risks.

2. The authors of the passage would be most likely to agree that the primary purpose of risk communication should be to

    (A) explain rather than to persuade
    (B) promote rather than to justify
    (C) influence experts rather than to influence lay people
    (D) allay people's fears about mundane hazards rather than about exotic hazards
    (E) foster public acceptance of new technologies rather than to acknowledge people's ethical concerns

3. According to the passage, it is probable that which one of the following will occur when risk communicators attempt to communicate with lay people who have mistaken ideas about a particular technology?

   (A) The lay people, perceiving that the risk communicators have provided more-reliable information, will discard their mistaken notions.
   (B) The lay people will only partially revise their ideas on the basis of the new information.
   (C) The lay people, fitting the new information into their existing framework, will interpret the communication differently than the risk communicators had intended.
   (D) The lay people, misunderstanding the new information, will further distort the information when they communicate it to other lay people.
   (E) The lay people will ignore any communication about a technology they consider potentially dangerous.

4. Which one of the following is most clearly an example of the kind of risk perception discussed in the "studies" mentioned in line 8?

   (A) A skydiver checks the lines on her parachute several times before a jump because tangled lines often keep the parachutes from opening properly.
   (B) A person decides to quit smoking in order to lessen the probability of lung damage to himself and his family.
   (C) A homeowner who decides to have her house tested for radon also decides not to allow anyone to smoke in her house.
   (D) A person who often weaves in and out of traffic while driving his car at excessive speeds worries about meteorites hitting his house.
   (E) A group of townspeople opposes the building of a nuclear waste dump outside their town and proposes that the dump be placed in another town.

5. It can be inferred that the authors of the passage would be more likely than would the risk communicators discussed in the first paragraph to emphasize which one of the following?

   (A) lay people's tendency to become alarmed about technologies that they find new or strange
   (B) lay people's tendency to compare risks that experts would not consider comparable
   (C) the need for lay people to adopt scientists' advice about technological risk
   (D) the inability of lay people to rank hazards by the number of fatalities caused annually
   (E) the impact of lay people's value systems on their perceptions of risk

6. According to the passage, many lay people believe which one of the following about risk communication?

   (A) It focuses excessively on mundane hazards.
   (B) It is a tool used to manipulate the public.
   (C) It is a major cause of inaccuracies in public knowledge about science.
   (D) It most often functions to help people make informed decisions.
   (E) Its level of effectiveness depends on the level of knowledge its audience already has.

Passage #3: December 1997 Questions 14-20

In recent years, scholars have begun to use social science tools to analyze court opinions. These scholars have justifiably criticized traditional legal research for its focus on a few cases that may not be representative
(5) and its fascination with arcane matters that do not affect real people with real legal problems. Zirkel and Schoenfeld, for example, have championed the application of social science tools to the analysis of case law surrounding discrimination against women in
(10) higher education employment. Their studies have demonstrated how these social science tools may be used to serve the interests of scholars, lawyers, and prospective plaintiffs as well. However, their enthusiasm for the "outcomes analysis" technique
(15) seems misguided.

Of fundamental concern is the outcomes analysts' assumption that simply counting the number of successful and unsuccessful plaintiffs will be useful to prospective plaintiffs. Although the odds are clearly
(20) against the plaintiff in sex discrimination cases, plaintiffs who believe that their cause is just and that they will prevail are not swayed by such evidence. In addition, because lawsuits are so different in the details of the case, in the quality of the evidence the plaintiff
(25) presents, and in the attitude of the judge toward academic plaintiffs, giving prospective plaintiffs statistics about overall outcomes without analyzing the reason for these outcomes is of marginal assistance. Outcomes analysis, for example, ignores the fact that in
(30) certain academic sex discrimination cases— those involving serious procedural violations or incriminating evidence in the form of written admissions of discriminatory practices—plaintiffs are much more likely to prevail.

(35) Two different approaches offer more useful applications of social science tools in analyzing sex discrimination cases. One is a process called "policy capturing," in which the researcher reads each opinion; identifies variables discussed in the opinion, such as
(40) the regularity of employer evaluations of the plaintiff's performance, training of evaluators, and the kind of evaluation instrument used; and then uses multivariate analysis to determine whether these variables predict the outcome of the lawsuit. The advantage of policy-
(45) capturing research is that it attempts to explain the reason for the outcome, rather than simply reporting the outcome, and identifies factors that contribute to a plaintiff's success or failure. Taking a slightly different approach, other scholars have adopted a technique that
(50) requires reading complete transcripts of all sex discrimination cases litigated during a certain time period to identify variables such as the nature of the allegedly illegal conduct, the consequences for employers, and the nature of the remedy, as well as the
(55) factors that contributed to the verdict and the kind of evidence necessary for the plaintiff to prevail. While the findings of these studies are limited to the period covered, they assist potential plaintiffs and defendants in assessing their cases.

14. Which one of the following best expresses the main idea of the passage?

(A) The analysis of a limited number of atypical discrimination suits is of little value to potential plaintiffs.
(B) When the number of factors analyzed in a sex discrimination suit is increased, the validity of the conclusions drawn becomes suspect.
(C) Scholars who are critical of traditional legal research frequently offer alternative approaches that are also seriously flawed.
(D) Outcomes analysis has less predictive value in sex discrimination cases than do certain other social science techniques.
(E) Given adequate information, it is possible to predict with considerable certainty whether a plaintiff will be successful in a discrimination suit.

15. It can be inferred from the author's discussion of traditional legal research that the author is

(A) frustrated because traditional legal research has not achieved its full potential
(B) critical because traditional legal research has little relevance to those actually involved in cases
(C) appreciative of the role traditional legal research played in developing later, more efficient approaches
(D) derisive because traditional legal research has outlasted its previously significant role
(E) grateful for the ability of traditional legal research to develop unique types of evidence

16. Which one of the following statements about Zirkel and Schoenfeld can be inferred from the passage?

    (A) They were the first scholars to use social science tools in analyzing legal cases.
    (B) They confined their studies to the outcomes analysis technique.
    (C) They saw no value in the analysis provided by traditional legal research.
    (D) They rejected policy capturing as being too limited in scope.
    (E) They believed that the information generated by outcomes analysis would be relevant for plaintiffs.

17. The author's characterization of traditional legal research in the first paragraph is intended to

    (A) provide background information for the subsequent discussion
    (B) summarize an opponent's position
    (C) argue against the use of social science tools in the analysis of sex discrimination cases
    (D) emphasize the fact that legal researchers act to the detriment of potential plaintiffs
    (E) reconcile traditional legal researchers to the use of social science tools

18. The information in the passage suggests that plaintiffs who pursue sex discrimination cases despite the statistics provided by outcomes analysis can best be likened to

    (A) athletes who continue to employ training techniques despite their knowledge of statistical evidence indicating that these techniques are unlikely to be effective
    (B) lawyers who handle lawsuits for a large number of clients in the hope that some percentage will be successful
    (C) candidates for public office who are more interested in making a political statement than in winning an election
    (D) supporters of a cause who recruit individuals sympathetic to it in the belief that large numbers of supporters will lend the cause legitimacy
    (E) purchasers of a charity's raffle tickets who consider the purchase a contribution because the likelihood of winning is remote

19. The policy-capturing approach differs from the approach described in lines 50-62 in that the latter approach

    (A) makes use of detailed information on a greater number of cases
    (B) focuses more directly on issues of concern to litigants
    (C) analyzes information that is more recent and therefore reflects current trends
    (D) allows assessment of aspects of a case that are not specifically mentioned in a judge's opinion
    (E) eliminates any distortion due to personal bias on the part of the researcher

20. Which one of the following best describes the organization of the passage?

    (A) A technique is introduced, its shortcomings are summarized, and alternatives are described.
    (B) A debate is introduced, evidence is presented, and a compromise is reached.
    (C) A theory is presented, clarification is provided, and a plan of further evaluation is suggested.
    (D) Standards are established, hypothetical examples are analyzed, and the criteria are amended.
    (E) A position is challenged, its shortcomings are categorized, and the challenge is revised.

Passage #4: June 1998 Questions 22-26

Scientists typically advocate the analytic method of studying complex systems: systems are divided into component parts that are investigated separately. But nineteenth-century critics of this method claimed that
(5) when a system's parts are isolated its complexity tends to be lost. To address the perceived weaknesses of the analytic method these critics put forward a concept called organicism, which posited that the whole determines the nature of its parts and that the parts of a
(10) whole are interdependent.

Organicism depended upon the theory of internal relations, which states that relations between entities are possible only within some whole that embraces them, and that entities are altered by the relationships
(15) into which they enter. If an entity stands in a relationship with another entity, it has some property as a consequence. Without this relationship, and hence without the property, the entity would be different— and so would be another entity. Thus, the property is
(20) one of the entity's defining characteristics. Each of an entity's relationships likewise determines a defining characteristic of the entity.

One problem with the theory of internal relations is that not all properties of an entity are defining
(25) characteristics: numerous properties are accompanying characteristics—even if they are always present, their presence does not influence the entity's identity. Thus, even if it is admitted that every relationship into which an entity enters determines some characteristic of the
(30) entity, it is not necessarily true that such characteristics will define the entity; it is possible for the entity to enter into a relationship yet remain essentially unchanged.

The ultimate difficulty with the theory of internal
(35) relations is that it renders the acquisition of knowledge impossible. To truly know an entity, we must know all of its relationships; but because the entity is related to everything in each whole of which it is a part, these wholes must be known completely before the entity
(40) can be known. This seems to be a prerequisite impossible to satisfy.

Organicists' criticism of the analytic method arose from their failure to fully comprehend the method. In rejecting the analytic method, organicists overlooked
(45) the fact that before the proponents of the method analyzed the component parts of a system, they first determined both the laws applicable to the whole system and the initial conditions of the system; proponents of the method thus did not study parts of a
(50) system in full isolation from the system as a whole. Since organicists failed to recognize this, they never advanced any argument to show that laws and initial conditions of complex systems cannot be discovered. Hence, organicists offered no valid reason for rejecting
(55) the analytic method or for adopting organicism as a replacement for it.

22. Which one of the following most completely and accurately summarizes the argument of the passage?

(A) By calling into question the possibility that complex systems can be studied in their entirety, organicists offered an alternative to the analytic method favored by nineteenth-century scientists.
(B) Organicists did not offer a useful method of studying complex systems because they did not acknowledge that there are relationships into which an entity may enter that do not alter the entity's identity.
(C) Organicism is flawed because it relies on a theory that both ignores the fact that not all characteristics of entities are defining and ultimately makes the acquisition of knowledge impossible.
(D) Organicism does not offer a valid challenge to the analytic method both because it relies on faulty theory and because it is based on a misrepresentation of the analytic method.
(E) In criticizing the analytic method, organicists neglected to disprove that scientists who employ the method are able to discover the laws and initial conditions of the systems they study.

23. According to the passage, organicists' chief objection to the analytic method was that the method

(A) oversimplified systems by isolating their components
(B) assumed that a system can be divided into component parts
(C) ignored the laws applicable to the system as a whole
(D) claimed that the parts of a system are more important than the system as a whole
(E) denied the claim that entities enter into relationships

24. The passage offers information to help answer each of the following questions EXCEPT:

    (A) Why does the theory of internal relations appear to make the acquisition of knowledge impossible?
    (B) Why did the organicists propose replacing the analytic method?
    (C) What is the difference between a defining characteristic and an accompanying characteristic?
    (D) What did organicists claim are the effects of an entity's entering into a relationship with another entity?
    (E) What are some of the advantages of separating out the parts of a system for study?

25. The passage most strongly supports the ascription of which one of the following views to scientists who use the analytic method?

    (A) A complex system is best understood by studying its component parts in full isolation from the system as a whole.
    (B) The parts of a system should be studied with an awareness of the laws and initial conditions that govern the system.
    (C) It is not possible to determine the laws governing a system until the system's parts are separated from one another.
    (D) Because the parts of a system are interdependent, they cannot be studied separately without destroying the system's complexity.
    (E) Studying the parts of a system individually eliminates the need to determine which characteristics of the parts are defining characteristics.

26. Which one of the following is a principle upon which the author bases an argument against the theory of internal relations?

    (A) An adequate theory of complex systems must define the entities of which the system is composed.
    (B) An acceptable theory cannot have consequences that contradict its basic purpose.
    (C) An adequate method of study of complex systems should reveal the actual complexity of the systems it studies.
    (D) An acceptable theory must describe the laws and initial conditions of a complex system.
    (E) An acceptable method of studying complex systems should not study parts of the system in isolation from the system as a whole.

Passage #5: December 1998 Questions 22-26

Freud's essay on "The Uncanny" can be said to have defined, for our century, what literary criticism once called the Sublime. This apprehension of a beyond or of a dæmonic—a sense of transcendence—
(5) appears in literature or life, according to Freud, when we feel that something uncanny is being represented, or conjured up, or at least intimated. Freud locates the source of the uncanny in our tendency to believe in the "omnipotence of thought," that is, in the power of our
(10) own or of others' minds over the natural world. The uncanny is, thus, a return to animistic conceptions of the universe, and is produced by the psychic defense mechanisms Freud called repression.

It would have seemed likely for Freud to find his
(15) literary instances of the uncanny, or at least some of them, in fairy tales, since as much as any other fictions they seem to be connected with repressed desires and archaic forms of thought. But Freud specifically excluded fairy tales from the realm of the uncanny.
(20) "Who would be so bold," Freud asks, "as to call it an uncanny moment, for instance, when Snow White opens her eyes once more?" Why not? Because, he goes on to say, in those stories everything is possible, so nothing is incredible, and, therefore, no conflicts in
(25) the reader's judgment are provoked. Thus Freud, alas, found fairy tales to be unsuited to his own analysis.

However, the psychoanalyst Bruno Bettelheim, with a kind of wise innocence, has subjected fairy tales to very close, generally orthodox, and wholly reductive
(30) Freudian interpretations. Bettelheim's book, although written in apparent ignorance of the vast critical traditions of interpreting literary romance, is nevertheless a splendid achievement, brimming with useful ideas and insights into how young children read
(35) and understand.

Bruno Bettelheim's major therapeutic concern has been with autistic children, so inevitably his interpretive activity is directed against a child's tendency to withdraw defensively or abnormally.
(40) According to Bettelheim, a child's desperate isolation, loneliness, and inarticulate anxieties are addressed directly by fairy tales. By telling the child such stories themselves, parents strengthen the therapeutic effect of fairy tales, for in the telling, parents impart to the child
(45) their approval of the stories.

But why should fairy tales, in themselves, be therapeutic? Bettelheim's answer depends on the child's being an interpreter: "The fairy tale is therapeutic because children find their own solutions,
(50) through contemplating what the story seems to imply about their inner conflicts at this moment in their lives." Bettelheim proceeds on the basis of two complementary assumptions: that children will interpret a story benignly, for their own good; and that

(55) Freudian interpretations will yield an accurate account of children's interpretations. The child, questing for help, and the analyst, attempting to find helpful patterns in the stories, thus read alike, though in different vocabularies.

22. According to the author, Bettelheim believes that fairy tales help troubled children by

(A) creating fantasy worlds into which they can escape
(B) helping them find solutions to their own problems
(C) providing a means of communication with their parents
(D) showing them other problems worse than their own
(E) solving their problems for them

23. According to the passage, Bettelheim believes that parents' telling fairy tales to troubled children strengthens the tales' therapeutic effect because

(A) most troubled children do not read independently
(B) most children believe whatever their parents tell them
(C) the parents' telling the stories imparts to the children the parents' sanction of the tales
(D) the parents can help the children interpret the stories according to the parents' belief
(E) the parents can reassure the children that the tales are imaginary

24. It can be inferred from the passage that Freud believed that in fairy tales, "nothing is incredible" (line 24) because, in his view,

    (A) fairy tales can be read and understood even by young children
    (B) everything in fairy tales is purely imaginary
    (C) fairy tales are so fantastic that in them nothing seems out of the ordinary
    (D) it is uncanny how the patterns of fairy tales fit our unconscious expectations and wishes
    (E) the reader represses those elements of fairy tales which might conflict with his or her judgment

25. According to the passage, Bettelheim believes that when children interpret a story benignly, they

    (A) find in fairy tales answers to their own needs
    (B) do not associate fairy tales with the uncanny
    (C) do not find underlying meanings in fairy tales
    (D) are aware that fairy tales are fictions
    (E) are reassured by parental approval

26. Which one of the following best describes the author's attitude toward Bettelheim's work?

    (A) approving of Bettelheim's rejection of orthodox and reductive Freudian interpretations of fairy tales
    (B) appalled at Bettelheim's ignorance of the critical traditions of interpreting literary romance
    (C) unimpressed with Bettelheim's research methods
    (D) skeptical of Bettelheim's claim that fairy tales are therapeutic
    (E) appreciative of Bettelheim's accomplishment and practical insights

Passage #6: June 2000 Questions 1-5

By the year 2030, the Earth's population is expected to increase to 10 billion; ideally, all would enjoy standards of living equivalent to those of present-day industrial democracies. However, if 10 billion
(5) people consume critical natural resources such as copper, nickel, and petroleum at the current per capita rates of industrialized countries, and if new resources are not discovered or substitutes developed, such an ideal would last a decade or less. Moreover, projections
(10) based on the current rate of waste production in many industrialized countries suggest that 10 billion people would generate enough solid waste every year to bury a large city and its surrounding suburbs 100 meters deep.

These estimates are not meant to predict a grim
(15) future. Instead they emphasize the incentives for recycling, conservation, and a switch to alternative materials. They also suggest that the traditional model of industrial activity, in which individual manufacturing processes take in raw materials and
(20) generate products to be sold plus waste to be disposed of, should be transformed into a more integrated model: an industrial ecosystem. In such a system the consumption of energy and materials is optimized, wastes and pollution are minimized, and the effluents
(25) of one process—whether they are spent catalysts from petroleum refining or discarded plastic containers from consumer products—serve as the raw material for another process.

Materials in an ideal industrial ecosystem would
(30) not be depleted any more than are materials in a biological ecosystem, in which plants synthesize nutrients that feed herbivores, some of which in turn feed a chain of carnivores whose waste products and remains eventually feed further generations of plants.
(35) A chunk of steel could potentially show up one year in a tin can, the next year in an automobile, and 10 years later in the skeleton of a building. Some manufacturers are already making use of "designed offal" in the manufacture of metals and some plastics: tailoring the
(40) production of waste from a manufacturing process so that the waste can be fed directly back into that process or a related one. Such recycling still requires the expenditure of energy and the unavoidable generation of some wastes and harmful by-products, but at much
(45) lower levels than are typical today.

The ideal industrial ecosystem, in which there is an economically viable role for every product of a manufacturing process, will not be attained soon; current technology is often inadequate to the task.
(50) However, if industrialized nations embrace major and minor changes in their current industrial practices and developing nations bypass older, less ecologically sound technologies, it should be possible to develop a more closed industrial ecosystem that would be more
(55) sustainable than current industrial practices, especially in the face of decreasing supplies of raw materials and increasing problems of waste and pollution.

1. According to the passage, which one of the following is currently an obstacle to the implementation of an ideal industrial ecosystem?

    (A) the unwillingness of manufacturers to change their industrial practices
    (B) the unwillingness of industrialized countries to reduce their standards of living to a level that is sustainable for the entire world
    (C) the unwillingness of developing nations to adopt new technologies that are more ecologically sound than those used by industrialized countries
    (D) the inability of technology to provide a profitable use for every by-product of the manufacturing process
    (E) the failure of the industrial ecosystem approach to provide sufficient quantities of manufactured goods

2. The author of the passage would most probably agree with which one of the following statements about standards of living?

   (A) An increase in the standard of living in developing countries will be accompanied by a decrease in the standard of living in industrialized countries.
   (B) It is likely that the standard of living of both industrialized and developing countries will decrease substantially by the year 2030.
   (C) The current standard of living of industrialized countries cannot be sustained if the population of the world increases.
   (D) All countries could enjoy a high standard of living without depleting natural resources if industrialized and developing countries implemented an ideal industrial ecosystem.
   (E) Supplies of critical natural resources will be in serious danger of depletion by the year 2030 unless the current standard of living of both industrialized and developing countries is reduced.

3. The author of the passage would most probably agree with which one of the following statements about the use of "designed offal" (line 38)?

   (A) It is a harmful step that requires the consumption of critical natural resources and results in the generation of waste and harmful by-products.
   (B) It is not an entirely helpful step because it draws attention away from the central problems that still need to be solved.
   (C) It is a temporary solution that will not contribute to the establishment of an industrial ecosystem.
   (D) It is a promising step in the right direction, but it does not solve all of the problems that need to be addressed.
   (E) It is the most practical solution to the environmental problems facing the world.

4. The author mentions all of the following as advantages of replacing current industrial practices with an industrial ecosystem approach EXCEPT:

   (A) The amount of waste produced by industrial processes would be reduced.
   (B) The amount of harmful by-products produced by industrial processes would be reduced.
   (C) The use of alternative sources of energy to provide power for industrial processes would be increased.
   (D) The consumption of raw materials used in industrial processes would be optimized.
   (E) Better use would be made of the waste produced by industrial processes.

5. Of the following, which one is the best example of the use of "designed offal" (line 38) as it is defined in the passage?

   (A) A paper container manufacturer purchases recycled newspaper that is turned into pulp and used as the raw material for producing paper containers.
   (B) A demolition company strips brass fixtures from condemned buildings, reconditions the fixtures, and sells them to home renovation companies.
   (C) A steel company buys metal taken from discarded automobiles, melts it down, and uses it in the production of steel beams.
   (D) An automobile manufacturer turns the plastic left over from its production of automobile body panels into insulation for its automobile doors.
   (E) A plastics company receives recycled beverage containers, reprocesses the containers, and uses the reprocessed material to produce polyester fiber.

Passage #7: June 2002 Questions 22-26

Recent investigations into the psychology of decision making have sparked interest among scholars seeking to understand why governments sometimes take gambles that appear theoretically unjustifiable on
(5) the basis of expected costs and benefits. Researchers have demonstrated some significant discrepancies between objective measurements of possible decision outcomes and the ways in which people subjectively value such possible results. Many of these
(10) discrepancies relate to the observation that a possible outcome perceived as a loss typically motivates more strongly than the prospect of an equivalent gain. Risk-taking is thus a more common strategy for those who believe they will lose what they already possess than it
(15) is for those who wish to gain something they do not have.

Previously, the notion that rational decision makers prefer risk-avoiding choices was considered to apply generally, epitomized by the assumption of many
(20) economists that entrepreneurs and consumers will choose a risky venture over a sure thing only when the expected measurable value of the outcome is sufficiently high to compensate the decision maker for taking the risk. What is the minimum prize that would
(25) be required to make a gamble involving a 50 percent chance of losing $100 and a 50 percent chance of winning the prize acceptable? It is commonplace that the pleasure of winning a sum of money is much less intense than the pain of losing the same amount;
(30) accordingly, such a gamble would typically be accepted only when the possible gain greatly exceeds the possible loss. Research subjects do, in fact, commonly judge that a 50 percent chance to lose $100 is unacceptable unless it is combined with an equal
(35) chance to win more than $300. Nevertheless, the recent studies indicate that risk-accepting strategies are common when the alternative to a sure loss is a substantial chance of losing an even larger amount, coupled with some chance—even a small one—of
(40) losing nothing.

Such observations are quite salient to scholars of international conflict and crisis. For example, governments typically are cautious in foreign policy initiatives that entail risk, especially the risk of armed
(45) conflict. But nations also often take huge gambles to retrieve what they perceive to have been taken from them by other nations. This type of motivation, then, can lead states to take risks that far outweigh the objectively measurable value of the lost assets. For
(50) example, when Britain and Argentina entered into armed conflict in 1982 over possession of the Falkland Islands—or Malvinas, as they are called in Spanish— each viewed the islands as territory that had been taken from them by the other; thus each was willing to
(55) commit enormous resources—and risks—to recapturing them. In international affairs, it is vital that each actor in such a situation understand the other's subjective view of what is at stake.

22. Suppose that a country seizes a piece of territory with great mineral wealth that is claimed by a neighboring country, with a concomitant risk of failure involving moderate but easily tolerable harm in the long run. Given the information in the passage, the author would most likely say that

(A) the country's actions are consistent with previously accepted views of the psychology of risk-taking
(B) the new research findings indicate that the country from which the territory has been seized probably weighs the risk factors involved in the situation similarly to the way in which they are weighed by the aggressor nation
(C) in spite of surface appearances to the contrary, the new research findings suggest that the objective value of the potential gain is overridden by the risks
(D) the facts of the situation show that the government is motivated by factors other than objective calculation of the measurable risks and probable benefits
(E) the country's leaders most likely subjectively perceive the territory as having been taken from their country in the past

23. The question in lines 24-27 functions primarily as

    (A) the introduction to a thought experiment whose results the author expects will vary widely among different people
    (B) a rhetorical question whose assumed answer is in conflict with the previously accepted view concerning risk-taking behavior
    (C) the basis for an illustration of how the previously accepted view concerning risk-taking behavior applies accurately to some types of situations
    (D) a suggestion that the discrepancies between subjective and objective valuations of possible decision outcomes are more illusive than real
    (E) a transitional device to smooth an otherwise abrupt switch from discussion of previous theories to discussion of some previously unaccepted research findings

24. It can most reasonably be inferred from the passage that the author would agree with which one of the following statements?

    (A) When states try to regain losses through risky conflict, they generally are misled by inadequate or inaccurate information as to the risks that they run in doing so.
    (B) Government decision makers subjectively evaluate the acceptability of risks involving national assets in much the same way that they would evaluate risks involving personal assets.
    (C) A new method for predicting and mediating international conflict has emerged from a synthesis of the fields of economics and psychology.
    (D) Truly rational decision making is a rare phenomenon in international crises and can, ironically, lead to severe consequences for those who engage in it.
    (E) Contrary to previous assumptions, people are more likely to take substantial risks when their subjective assessments of expected benefits match or exceed the objectively measured costs.

25. The passage can be most accurately described as

    (A) a psychological analysis of the motives involved in certain types of collective decision making in the presence of conflict
    (B) a presentation of a psychological hypothesis which is then subjected to a political test case
    (C) a suggestion that psychologists should incorporate the findings of political scientists into their research
    (D) an examination of some new psychological considerations regarding risk and their application to another field of inquiry
    (E) a summary of two possible avenues for understanding international crises and conflicts

26. The passage most clearly suggests that the author would agree with which one of the following statements?

    (A) Researchers have previously been too willing to accept the claims that subjects make about their preferred choices in risk-related decision problems.
    (B) There is inadequate research support for the hypothesis that except when a gamble is the only available means for averting an otherwise certain loss, people typically are averse to risk-taking.
    (C) It can reasonably be argued that the risk that Britain accepted in its 1982 conflict with Argentina outweighed the potential objectively measurable benefit of that venture.
    (D) The new findings suggest that because of the subjective elements involved, governmental strategies concerning risks of loss in international crises will remain incomprehensible to outside observers.
    (E) Moderate risks in cases involving unavoidable losses are often taken on the basis of reasoning that diverges markedly from that which was studied in the recent investigations.

Passage #8: October 2002 Questions 15-20

In explaining the foundations of the discipline known as historical sociology—the examination of history using the methods of sociology—historical sociologist Philip Abrams argues that, while people are
(5) made by society as much as society is made by people, sociologists' approach to the subject is usually to focus on only one of these forms of influence to the exclusion of the other. Abrams insists on the necessity for sociologists to move beyond these one-sided
(10) approaches to understand society as an entity constructed by individuals who are at the same time constructed by their society. Abrams refers to this continuous process as "structuring."

Abrams also sees history as the result of
(15) structuring. People, both individually and as members of collectives, make history. But our making of history is itself formed and informed not only by the historical conditions we inherit from the past, but also by the prior formation of our own identities and capacities,
(20) which are shaped by what Abrams calls "contingencies"—social phenomena over which we have varying degrees of control. Contingencies include such things as the social conditions under which we come of age, the condition of our household's
(25) economy, the ideologies available to help us make sense of our situation, and accidental circumstances. The ways in which contingencies affect our individual or group identities create a structure of forces within which we are able to act, and that partially determines
(30) the sorts of actions we are able to perform.

In Abrams's analysis, historical structuring, like social structuring, is manifold and unremitting. To understand it, historical sociologists must extract from it certain significant episodes, or events, that their
(35) methodology can then analyze and interpret. According to Abrams, these events are points at which action and contingency meet, points that represent a cross section of the specific social and individual forces in play at a given time. At such moments, individuals stand forth
(40) as agents of history not simply because they possess a unique ability to act, but also because in them we see the force of the specific social conditions that allowed their actions to come forth. Individuals can "make their mark" on history, yet in individuals one also finds the
(45) convergence of wider social forces. In order to capture the various facets of this mutual interaction, Abrams recommends a fourfold structure to which he believes the investigations of historical sociologists should conform: first, description of the event itself; second,
(50) discussion of the social context that helped bring the event about and gave it significance; third, summary of the life history of the individual agent in the event; and fourth, analysis of the consequences of the event both for history and for the individual.

15. Which one of the following most accurately states the central idea of the passage?

(A) Abrams argues that historical sociology rejects the claims of sociologists who assert that the sociological concept of structuring cannot be applied to the interactions between individuals and history.
(B) Abrams argues that historical sociology assumes that, despite the views of sociologists to the contrary, history influences the social contingencies that affect individuals.
(C) Abrams argues that historical sociology demonstrates that, despite the views of sociologists to the contrary, social structures both influence and are influenced by the events of history.
(D) Abrams describes historical sociology as a discipline that unites two approaches taken by sociologists to studying the formation of societies and applies the resulting combined approach to the study of history.
(E) Abrams describes historical sociology as an attempt to compensate for the shortcomings of traditional historical methods by applying the methods established in sociology.

16. Given the passage's argument, which one of the following sentences most logically completes the last paragraph?

(A) Only if they adhere to this structure, Abrams believes, can historical sociologists conclude with any certainty that the events that constitute the historical record are influenced by the actions of individuals.
(B) Only if they adhere to this structure, Abrams believes, will historical sociologists be able to counter the standard sociological assumption that there is very little connection between history and individual agency.
(C) Unless they can agree to adhere to this structure, Abrams believes, historical sociologists risk having their discipline treated as little more than an interesting but ultimately indefensible adjunct to history and sociology.
(D) By adhering to this structure, Abrams believes, historical sociologists can shed light on issues that traditional sociologists have chosen to ignore in their one-sided approaches to the formation of societies.
(E) By adhering to this structure, Abrams believes, historical sociologists will be able to better portray the complex connections between human agency and history.

17. The passage states that a contingency could be each of the following EXCEPT:

    (A) a social phenomenon
    (B) a form of historical structuring
    (C) an accidental circumstance
    (D) a condition controllable to some extent by an individual
    (E) a partial determinant of an individual's actions

18. Which one of the following is most analogous to the ideal work of a historical sociologist as outlined by Abrams?

    (A) In a report on the enactment of a bill into law, a journalist explains why the need for the bill arose, sketches the biography of the principal legislator who wrote the bill, and ponders the effect that the bill's enactment will have both on society and on the legislator's career.
    (B) In a consultation with a patient, a doctor reviews the patient's medical history, suggests possible reasons for the patient's current condition, and recommends steps that the patient should take in the future to ensure that the condition improves or at least does not get any worse.
    (C) In an analysis of a historical novel, a critic provides information to support the claim that details of the work's setting are accurate, explains why the subject of the novel was of particular interest to the author, and compares the novel with some of the author's other books set in the same period.
    (D) In a presentation to stockholders, a corporation's chief executive officer describes the corporation's most profitable activities during the past year, introduces the vice president largely responsible for those activities, and discusses new projects the vice president will initiate in the coming year.
    (E) In developing a film based on a historical event, a filmmaker conducts interviews with participants in the event, bases part of the film's screenplay on the interviews, and concludes the screenplay with a sequence of scenes speculating on the outcome of the event had certain details been different.

19. The primary function of the first paragraph of the passage is to

    (A) outline the merits of Abrams's conception of historical sociology
    (B) convey the details of Abrams's conception of historical sociology
    (C) anticipate challenges to Abrams's conception of historical sociology
    (D) examine the roles of key terms used in Abrams's conception of historical sociology
    (E) identify the basis of Abrams's conception of historical sociology

20. Based on the passage, which one of the following is the LEAST illustrative example of the effect of a contingency upon an individual?

    (A) the effect of the fact that a person experienced political injustice on that person's decision to work for political reform
    (B) the effect of the fact that a person was raised in an agricultural region on that person's decision to pursue a career in agriculture
    (C) the effect of the fact that a person lives in a particular community on that person's decision to visit friends in another community
    (D) the effect of the fact that a person's parents practiced a particular religion on that person's decision to practice that religion
    (E) the effect of the fact that a person grew up in financial hardship on that person's decision to help others in financial hardship

SOCIAL SCIENCE

Hard Science

Hard Science Passages

Passage #1: December 1996 Questions 17-21 118
Passage #2: September 1998 Questions 14-21 120
Passage #3: December 1998 Questions 15-21 122
Passage #4: June 1999 Questions 6-13 124
Passage #5: October 1999 Questions 16-21 126
Passage #6: December 1999 Questions 1-6 128
Passage #7: October 2000 Questions 20-27 130
Passage #8: December 2000 Questions 15-22 132
Passage #9: June 2001 Questions 13-18 134
Passage #10: October 2001 Questions 15-20 136
Passage #11: December 2001 Questions 15-20 138
Passage #12: June 2002 Questions 8-13 140
Passage #13: December 2002 Questions 17-23 142
Passage #14: June 2003 Questions 13-19 144

Passage #1: December 1996 Questions 17-21

Since the early 1920s, most petroleum geologists have favored a biogenic theory for the formation of oil. According to this theory, organic matter became buried in sediments, and subsequent conditions of
(5) temperature and pressure over time transformed it into oil.
Since 1979 an opposing abiogenic theory about the origin of oil has been promulgated. According to this theory, what is now oil began as
(10) hydrocarbon compounds within the earth's mantle (the region between the core and the crust) during the formation of the earth. Oil was created when gases rich in methane, the lightest of the hydrocarbons, rose from the mantle through
(15) fractures and faults in the crust, carrying a significant amount of heavier hydrocarbons with them. As the gases encountered intermittent drops in pressure, the heavier hydrocarbons condensed, forming oil, and were deposited in reservoirs
(20) throughout the crust. Rock regions deformed by motions of the crustal plates provided the conduits and fractures necessary for the gases to rise through the crust.
Opponents of the abiogenic theory charge that
(25) hydrocarbons could not exist in the mantle, because high temperatures would destroy or break them down. Advocates of the theory, however, point out that other types of carbon exist in the mantle: unoxidized carbon must exist there, because
(30) diamonds are formed within the mantle before being brought to the surface by eruptive processes. Proponents of the abiogenic theory also point to recent experimental work that suggests that the higher pressures within the mantle tend to offset the
(35) higher temperatures, allowing hydrocarbons, like unoxidized carbon, to continue to exist in the mantle.
If the abiogenic theory is correct, vast undiscovered reservoirs of oil and gas—
(40) undiscovered because the biogenic model precludes their existence—may in actuality exist. One company owned by the Swedish government has found the abiogenic theory so persuasive that it has started exploratory drilling for gas or oil in a granite
(45) formation called the Siljan Ring—not the best place to look for gas or oil if one believes they are derived from organic compounds, because granite forms from magma (molten rock) and contains no organic sediments. The ring was formed about 360
(50) million years ago when a large meteorite hit the 600-million-year-old granite that forms the base of the continental crust. The impact fractured the granite, and the Swedes believe that if oil comes from the mantle, it could have risen with methane
(55) gas through this now permeable rock. Fueling their optimism further is the fact that prior to the start of drilling, methane gas had been detected rising through the granite.

17. Which one of the following statements best expresses the main idea of the passage?

(A) Although the new abiogenic theory about the origin of oil is derived from the conventional biogenic theory, it suggests new types of locations for oil drilling.

(B) The small number of drilling companies that have responded to the new abiogenic theory about the origin of oil reflects the minimal level of acceptance the theory has met with in the scientific community.

(C) Although the new abiogenic theory about the origin of oil fails to explain several enigmas about oil reservoirs, it is superior to the conventional biogenic theory.

(D) Although it has yet to receive either support or refutation by data gathered from a drilling project, the new abiogenic theory about the origin of oil offers a plausible alternative to the conventional biogenic theory.

(E) Having answered objections about higher pressures in the earth's core, proponents of the new abiogenic theory have gained broad acceptance for their theory in the scientific community.

18. Which one of the following best describes the function of the third paragraph?

    (A) It presents a view opposed to a theory and points out an internal contradiction in that opposing view.
    (B) It describes a criticism of a theory and provides countervailing evidence to the criticism.
    (C) It identifies a conflict between two views of a theory and revises both views.
    (D) It explains an argument against a theory and shows it to be a valid criticism.
    (E) It points out the correspondence between an argument against one theory and arguments against similar theories.

19. The passage suggests that the opponents of the abiogenic theory mentioned in the third paragraph would most probably agree with which one of the following statements?

    (A) The formation of oil does not involve the condensation of hydrocarbons released from the earth's mantle.
    (B) Large oil reserves are often found in locations that contain small amounts of organic matter.
    (C) The eruptive processes by which diamonds are brought to the earth's surface are similar to those that aid in the formation of oil.
    (D) Motions of the crustal plates often create the pressure necessary to transform organic matter into oil.
    (E) The largest known oil reserves may have resulted from organic matter combining with heavier hydrocarbons carried by methane gas.

20. Which one of the following is most analogous to the situation described in the final paragraph?

    (A) A new theory about the annual cycles of breeding and migration of the monarch butterfly has led scientists to look for similar patterns in other butterfly species.
    (B) A new theory about the stage at which a star collapses into a black hole has led astronomers to search for evidence of black holes in parts of the universe where they had not previously searched.
    (C) A new theory about how the emission of sulfur dioxide during coal-burning can be reduced has led several companies to develop desulfurization systems.
    (D) A new theory about photosynthesis has convinced a research team to explore in new ways the various functions of the cell membrane in plant cells.
    (E) A new theory about the distribution of metals in rock formations has convinced a silver-mining company to keep different types of records of its operations.

21. According to the passage, all of the following are true of the Siljan Ring EXCEPT:

    (A) It was formed from magma.
    (B) It does not contain organic sediments.
    (C) Its ring shape existed 500 million years ago.
    (D) Methane gas has been detected rising through it.
    (E) It was shaped from the granite that makes up the base of the continental crust.

Passage #2: September 1998 Questions 14-21

Between June 1987 and May 1988, the bodies of at least 740 bottlenose dolphins out of a total coastal population of 3,000 to 5,000 washed ashore on the Atlantic coast of the United States. Since some of the
(5) dead animals never washed ashore, the overall disaster was presumably worse; perhaps 50 percent of the population died. A dolphin die-off of this character and magnitude had never before been observed; furthermore, the dolphins exhibited a startling range of
(10) symptoms. The research team that examined the die-off noted the presence of both skin lesions and internal lesions in the liver, lung, pancreas, and heart, which suggested a massive opportunistic bacterial infection of already weakened animals.
(15) Tissues from the stricken dolphins were analyzed for a variety of toxins. Brevetoxin, a toxin produced by the blooming of the alga *Ptychodiscus brevis,* was present in eight out of seventeen dolphins tested. Tests for synthetic pollutants revealed that polychlorinated
(20) biphenyls (PCBs) were present in almost all animals tested.
The research team concluded that brevetoxin poisoning was the most likely cause of the illnesses that killed the dolphins. Although *P. brevis* is
(25) ordinarily not found along the Atlantic coast, an unusual bloom of this organism—such blooms are called "red tides" because of the reddish color imparted by the blooming algae—did occur in the middle of the affected coastline in October 1987. These researchers
(30) believe the toxin accumulated in the tissue of fish and then was ingested by dolphins that preyed on them. The emaciated appearance of many dolphins indicated that they were metabolizing their blubber reserves, thereby reducing their buoyancy and insulation (and
(35) adding to overall stress) as well as releasing stores of previously accumulated synthetic pollutants, such as PCBs, which further exacerbated their condition. The combined impact made the dolphins vulnerable to opportunistic bacterial infection, the ultimate cause of
(40) death.
For several reasons, however, this explanation is not entirely plausible. First, bottlenose dolphins and *P. brevis* red tides are both common in the Gulf of Mexico, yet no dolphin die-off of a similar magnitude
(45) has been noted there. Second, dolphins began dying in June, hundreds of miles north of and some months earlier than the October red tide bloom. Finally, the specific effects of brevetoxin on dolphins are unknown, whereas PCB poisoning is known to impair functioning
(50) of the immune system and liver and to cause skin lesions; all of these problems were observed in the diseased animals. An alternative hypothesis, which accounts for these facts, is that a sudden influx of pollutants, perhaps from offshore dumping, triggered a
(55) cascade of disorders in animals whose systems were already heavily laden with pollutants. Although brevetoxin may have been a contributing factor, the event that actually precipitated the die-off was a sharp increase in the dolphins' exposure to synthetic
(60) pollutants.

14. The passage is primarily concerned with assessing

   (A) the effects of a devastating bacterial infection in Atlantic coast bottlenose dolphins
   (B) the process by which illnesses in Atlantic coast bottlenose dolphins were correctly diagnosed
   (C) the weaknesses in the research methodology used to explore the dolphin die-off
   (D) possible alternative explanations for the massive dolphin die-off
   (E) relative effects of various marine pollutants on dolphin mortality

15. Which one of the following is mentioned in the passage as evidence for the explanation of the dolphin die-off offered in the final paragraph?

   (A) the release of stored brevetoxins from the dolphins' blubber reserves
   (B) the date on which offshore dumping was known to have occurred nearby
   (C) the presence of dumping sites for PCBs in the area
   (D) the synthetic pollutants that were present in the fish eaten by the dolphins
   (E) the effects of PCBs on liver function in dolphins

16. Which one of the following is most analogous to the approach taken by the author of the passage with regard to the research described in the third paragraph?

   (A) A physics teacher accepts the data from a student's experiment but questions the student's conclusions.
   (B) An astronomer provides additional observations to support another astronomer's theory.
   (C) A cook revises a traditional recipe by substituting modern ingredients for those used in the original.
   (D) A doctor prescribes medication for a patient whose illness was misdiagnosed by another doctor.
   (E) A microbiologist sets out to replicate the experiment that yielded a classic theory of cell structure.

17. Which one of the following most accurately describes the organization of the last paragraph?

    (A) One explanation is criticized and a different explanation is proposed.
    (B) An argument is advanced and then refuted by means of an opposing argument.
    (C) Objections against a hypothesis are advanced, the hypothesis is explained more fully, and then the objections are rejected.
    (D) New evidence in favor of a theory is described, and then the theory is reaffirmed.
    (E) Discrepancies between two explanations are noted, and a third explanation is proposed.

18. It can be inferred from the passage that the author would most probably agree with which one of the following statements about brevetoxin?

    (A) It may have been responsible for the dolphins' skin lesions but could not have contributed to the bacterial infection.
    (B) It forms more easily when both P. brevis and synthetic pollutants are present in the environment simultaneously.
    (C) It damages liver function and immune system responses in bottlenose dolphins but may not have triggered this particular dolphin die-off.
    (D) It is unlikely to be among the factors that contributed to the dolphin die-off.
    (E) It is unlikely to have caused the die-off because it was not present in the dolphins' environment when the die-off began.

19. The explanation for the dolphin die-off given by the research team most strongly supports which one of the following?

    (A) The biological mechanism by which brevetoxin affects dolphins is probably different from that by which it affects other marine animals.
    (B) When P. brevis blooms in an area where it does not usually exist, it is more toxic than it is in its usual habitat.
    (C) Opportunistic bacterial infection is usually associated with brevetoxin poisoning in bottlenose dolphins.
    (D) The dolphins' emaciated state was probably a symptom of PCB poisoning rather than of brevetoxin poisoning.
    (E) When a dolphin metabolizes its blubber, the PCBs released may be more dangerous to the dolphin than they were when stored in the blubber.

20. The author refers to dolphins in the Gulf of Mexico in the last paragraph in order to

    (A) refute the assertion that dolphins tend not to inhabit areas where P. brevis is common
    (B) compare the effects of synthetic pollutants on these dolphins and on Atlantic coast dolphins
    (C) cast doubt on the belief that P. brevis contributes substantially to dolphin die-offs
    (D) illustrate the fact that dolphins in relatively pollution-free waters are healthier than dolphins in polluted waters
    (E) provide evidence for the argument that P. brevis was probably responsible for the dolphins' deaths

21. Which one of the following factors is explicitly cited as contributing to the dolphins' deaths in both theories discussed in the passage?

    (A) the dolphins' diet
    (B) the presence of P. brevis in the Gulf of Mexico
    (C) the wide variety of toxins released by the red tide bloom of October 1987
    (D) the presence of synthetic pollutants in the dolphins' bodies
    (E) the bacterial infection caused by a generalized failure of the dolphins' immune systems

Passage #3: December 1998 Questions 15-21

Homing pigeons can be taken from their lofts and transported hundreds of kilometers in covered cages to unfamiliar sites and yet, when released, be able to choose fairly accurate homeward bearings within a
(5) minute and fly home. Aside from reading the minds of the experimenters (a possibility that has not escaped investigation), there are two basic explanations for the remarkable ability of pigeons to "home": the birds might keep track of their outward displacement (the
(10) system of many short-range species such as honeybees); or they might have some sense, known as a "map sense," that would permit them to construct an internal image of their environment and then "place" themselves with respect to home on some internalized
(15) coordinate system.

The first alternative seems unlikely. One possible model for such an inertial system might involve an internal magnetic compass to measure the directional leg of each journey. Birds transported to the release site
(20) wearing magnets or otherwise subjected to an artificial magnetic field, however, are only occasionally affected. Alternately, if pigeons measure their displacement by consciously keeping track of the direction and degree of acceleration and deceleration of
(25) the various turns, and timing the individual legs of the journey, simply transporting them in the dark, with constant rotations, or under complete anesthesia ought to impair or eliminate their ability to orient. These treatments, however, have no effect. Unfortunately, no
(30) one has yet performed the crucial experiment of transporting pigeons in total darkness, anesthetized, rotating, and with the magnetic field reversed all at the same time.

The other alternative, that pigeons have a "map
(35) sense," seems more promising, yet the nature of this sense remains mysterious. Papi has posited that the map sense is olfactory: that birds come to associate odors borne on the wind with the direction in which the wind is blowing, and so slowly build up an olfactory
(40) map of their surroundings. When transported to the release site, then, they only have to sniff the air en route and/or at the site to know the direction of home. Papi conducted a series of experiments showing that pigeons whose nostrils have been plugged are poorly
(45) oriented at release and home slowly.

One problem with the hypothesis is that Schmidt-Koenig and Phillips failed to detect any ability in pigeons to distinguish natural air (presumably laden with olfactory map information) from pure, filtered air.
(50) Papi's experimental results, moreover, admit of simpler, nonolfactory explanations. It seems likely that the behavior of nostril-plugged birds results from the distracting and traumatic nature of the experiment. When nasal tubes are used to bypass the olfactory
(55) chamber but allow for comfortable breathing, no disorientation is evident. Likewise, when the olfactory epithelium is sprayed with anesthetic to block smell-detection but not breathing, orientation is normal.

15. Which one of the following best states the main idea of the passage?

(A) The ability of pigeons to locate and return to their homes from distant points is unlike that of any other species.
(B) It is likely that some map sense accounts for the homing ability of pigeons, but the nature of that sense has not been satisfactorily identified.
(C) The majority of experiments on the homing ability of pigeons have been marked by design flaws.
(D) The mechanisms underlying the homing ability of pigeons can best be identified through a combination of laboratory research and field experimentation.
(E) The homing ability of pigeons is most likely based on a system similar to that used by many short-range species.

16. According to the passage, which one of the following is ordinarily true regarding how homing pigeons "home"?

(A) Each time they are released at a specific site they fly home by the same route.
(B) When they are released they take only a short time to orient themselves before selecting their route home.
(C) Each time they are released at a specific site they take a shorter amount of time to orient themselves before flying home.
(D) They travel fairly long distances in seemingly random patterns before finally deciding on a route home.
(E) Upon release they travel briefly in the direction opposite to the one they eventually choose.

17. Which one of the following experiments would best test the "possibility" referred to in line 6?

    (A) an experiment in which the handlers who transported, released, and otherwise came into contact with homing pigeons released at an unfamiliar site were unaware of the location of the pigeons' home
    (B) an experiment in which the handlers who transported, released, and otherwise came into contact with homing pigeons released at an unfamiliar site were asked not to display any affection toward the pigeons
    (C) an experiment in which the handlers who transported, released, and otherwise came into contact with homing pigeons released at an unfamiliar site were asked not to speak to each other throughout the release process
    (D) an experiment in which all the homing pigeons released at an unfamiliar site had been raised and fed by individual researchers rather than by teams of handlers
    (E) an experiment in which all the homing pigeons released at an unfamiliar site were exposed to a wide variety of unfamiliar sights and sounds

18. Information in the passage supports which one of the following statements regarding the "first alternative" (line 16) for explaining the ability of pigeons to "home"?

    (A) It has been conclusively ruled out by the results of numerous experiments.
    (B) It seems unlikely because there are no theoretical models that could explain how pigeons track displacement.
    (C) It has not, to date, been supported by experimental data, but neither has it been definitively ruled out.
    (D) It seems unlikely in theory, but recent experimental results show that it may in fact be correct.
    (E) It is not a useful theory because of the difficulty in designing experiments by which it might be tested.

19. The author refers to "the system of many short-range species such as honeybees" (lines 9-11) most probably in order to

    (A) emphasize the universality of the ability to home
    (B) suggest that a particular explanation of pigeons' homing ability is worthy of consideration
    (C) discredit one of the less convincing theories regarding the homing ability of pigeons
    (D) criticize the techniques utilized by scientists investigating the nature of pigeons' homing ability
    (E) illustrate why a proposed explanation of pigeons' homing ability is correct

20. Which one of the following, if true, would most weaken Papi's theory regarding homing pigeons' homing ability?

    (A) Even pigeons that have been raised in several different lofts in a variety of territories can find their way to their current home when released in unfamiliar territory.
    (B) Pigeons whose sense of smell has been partially blocked find their way home more slowly than do pigeons whose sense of smell has not been affected.
    (C) Even pigeons that have been raised in the same loft frequently take different routes home when released in unfamiliar territory.
    (D) Even pigeons that have been transported well beyond the range of the odors detectable in their home territories can find their way home.
    (E) Pigeons' sense of smell is no more acute than that of other birds who do not have the ability to "home."

21. Given the information in the passage, it is most likely that Papi and the author of the passage would both agree with which one of the following statements regarding the homing ability of pigeons?

    (A) The map sense of pigeons is most probably related to their olfactory sense.
    (B) The mechanism regulating the homing ability of pigeons is most probably similar to that utilized by honeybees.
    (C) The homing ability of pigeons is most probably based on a map sense.
    (D) The experiments conducted by Papi himself have provided the most valuable evidence yet collected regarding the homing ability of pigeons.
    (E) The experiments conducted by Schmidt-Koenig and Phillips have not substantially lessened the probability that Papi's own theory is correct.

Passage #4: June 1999 Questions 6-13

Long after the lava has cooled, the effects of a major volcanic eruption may linger on. In the atmosphere a veil of fine dust and sulfuric acid droplets can spread around the globe and persist for years.
(5) Researchers have generally thought that this veil can block enough sunlight to have a chilling influence on Earth's climate. Many blame the cataclysmic eruption of the Indonesian volcano Tambora in 1815 for the ensuing "year without a summer" of 1816—when parts
(10) of the northeastern United States and southeastern Canada were hit by snowstorms in June and frosts in August.

The volcano-climate connection seems plausible, but, say scientists Clifford Mass and David Portman, it
(15) is not as strong as previously believed. Mass and Portman analyzed global temperature data for the years before and after nine volcanic eruptions, from Krakatau in 1883 to El Chichon in 1982. In the process they tried to filter out temperature changes caused by the cyclic
(20) weather phenomenon known as the El Nino-Southern Oscillation, which warms the sea surface in the equatorial Pacific and thereby warms the atmosphere. Such warming can mask the cooling brought about by an eruption, but it can also mimic volcanic cooling if
(25) the volcano happens to erupt just as an El Nino-induced warm period is beginning to fade.

Once El Nino effects had been subtracted from the data, the actual effects of the eruptions came through more clearly. Contrary to what earlier studies had
(30) suggested, Mass and Portman found that minor eruptions have no discernible effect on temperature. And major, dust-spitting explosions, such as Krakatau or El Chichon, cause a smaller drop than expected in the average temperature in the hemisphere (Northern or
(35) Southern) of the eruption—only half a degree centigrade or less—with a correspondingly smaller drop in the opposite hemisphere.

Other researchers, however, have argued that even a small temperature drop could result in a significant
(40) regional fluctuation in climate if its effects were amplified by climatic feedback loops. For example, a small temperature drop in the northeastern U.S. and southeastern Canada in early spring might delay the melting of snow, and the unmelted snow would
(45) continue to reflect sunlight away from the surface, amplifying the cooling. The cool air over the region could, in turn, affect the jet stream. The jet stream tends to flow at the boundary between cool northern air and warm southern air, drawing its power from the
(50) sharp temperature contrast and the consequent difference in pressure. An unusual cooling in the region could cause the stream to wander farther south than normal, allowing more polar air to come in behind it and deepen the region's cold snap. Through such a
(55) series of feedbacks a small temperature drop could be blown up into a year without a summer.

6. Which one of the following most accurately expresses the main idea of the passage?

(A) The effect of volcanic eruptions on regional temperature is greater than it was once thought to be.
(B) The effect of volcanic eruptions on regional temperature is smaller than the effect of volcanic eruptions on global temperature.
(C) The effect of volcanic eruptions on global temperature appears to be greater than was previously supposed.
(D) Volcanic eruptions appear not to have the significant effect on global temperature they were once thought to have but might have a significant effect on regional temperature.
(E) Researchers tended to overestimate the influence of volcanic eruptions on global temperature because they exaggerated the effect of cyclical weather phenomena in making their calculations.

7. Not taking the effects of El Nino into account when figuring the effect of volcanic eruptions on Earth's climate is most closely analogous to not taking into account the

(A) weight of a package as a whole when determining the weight of its contents apart from the packing material
(B) monetary value of the coins in a pile when counting the number of coins in the pile
(C) magnification of a lens when determining the shape of an object seen through the lens
(D) number of false crime reports in a city when figuring the average annual number of crimes committed in that city
(E) ages of new immigrants to a country before attributing a change in the average age of the country's population to a change in the number of births

8. The passage indicates that each of the following can be an effect of the El Nino phenomenon EXCEPT:

(A) making the cooling effect of a volcanic eruption appear to be more pronounced than it actually is
(B) making the cooling effect of a volcanic eruption appear to be less pronounced than it actually is
(C) increasing atmospheric temperature through cyclic warming of equatorial waters
(D) initiating a feedback loop that masks cooling brought about by an eruption
(E) confounding the evidence for a volcano-climate connection

9. Which one of the following most accurately characterizes what the author of the passage means by a "minor" volcanic eruption (line 30)?

    (A) an eruption that produces less lava than either Krakatau or El Chichon did
    (B) an eruption that has less of an effect on global temperature than either Krakatau or El Chichon did
    (C) an eruption whose effect on regional temperature can be masked by conditions in the hemisphere of the eruption
    (D) an eruption that introduces a relatively small amount of debris into the atmosphere
    (E) an eruption that causes average temperature in the hemisphere of the eruption to drop by less than half a degree centigrade

10. To which one of the following situations would the concept of a feedback loop, as it is employed in the passage, be most accurately applied?

    (A) An increase in the amount of decaying matter in the soil increases the amount of nutrients in the soil, which increases the number of plants, which further increases the amount of decaying matter in the soil.
    (B) An increase in the number of wolves in an area decreases the number of deer, which decreases the grazing of shrubs, which increases the amount of food available for other animals, which increases the number of other animals in the area.
    (C) An increase in the amount of rain in an area increases the deterioration of the forest floor, which makes it harder for wolves to prey on deer, which increases the number of deer, which gives wolves more opportunities to prey upon deer.
    (D) An increase in the amount of sunlight on the ocean increases the ocean temperature, which increases the number of phytoplankton in the ocean, which decreases the ocean temperature by blocking sunlight.
    (E) An increase in the number of outdoor electric lights in an area increases the number of insects in the area, which increases the number of bats in the area, which decreases the number of insects in the area, which decreases the number of bats in the area.

11. The author of the passage would be most likely to agree with which one of the following hypotheses?

    (A) Major volcanic eruptions sometimes cause average temperature in the hemisphere of the eruption to drop by more than a degree centigrade.
    (B) Major volcanic eruptions can induce the El Nino phenomenon when it otherwise might not occur.
    (C) Major volcanic eruptions do not directly cause unusually cold summers.
    (D) The climatic effects of minor volcanic eruptions differ from those of major eruptions only in degree.
    (E) El Nino has no discernible effect on average hemispheric temperature.

12. The information in the passage provides the LEAST support for which one of the following claims?

    (A) Major volcanic eruptions have a discernible effect on global temperature.
    (B) The effect of major volcanic eruptions on global temperature is smaller than was previously thought.
    (C) Major volcanic eruptions have no discernible effect on regional temperature.
    (D) Minor volcanic eruptions have no discernible effect on temperature in the hemisphere in which they occur.
    (E) Minor volcanic eruptions have no discernible effect on temperature in the hemisphere opposite the hemisphere of the eruption.

13. The primary purpose of the last paragraph of the passage is to

    (A) describe how the "year without a summer" differs from other examples of climatic feedback loops
    (B) account for the relatively slight hemispheric cooling effect of a major volcanic eruption
    (C) explain how regional climatic conditions can be significantly affected by a small drop in temperature
    (D) indicate how researchers are sometimes led to overlook the effects of El Nino on regional temperature
    (E) suggest a modification to the current model of how feedback loops produce changes in regional temperature

Passage #5: October 1999 Questions 16-21

Scientists have long known that the soft surface of the bill of the platypus is perforated with openings that contain sensitive nerve endings. Only recently, however, have biologists concluded on the basis of new
(5) evidence that the animal uses its bill to locate its prey while underwater, a conclusion suggested by the fact that the animal's eyes, ears, and nostrils are sealed when it is submerged. The new evidence comes from neurophysiological studies, which have recently
(10) revealed that within the pores on the bill there are two kinds of sensory receptors: mechanoreceptors, which are tiny pushrods that respond to tactile pressure, and electroreceptors, which respond to weak electrical fields. Having discovered that tactile stimulation of the
(15) pushrods sends nerve impulses to the brain, where they evoke an electric potential over an area of the neocortex much larger than the one stimulated by input from the limbs, eyes, and ears, Bohringer concluded that the bill must be the primary sensory organ for the
(20) platypus. Her finding was supported by studies showing that the bill is extraordinarily sensitive to tactile stimulation: stimulation with a fine glass stylus sent a signal by way of the fifth cranial nerve to the neocortex and from there to the motor cortex.
(25) Presumably nerve impulses from the motor cortex then induced a snapping movement of the bill. But Bohringer's investigations did not explain how the animal locates its prey at a distance.

Scheich's neurophysiological studies contribute to
(30) solving this mystery. His initial work showed that when a platypus feeds, it swims along, steadily wagging its bill from side to side until prey is encountered. It thereupon switches to searching behavior, characterized by erratic movements of the
(35) bill over a small area at the bottom of a body of water, which is followed by homing in on the object and seizing it. In order to determine how the animal senses prey and then distinguishes it from other objects on the bottom, Scheich hypothesized that a sensory system
(40) based on electroreception similar to that found in sharks might exist in the platypus. In further experiments he found he could trigger the switch from patrolling to searching behavior in the platypus by creating a dipole electric field in the water with the aid
(45) of a small 1.5-volt battery. The platypus, sensitive to the weak electric current that was created, rapidly oriented toward the battery at a distance of 10 centimeters and sometimes as much as 30 centimeters. Once the battery was detected, the
(50) platypus would inevitably attack it as if it were food. Scheich then discovered that the tail flicks of freshwater shrimp, a common prey of the platypus, also produce weak electric fields and elicit an identical response. Scheich and his colleagues believe that it is
(55) reasonable to assume that all the invertebrates on which the platypus feeds must produce electric fields.

16. The primary purpose of the passage is to

(A) explain how the platypus locates prey at a distance
(B) present some recent scientific research on the function of the platypus's bill
(C) assess the results of Bohringer's experimental work about the platypus
(D) present Scheich's contributions to scientific work about the platypus
(E) describe two different kinds of pores on the platypus's bill

17. Which one of the following statements best expresses the main idea of the passage?

(A) Neurophysiological studies have established that the bill of the platypus is one of its primary sensory organs.
(B) Neurophysiological studies have established that the platypus uses its bill to locate its prey underwater.
(C) Bohringer's neurophysiological studies have established that sensory receptors in the bill of the platypus respond to electrical stimulation.
(D) Biologists have concluded that the surface of the bill of the platypus is perforated with openings that contain sensitive nerve endings.
(E) Biologists have concluded that the hunting platypus responds to weak electric fields emitted by freshwater invertebrates.

18. During the studies supporting Bohringer's finding, as they are described in the passage, which one of the following occurred before a nerve impulse reached the motor cortex of the platypus?

    (A) The electroreceptors sent the nerve impulse to the fifth cranial nerve.
    (B) The neocortex induced a snapping movement of the bill.
    (C) The mechanoreceptors sent the nerve impulse via the fifth cranial nerve to the electroreceptors.
    (D) The platypus opened the pores on its bill.
    (E) The fifth cranial nerve carried the nerve impulse to the neocortex.

19. Which one of the following strategies is most similar to Scheich's experimental strategy as it is described in the passage?

    (A) To determine the mating habits of birds, a biologist places decoys near the birds' nests that resemble the birds and emit bird calls.
    (B) To determine whether certain animals find their way by listening for echoes to their cries, a biologist plays a tape of the animals' cries in their vicinity.
    (C) To determine whether an animal uses heat sensitivity to detect prey, a biologist places a heat-generating object near the animal's home.
    (D) A fisherman catches fish by dangling in the water rubber replicas of the fishes' prey that have been scented with fish oil.
    (E) A game warden captures an animal by baiting a cage with a piece of meat that the animal will want to eat.

20. It can be inferred from the passage that during patrolling behavior, the platypus is attempting to

    (A) capture prey that it has detected
    (B) distinguish one kind of prey from another
    (C) detect electric fields produced by potential prey
    (D) stimulate its mechanoreceptors
    (E) pick up the scent of its prey

21. Which one of the following best describes the organization of the passage?

    (A) A hypothesis is presented and defended with supporting examples.
    (B) A conclusion is presented and the information supporting it is provided.
    (C) A thesis is presented and defended with an argument.
    (D) Opposing views are presented, discussed, and then reconciled.
    (E) A theory is proposed, considered, and then amended.

Passage #6: December 1999 Questions 1-6

The okapi, a forest mammal of central Africa, has presented zoologists with a number of difficult questions since they first learned of its existence in 1900. The first was how to classify it. Because it was
(5) horselike in dimension, and bore patches of striped hide similar to a zebra's (a relative of the horse), zoologists first classified it as a member of the horse family. But further studies showed that, despite okapis' coloration and short necks, their closest relatives were
(10) giraffes. The okapi's rightful place within the giraffe family is confirmed by its skin-covered horns (in males), two-lobed canine teeth, and long prehensile tongue.

The next question was the size of the okapi
(15) population. Because okapis were infrequently captured by hunters, some zoologists believed that they were rare; however, others theorized that their habits simply kept them out of sight. It was not until 1985, when zoologists started tracking okapis by affixing collars
(20) equipped with radio transmitters to briefly captured specimens, that reliable information about okapi numbers and habits began to be collected. It turns out that while okapis are not as rare as some zoologists suspected, their population is concentrated in an
(25) extremely limited chain of forestland in northeastern central Africa, surrounded by savanna.

One reason for their seeming scarcity is that their coloration allows okapis to camouflage themselves even at close range. Another is that okapis do not travel
(30) in groups or with other large forest mammals, and neither frequent open riverbanks nor forage at the borders of clearings, choosing instead to keep to the forest interior. This is because okapis, unlike any other animal in the central African forest, subsist entirely on
(35) leaves: more than one hundred species of plants have been identified as part of their diet, and about twenty of these are preferred. Okapis never eat one plant to the exclusion of others; even where preferred foliage is abundant, okapis will leave much of it uneaten,
(40) choosing to move on and sample other leaves. Because of this, and because of the distribution of their food, okapis engage in individual rather than congregated foraging.

But other questions about okapi behavior arise.
(45) Why, for example, do they prefer to remain within forested areas when many of their favorite plants are found in the open border between forest and savanna? One possibility is that this is a defense against predators; another is that the okapi was pushed into the
(50) forest by competition with other large, hoofed animals, such as the bushbuck and bongo, that specialize on the forest edges and graze them more efficiently. Another question is why okapis are absent from other nearby forest regions that would seem hospitable to them.
(55) Zoologists theorize that okapis are relics of an era when forestland was scarce and that they continue to respect those borders even though available forestland has long since expanded.

1. Which one of the following most completely and accurately expresses the main idea of the passage?

(A) Information gathered by means of radio-tracking collars has finally provided answers to the questions about okapis that zoologists have been attempting to answer since they first learned of the mammal's existence.

(B) Because of their physical characteristics and their infrequent capture by hunters, okapis presented zoologists with many difficult questions at the start of the twentieth century.

(C) Research concerning okapis has answered some of the questions that have puzzled zoologists since their discovery, but has also raised other questions regarding their geographic concentration and feeding habits.

(D) A new way of tracking okapis using radio-tracking collars reveals that their apparent scarcity is actually a result of their coloration, their feeding habits, and their geographic concentration.

(E) Despite new research involving radio tracking, the questions that have puzzled zoologists about okapis since their discovery at the start of the twentieth century remain mostly unanswered.

2. The function of the third paragraph is to

   (A) pose a question about okapi behavior
   (B) rebut a theory about okapi behavior
   (C) counter the assertion that okapis are rare
   (D) explain why okapis appeared to be rare
   (E) support the belief that okapis are rare

3. Based on the passage, in its eating behavior the okapi is most analogous to

   (A) a child who eats one kind of food at a time, consuming all of it before going on to the next kind
   (B) a professor who strictly follows the outline in the syllabus, never digressing to follow up on student questions
   (C) a student who delays working on homework until the last minute, then rushes to complete it
   (D) a newspaper reader who skips from story to story, just reading headlines and eye-catching paragraphs
   (E) a deer that ventures out of the woods only at dusk and dawn, remaining hidden during the rest of the day

4. Suppose that numerous okapis are discovered living in a remote forest region in northeastern central Africa that zoologists had not previously explored. Based on their current views, which one of the following would the zoologists be most likely to conclude about this discovery?

   (A) Okapis were pushed into this forest region by competition with mammals in neighboring forests.
   (B) Okapis in this forest region forage in the border between forest and savanna.
   (C) Okapis in this forest region are not threatened by the usual predators of okapis.
   (D) Okapis moved into this forest region because their preferred foliage is more abundant there than in other forests.
   (E) Okapis lived in this forest region when forestland in the area was scarce.

5. The passage provides information intended to help explain each of the following EXCEPT:

   (A) why zoologists once believed that okapis were rare
   (B) why zoologists classified the okapi as a member of the giraffe family
   (C) why okapis choose to limit themselves to the interiors of forests
   (D) why okapis engage in individual rather than congregated foraging
   (E) why okapis leave much preferred foliage uneaten

6. Based on the passage, the author would be most likely to agree with which one of the following statements?

   (A) The number of okapis is many times larger than zoologists had previously believed it to be.
   (B) Radio-tracking collars have enabled scientists to finally answer all the questions about the okapi.
   (C) Okapis are captured infrequently because their habits and coloration make it difficult for hunters to find them.
   (D) Okapis are concentrated in a limited geographic area because they prefer to eat one plant species to the exclusion of others.
   (E) The number of okapis would steadily increase if okapis began to forage in the open border between forest and savanna.

Passage #7: October 2000 Questions 20-27

Most scientists who study the physiological effects of alcoholic beverages have assumed that wine, like beer or distilled spirits, is a drink whose only active ingredient is alcohol. Because of this assumption, these
(5) scientists have rarely investigated the effects of wine as distinct from other forms of alcoholic beverages. Nevertheless, unlike other alcoholic beverages, wine has for centuries been thought to have healthful effects that these scientists—who not only make no distinction
(10) among wine, beer, and distilled spirits but also study only the excessive or abusive intake of these beverages—have obscured.

Recently, a small group of researchers has questioned this assumption and investigated the effects
(15) of moderate wine consumption. While alcohol has been shown conclusively to have negative physiological effects—for example, alcohol strongly affects the body's processing of lipids (fats and other substances including cholesterol), causing dangerous increases in
(20) the levels of these substances in the blood, increases that are a large contributing factor in the development of premature heart disease—the researchers found that absorption of alcohol into the bloodstream occurs much more slowly when subjects drink wine than when they
(25) drink distilled spirits. More remarkably, it was discovered that deaths due to premature heart disease in the populations of several European countries decreased dramatically as the incidence of moderate wine consumption increased. One preliminary study
(30) linked this effect to red wine, but subsequent research has shown identical results whether the wine was white or red. What could explain such apparently healthful effects?

For one thing, the studies show increased activity
(35) of a natural clot breaking compound used by doctors to restore blood flow through blocked vessels in victims of heart disease. In addition, the studies of wine drinkers indicate increased levels of certain compounds that may help to prevent damage from high lipid levels.
(40) And although the link between lipid processing and premature heart disease is one of the most important discoveries in modern medicine, in the past 20 years researchers have found several additional important contributing factors. We now know that endothelial
(45) cell reactivity (which affects the thickness of the innermost walls of blood vessels) and platelet adhesiveness (which influences the degree to which platelets cause blood to clot) are each linked to the development of premature heart disease. Studies show
(50) that wine appears to have ameliorating effects on both of these factors: it decreases the thickness of the innermost walls of blood vessels, and it reduces platelet adhesiveness. One study demonstrated a decrease in platelet adhesiveness among individuals who drank
(55) large amounts of grape juice. This finding may be the first step in confirming speculation that the potentially healthful effects of moderate wine intake may derive from the concentration of certain natural compounds found in grapes and not present in other alcoholic
(60) beverages.

20. Which one of the following most accurately states the author's main point in the passage?

(A) Because of their assumption that alcohol is the only active ingredient in wine, beer, and distilled spirits, scientists have previously studied these beverages in ways that obscure their healthful effects.
(B) A new study of moderate wine consumption calls into question the belief that premature heart disease is caused solely by the presence of high lipid levels in the bloodstream.
(C) Researchers have found that alcohol from moderate wine consumption is absorbed into the bloodstream more slowly than is alcohol from other alcoholic beverages.
(D) Although it has long been held that moderate wine consumption has healthful effects, scientific studies have yet to prove such effects definitively.
(E) Wine, unlike other alcoholic beverages, appears to have a number of significant healthful effects that may be tied to certain natural compounds found in grapes.

21. In the first paragraph, the author most likely refers to the centuries old belief that wine has healthful effects in order to

(A) demonstrate that discoveries in the realm of science often bear out popular beliefs
(B) provide evidence for the theory that moderate wine consumption ameliorates factors that contribute to premature heart disease
(C) argue that traditional beliefs are no less important than scientific evidence when investigating health matters
(D) suggest that a prevailing scientific assumption might be mistaken
(E) refute the argument that science should take cues from popular beliefs

22. According to the passage, each of the following might help to prevent premature heart disease EXCEPT:

    (A) an increase in the degree to which platelets cause blood to clot
    (B) an increase in the body's ability to remove lipids from the bloodstream
    (C) an increase in the amount of time it takes alcohol to be absorbed into the bloodstream
    (D) increased activity of a natural compound that reduces blood clotting
    (E) increased levels of compounds that prevent damage from high lipid levels

23. Which one of the following, if true, would most strengthen the passage's position concerning the apparently healthful effects of moderate wine consumption?

    (A) Subjects who consumed large amounts of grape juice exhibited decreased thickness of the innermost walls of their blood vessels.
    (B) Subjects who were habitual drinkers of wine and subjects who were habitual drinkers of beer exhibited similar lipid levels in their bloodstreams.
    (C) Subjects who drank grape juice exhibited greater platelet adhesiveness than did subjects who drank no grape juice.
    (D) Subjects who drank excessive amounts of wine suffered from premature heart disease at roughly the same rate as moderate wine drinkers.
    (E) Subjects who possess a natural clot breaking compound were discovered to have a certain gene that is absent from subjects who do not possess the compound.

24. It can be inferred from the passage that the author would most likely agree with which one of the following statements?

    (A) Scientists should not attempt to study the possible healthful effects of moderate consumption of beer and distilled spirits.
    (B) The conclusion that alcohol affects lipid processing should be questioned in light of studies of moderate wine consumption.
    (C) Moderate consumption of wine made from plums or apples rather than grapes would be unlikely to reduce the risk of premature heart disease.
    (D) Red wine consumption has a greater effect on reducing death rates from premature heart disease than does white wine consumption.
    (E) Beer and distilled spirits contain active ingredients other than alcohol whose effects tend to be beneficial.

25. Based on the passage, the author's attitude toward the scientists discussed in the first paragraph can most accurately be described as

    (A) highly enthusiastic
    (B) tacitly approving
    (C) grudgingly accepting
    (D) overtly critical
    (E) clearly outraged

26. In the passage, the author is primarily concerned with doing which one of the following?

    (A) advocating a particular method of treatment
    (B) criticizing popular opinion
    (C) correcting a scientific misconception
    (D) questioning the relevance of newly discovered evidence
    (E) countering a revolutionary hypothesis

27. The author suggests each of the following in the passage EXCEPT:

    (A) Greater platelet adhesiveness increases the risk of premature heart disease.
    (B) The body's ability to process lipids is compromised by the presence of alcohol in the bloodstream.
    (C) Doctors have access to a natural compound that breaks down blood clots.
    (D) High lipid levels are dangerous because they lead to increased endothelial cell reactivity and platelet adhesiveness.
    (E) Moderate wine consumption appears to decrease the thickness of the interior walls of blood vessels.

Passage #8: December 2000 Questions 15-22

Experts anticipate that global atmospheric concentrations of carbon dioxide (CO_2) will have doubled by the end of the twenty-first century. It is known that CO_2 can contribute to global warming by
(5) trapping solar energy that is being reradiated as heat from the Earth's surface. However, some research has suggested that elevated CO_2 levels could enhance the photosynthetic rates of plants, resulting in a lush world of agricultural abundance, and that this CO_2
(10) fertilization effect might eventually decrease the rate of global warming. The increased vegetation in such an environment could be counted on to draw more CO_2 from the atmosphere. The level of CO_2 would thus increase at a lower rate than many experts have
(15) predicted.

However, while a number of recent studies confirm that plant growth would be generally enhanced in an atmosphere rich in CO_2, they also suggest that increased CO_2 would differentially increase the growth
(20) rate of different species of plants, which could eventually result in decreased agricultural yields. Certain important crops such as corn and sugarcane that currently have higher photosynthetic efficiencies than other plants may lose that edge in an atmosphere
(25) rich in CO_2. Patterson and Flint have shown that these important crops may experience yield reductions because of the increased performance of certain weeds. Such differences in growth rates between plant species could also alter ecosystem stability. Studies have
(30) shown that within rangeland regions, for example, a weedy grass grows much better with plentiful CO_2 than do three other grasses. Because this weedy grass predisposes land to burning, its potential increase may lead to greater numbers of and more severe wildfires in
(35) future rangeland communities.

It is clear that the CO_2 fertilization effect does not guarantee the lush world of agricultural abundance that once seemed likely, but what about the potential for the increased uptake of CO_2 to decrease the rate of global
(40) warming? Some studies suggest that the changes accompanying global warming will not improve the ability of terrestrial ecosystems to absorb CO_2. Billings' simulation of global warming conditions in wet tundra grasslands showed that the level of CO_2
(45) actually increased. Plant growth did increase under these conditions because of warmer temperatures and increased CO_2 levels. But as the permafrost melted, more peat (accumulated dead plant material) began to decompose. This process in turn liberated more CO_2 to
(50) the atmosphere. Billings estimated that if summer temperatures rose four degrees Celsius, the tundra would liberate 50 percent more CO_2 than it does currently. In a warmer world, increased plant growth, which could absorb CO_2 from the atmosphere, would
(55) not compensate for this rapid increase in decomposition rates. This observation is particularly important because high-latitude habitats such as the tundra are expected to experience the greatest temperature increase.

15. Which one of the following best states the main point of the passage?

(A) Elevated levels of CO_2 would enhance photosynthetic rates, thus increasing plant growth and agricultural yields.
(B) Recent studies have yielded contradictory findings about the benefits of increased levels of CO_2 on agricultural productivity.
(C) The possible beneficial effects of increased levels of CO_2 on plant growth and global warming have been overstated.
(D) Increased levels of CO_2 would enhance the growth rates of certain plants, but would inhibit the growth rates of other plants.
(E) Increased levels of CO_2 would increase plant growth, but the rate of global warming would ultimately increase.

16. The passage suggests that the hypothesis mentioned in the first paragraph is not entirely accurate because it fails to take into account which one of the following in predicting the effects of increased vegetation on the rate of global warming?

(A) Increased levels of CO_2 will increase the photosynthetic rates of many species of plants.
(B) Increased plant growth cannot compensate for increased rates of decomposition caused by warmer temperatures.
(C) Low-latitude habitats will experience the greatest increases in temperature in an atmosphere high in CO_2.
(D) Increased levels of CO_2 will change patterns of plant growth and thus will alter the distribution of peat.
(E) Increases in vegetation can be counted on to draw more CO_2 from the atmosphere.

17. Which one of the following best describes the function of the last paragraph of the passage?

(A) It presents research that may undermine a hypothesis presented in the first paragraph.
(B) It presents solutions for a problem discussed in the first and second paragraphs.
(C) It provides an additional explanation for a phenomenon described in the first paragraph.
(D) It provides experimental data in support of a theory described in the preceding paragraph.
(E) It raises a question that may cast doubt on information presented in the preceding paragraph.

18. The passage suggests that Patterson and Flint would be most likely to agree with which one of the following statements about increased levels of CO_2 in the Earth's atmosphere?

    (A) They will not increase the growth rates of most species of plants.
    (B) They will inhibit the growth of most crops, thus causing substantial decreases in agricultural yields.
    (C) They are unlikely to increase the growth rates of plants with lower photosynthetic efficiencies.
    (D) They will increase the growth rates of certain species of plants more than the growth rates of other species of plants.
    (E) They will not affect the photosynthetic rates of plants that currently have the highest photosynthetic efficiencies.

19. The author would be most likely to agree with which one of the following statements about the conclusions drawn on the basis of the research on plant growth mentioned in the first paragraph of the passage?

    (A) The conclusions are correct in suggesting that increased levels of CO_2 will increase the photosynthetic rates of certain plants.
    (B) The conclusions are correct in suggesting that increased levels of CO_2 will guarantee abundances of certain important crops.
    (C) The conclusions are correct in suggesting that increased plant growth will reverse the process of global warming.
    (D) The conclusions are incorrect in suggesting that enhanced plant growth could lead to abundances of certain species of plants.
    (E) The conclusions are incorrect in suggesting that vegetation can draw CO_2 from the atmosphere.

20. The passage supports which one of the following statements about peat in wet tundra grasslands?

    (A) More of it would decompose if temperatures rose four degrees Celsius.
    (B) It could help absorb CO_2 from the atmosphere if temperatures rose four degrees Celsius.
    (C) It will not decompose unless temperatures rise four degrees Celsius.
    (D) It decomposes more quickly than peat found in regions at lower latitudes.
    (E) More of it accumulates in regions at lower latitudes.

21. Which one of the following, if true, is LEAST consistent with the hypothesis mentioned in lines 22-25 of the passage?

    (A) The roots of a certain tree species grow more rapidly when the amount of CO_2 in the atmosphere increases, thus permitting the trees to expand into habitats formerly dominated by grasses with high photosynthetic efficiencies.
    (B) When grown in an atmosphere high in CO_2, certain weeds with low photosynthetic efficiencies begin to thrive in cultivated farmlands formerly dominated by agricultural crops.
    (C) When trees of a species with a high photosynthetic efficiency and grasses of a species with a low photosynthetic efficiency were placed in an atmosphere high in CO_2, the trees grew more quickly than the grasses.
    (D) When two different species of grass with equivalent photosynthetic efficiency were placed in an atmosphere high in CO_2, one species grew much more rapidly and crowded the slower-growing species out of the growing area.
    (E) The number of leguminous plants decreased in an atmosphere rich in CO_2, thus diminishing soil fertility and limiting the types of plant species that could thrive in certain habitats.

22. According to the passage, Billings' research addresses which one of the following questions?

    (A) Which kind of habitat will experience the greatest temperature increase in an atmosphere high in CO_2?
    (B) How much will summer temperatures rise if levels of CO_2 double by the end of the twenty-first century?
    (C) Will enhanced plant growth necessarily decrease the rate of global warming that has been predicted by experts?
    (D) Would plant growth be differentially enhanced if atmospheric concentrations of CO_2 were to double by the end of the twenty-first century?
    (E) Does peat decompose more rapidly in wet tundra grasslands than it does in other types of habitats when atmospheric concentrations of CO_2 increase?

Passage #9: June 2001 Questions 13-18

In the eighteenth century the French naturalist Jean Baptiste de Lamarck believed that an animal's use or disuse of an organ affected that organ's development in the animal's offspring. Lamarck claimed that the
(5) giraffe's long neck, for example, resulted from its ancestors stretching to reach distant leaves. But because biologists could find no genetic mechanism to make the transmission of environmentally induced adaptations seem plausible, they have long held that
(10) inheritance of acquired characteristics never occurs. Yet new research has uncovered numerous examples of the phenomenon.

In bacteria, for instance, enzymes synthesize and break down rigid cell walls as necessary to
(15) accommodate the bacteria's growth. But if an experimenter completely removes the cell wall from a bacterium, the process of wall synthesis and breakdown is disrupted, and the bacterium continues to grow—and multiply indefinitely—without walls. This
(20) inherited absence of cell walls in bacteria results from changes in the interactions among genes, without any attendant changes in the genes themselves.

A fundamentally different kind of environmentally induced heritable characteristic occurs when specific
(25) genes are added to or eliminated from an organism. For example, a certain virus introduces a gene into fruit flies that causes the flies to be vulnerable to carbon dioxide poisoning, and fruit flies infected with the virus will pass the gene to their offspring. But if infected
(30) flies are kept warm while they are producing eggs, the virus is eliminated from the eggs and the offspring are resistant to carbon dioxide. Similarly, if an *Escherichia coli* bacterium carrying a certain plasmid—a small ring of genetic material—comes into contact with an *E. coli*
(35) bacterium lacking the plasmid, the plasmid will enter the second bacterium and become part of its genetic makeup, which it then passes to its offspring. The case of the *E. coli* is especially noteworthy for its suggestion that inheritance of acquired characteristics may have
(40) helped to speed up evolution: for example, many complex cells may have first acquired the ability to carry out photosynthesis by coming into contact with a bacterium possessing the gene for that trait, an ability that normally would have taken eons to develop
(45) through random mutation and natural selection.

The new evidence suggests that genes can be divided into two groups. Most are inherited "vertically," from ancestors. Some, however, seem to have been acquired "horizontally," from viruses,
(50) plasmids, bacteria, or other environmental agents. The evidence even appears to show that genes can be transmitted horizontally between organisms that are considered to be unrelated: from bacteria to plants, for example, or from bacteria to yeast. Such horizontal
(55) transmission may well be the mechanism for inheritance of acquired characteristics that has long eluded biologists, and that may eventually prove Lamarck's hypothesis to be correct.

13. The passage suggests that many biologists no longer believe which one of the following?

(A) An organ's use or disuse can affect that organ's development.
(B) Some but not all genes are inherited horizontally.
(C) All genes are inherited horizontally.
(D) Some but not all genes are inherited vertically.
(E) All genes are inherited vertically.

14. According to the passage, which one of the following is an acquired characteristic transmitted by altering the interaction among genes rather than by adding or eliminating a gene?

(A) invulnerability to carbon dioxide poisoning
(B) susceptibility to carbon dioxide poisoning
(C) lack of cell walls
(D) presence of cell walls
(E) possession of certain plasmids

15. The primary purpose of the last paragraph is to

(A) suggest a modification to Lamarck's hypothesis
(B) demonstrate the correctness of Lamarck's hypothesis
(C) illustrate the significance of Lamarck's hypothesis
(D) criticize scientists' rejection of Lamarck's hypothesis
(E) explain how recent discoveries may support Lamarck's hypothesis

16. Which one of the following, if true, offers the most support for Lamarck's hypothesis?

    (A) Deer have antlers because antlers make deer more likely to survive and reproduce.
    (B) Anteaters developed long snouts because the anteater stretches its snout in order to reach ants hidden well below ground.
    (C) Potatoes produced from synthetic genes tend to be more resistant to disease than are potatoes produced from natural genes.
    (D) Lions raised in captivity tend to have a weaker sense of direction than do lions raised in the wild.
    (E) Pups born to wild dogs tend to be more aggressive than are pups born to dogs bred for hunting.

17. According to the passage, the inheritance of acquired characteristics is particularly significant because this phenomenon

    (A) may affect the speed at which photosynthesis occurs
    (B) may help to explain the process of natural selection
    (C) may occur without affecting the composition of genes
    (D) may influence the rate at which evolution progresses
    (E) may be changed or stopped under experimental conditions

18. Which one of the following can be inferred from the passage about the absence of cell walls in some bacteria?

    (A) It can be reversed by introducing the appropriate gene.
    (B) It can be brought about by a virally introduced gene.
    (C) It can be caused by the loss of a cell wall in a single bacterium.
    (D) It can be halted, but not reversed, by restoring cell walls to a group of bacteria.
    (E) It can be transmitted horizontally to other bacteria.

Passage #10: October 2001 Questions 15-20

Philosophers of science have long been uneasy with biology, preferring instead to focus on physics. At the heart of this preference is a mistrust of uncertainty. Science is supposed to be the study of what is true
(5) everywhere and for all times, and the phenomena of science are supposed to be repeatable, arising from universal laws, rather than historically contingent. After all, if something pops up only on occasional Tuesdays or Thursdays, it is not classified as science
(10) but as history. Philosophers of science have thus been fascinated with the fact that elephants and mice would fall at the same rate if dropped from the Tower of Pisa, but not much interested in how elephants and mice got to be such different sizes in the first place.
(15) Philosophers of science have not been alone in claiming that science must consist of universal laws. Some evolutionary biologists have also acceded to the general intellectual disdain for the merely particular and tried to emulate physicists, constructing their
(20) science as a set of universal laws. In formulating the notion of a universal "struggle for existence" that is the engine of biological history or in asserting that virtually all DNA evolves at a constant clocklike rate, they have attempted to find their own versions of the
(25) law of gravity. Recently, however, some biologists have questioned whether biological history is really the necessary unfolding of universal laws of life, and they have raised the possibility that historical contingency is an integral factor in biology.
(30) To illustrate the difference between biologists favoring universal, deterministic laws of evolutionary development and those leaving room for historical contingency, consider two favorite statements of philosophers (both of which appear, at first sight, to be
(35) universal assertions): "All planets move in ellipses" and "All swans are white." The former is truly universal because it applies not only to those planets that actually do exist, but also to those that could exist—for the shape of planetary orbits is a necessary
(40) consequence of the laws governing the motion of objects in a gravitational field.
Biological determinists would say that "All swans are white" is universal in the same way, since, if all swans were white, it would be because the laws of
(45) natural selection make it impossible for swans to be otherwise: natural selection favors those characteristics that increase the average rate of offspring production, and so traits that maximize flexibility and the ability to manipulate nature will
(50) eventually appear. Nondeterminist biologists would deny this, saying that "swans" is merely the name of a finite collection of historical objects that may happen all to be white, but not of necessity. The history of evolutionary theory has been the history of the struggle
(55) between these two views of swans.

15. Which one of the following best summarizes the main idea of the passage?

(A) Just as philosophers of science have traditionally been reluctant to deal with scientific phenomena that are not capable of being explained by known physical laws, biologists have tended to shy away from confronting philosophical questions.
(B) While science is often considered to be concerned with universal laws, the degree to which certain biological phenomena can be understood as arising from such laws is currently in dispute.
(C) Although biologists have long believed that the nature of their field called for a theoretical approach different from that taken by physicists, some biologists have recently begun to emulate the methods of physicists.
(D) Whereas physicists have achieved a far greater degree of experimental precision than has been possible in the field of biology, the two fields employ similar theoretical approaches.
(E) Since many biologists are uncomfortable with the emphasis placed by philosophers of science on the need to construct universal laws, there has been little interaction between the two disciplines.

16. The reference to the formulation of the notion of a universal "struggle for existence" (line 21) serves primarily to

(A) identify one of the driving forces of biological history
(B) illustrate one context in which the concept of uncertainty has been applied
(C) highlight the chief cause of controversy among various schools of biological thought
(D) provide an example of the type of approach employed by determinist biologists
(E) provide an example of a biological phenomenon that illustrates historical contingency

17. Which one of the following statements about biology is most consistent with the view held by determinist biologists, as that view is presented in the passage?

    (A) The appearance of a species is the result of a combination of biological necessity and historical chance.
    (B) The rate at which physiological characteristics of a species change fluctuates from generation to generation.
    (C) The causes of a given evolutionary phenomenon can never be understood by biological scientists.
    (D) The qualities that define a species have been developed according to some process that has not yet been identified.
    (E) The chief physical characteristics of a species are inevitable consequences of the laws governing natural selection.

18. It can be inferred from the passage that philosophers of science view the laws of physics as

    (A) analogous to the laws of history
    (B) difficult to apply because of their uncertainty
    (C) applicable to possible as well as actual situations
    (D) interesting because of their particularity
    (E) illustrative of the problem of historical contingency

19. It can be inferred from the passage that determinist biologists have tried to emulate physicists because these biologists believe that

    (A) the methods of physicists are more easily understood by nonscientists
    (B) physicists have been accorded more respect by their fellow scientists than have biologists
    (C) biology can only be considered a true science if universal laws can be constructed to explain its phenomena
    (D) the specific laws that have helped to explain the behavior of planets can be applied to biological phenomena
    (E) all scientific endeavors benefit from intellectual exchange between various scientific disciplines

20. The passage suggests that the preference of many philosophers of science for the field of physics depends primarily upon the

    (A) belief that biological laws are more difficult to discover than physical laws
    (B) popular attention given to recent discoveries in physics as opposed to those in biology
    (C) bias shown toward the physical sciences in the research programs of many scientific institutions
    (D) teaching experiences of most philosophers of science
    (E) nature of the phenomena that physicists study

Passage #11: December 2001 Questions 15-20

Discussions of how hormones influence behavior have generally been limited to the effects of gonadal hormones on reproductive behavior and have emphasized the parsimonious arrangement whereby the
(5) same hormones involved in the biology of reproduction also influence sexual behavior. It has now become clear, however, that other hormones, in addition to their recognized influence on biological functions, can affect behavior. Specifically, peptide and steroid hormones
(10) involved in maintaining the physiological balance, or homeostasis, of body fluids also appear to play an important role in the control of water and salt consumption. The phenomenon of homeostasis in animals depends on various mechanisms that promote
(15) stability within the organism despite an inconstant external environment; the homeostasis of body fluids, whereby the osmolality (the concentration of solutes) of blood plasma is closely regulated, is achieved primarily through alterations in the intake and
(20) excretion of water and sodium, the two principal components of the fluid matrix that surrounds body cells. Appropriate compensatory responses are initiated when deviations from normal are quite small, thereby maintaining plasma osmolality within relatively narrow
(25) ranges.
In the osmoregulation of body fluids, the movement of water across cell membranes permits minor fluctuations in the concentration of solutes in extracellular fluid to be buffered by corresponding
(30) changes in the relatively larger volume of cellular water. Nevertheless, the concentration of solutes in extracellular fluid may at times become elevated or reduced by more than the allowed tolerances of one or two percent. It is then that complementary
(35) physiological and behavioral responses come into play to restore plasma osmolality to normal. Thus, for example, a decrease in plasma osmolality, such as that which occurs after the consumption of water in excess of need, leads to the excretion of surplus body water in
(40) the urine by inhibiting secretion from the pituitary gland of vasopressin, a peptide hormone that promotes water conservation in the kidneys. As might be expected, thirst also is inhibited then, to prevent further dilution of body fluids. Conversely, an increase in
(45) plasma osmolality, such as that which occurs after one eats salty foods or after body water evaporates without being replaced, stimulates the release of vasopressin, increasing the conservation of water and the excretion of solutes in urine. This process is accompanied by
(50) increased thirst, with the result of making plasma osmolality more dilute through the consumption of water. The threshold for thirst appears to be slightly higher than for vasopressin secretion, so that thirst is stimulated only after vasopressin has been released in
(55) amounts sufficient to produce maximal water retention by the kidneys—that is, only after osmotic dehydration exceeds the capacity of the animal to deal with it physiologically.

15. Which one of the following best states the main idea of the passage?

(A) Both the solute concentration and the volume of an animal's blood plasma must be kept within relatively narrow ranges.
(B) Behavioral responses to changes in an animal's blood plasma can compensate for physiological malfunction, allowing the body to avoid dehydration.
(C) The effect of hormones on animal behavior and physiology has only recently been discovered.
(D) Behavioral and physiological responses to major changes in osmolality of an animal's blood plasma are hormonally influenced and complement one another.
(E) The mechanisms regulating reproduction are similar to those that regulate thirst and sodium appetite.

16. The author of the passage cites the relationship between gonadal hormones and reproductive behavior in order to

(A) review briefly the history of research into the relationships between gonadal and peptide hormones that has led to the present discussion
(B) decry the fact that previous research has concentrated on the relatively minor issue of the relationships between hormones and behavior
(C) establish the emphasis of earlier research into the connections between hormones and behavior before elaborating on the results described in the passage
(D) introduce a commonly held misconception about the relationships between hormones and behavior before refuting it with the results described in the passage
(E) summarize the main findings of recent research described in the passage before detailing the various procedures that led to those findings

17. It can be inferred from the passage that which one of the following is true of vasopressin?

    (A) The amount secreted depends on the level of steroid hormones in the blood.
    (B) The amount secreted is important for maintaining homeostasis in cases of both increased and decreased osmolality.
    (C) It works in conjunction with steroid hormones in increasing plasma volume.
    (D) It works in conjunction with steroid hormones in regulating sodium appetite.
    (E) It is secreted after an animal becomes thirsty, as a mechanism for diluting plasma osmolality.

18. The primary function of the passage as a whole is to

    (A) present new information
    (B) question standard assumptions
    (C) reinterpret earlier findings
    (D) advocate a novel theory
    (E) outline a new approach

19. According to the passage, all of the following typically occur in the homeostasis of blood-plasma osmolality EXCEPT:

    (A) Hunger is diminished.
    (B) Thirst is initiated.
    (C) Vasopressin is secreted.
    (D) Water is excreted.
    (E) Sodium is consumed.

20. According to the passage, the withholding of vasopressin fulfills which one of the following functions in the restoration of plasma osmolality to normal levels?

    (A) It increases thirst and stimulates sodium appetite.
    (B) It helps prevent further dilution of body fluids.
    (C) It increases the conservation of water in the kidneys.
    (D) It causes minor changes in plasma volume.
    (E) It helps stimulate the secretion of steroid hormones.

Passage #12: June 2002 Questions 8-13

Spurred by the discovery that a substance containing uranium emitted radiation, Marie Curie began studying radioactivity in 1897. She first tested gold and copper for radiation but found none. She then
(5) tested pitchblende, a mineral that was known to contain uranium, and discovered that it was more radioactive than uranium. Acting on the hypothesis that pitchblende must contain at least one other radioactive element, Curie was able to isolate a pair of previously
(10) unknown elements, polonium and radium. Turning her attention to the rate of radioactive emission, she discovered that uranium emitted radiation at a consistent rate, even if heated or dissolved. Based on these results, Curie concluded that the emission rate for
(15) a given element was constant. Furthermore, because radiation appeared to be spontaneous, with no discernible difference between radiating and nonradiating elements, she was unable to postulate a mechanism by which to explain radiation.
(20) It is now known that radiation occurs when certain isotopes (atoms of the same element that differ slightly in their atomic structure) decay, and that emission rates are not constant but decrease very slowly with time. Some critics have recently faulted Curie for not
(25) reaching these conclusions herself, but it would have been impossible for Curie to do so given the evidence available to her. While relatively light elements such as gold and copper occasionally have unstable (i.e., radioactive) isotopes, radioactive isotopes of most of
(30) these elements are not available in nature because they have largely finished decaying and so have become stable. Conversely, heavier elements such as uranium, which decay into lighter elements in a process that takes billions of years, are present in nature exclusively
(35) in radioactive form.
Furthermore, we must recall that in Curie's time the nature of the atom itself was still being debated. Physicists believed that matter could not be divided indefinitely but instead would eventually be reduced to
(40) its indivisible components. Chemists, on the other hand, observing that chemical reactions took place as if matter was composed of atomlike particles, used the atom as a foundation for conceptualizing and describing such reactions—but they were not
(45) ultimately concerned with the question of whether or not such indivisible atoms actually existed.
As a physicist, Curie conjectured that radiating substances might lose mass in the form of atoms, but this idea is very different from the explanation
(50) eventually arrived at. It was not until the 1930s that advances in quantum mechanics overthrew the earlier understanding of the atom and showed that radiation occurs because the atoms themselves lose mass—a hypothesis that Curie, committed to the indivisible
(55) atom, could not be expected to have conceived of. Moreover, not only is Curie's inability to identify the mechanism by which radiation occurs understandable, it is also important to recognize that it was Curie's investigation of radiation that paved the way for the
(60) later breakthroughs.

8. Which one of the following most accurately states the central idea of the passage?

(A) It is unlikely that quantum mechanics would have been developed without the theoretical contributions of Marie Curie toward an understanding of the nature of radioactivity.
(B) Although later shown to be incomplete and partially inaccurate, Marie Curie's investigations provided a significant step forward on the road to the eventual explanation of radioactivity.
(C) Though the scientific achievements of Marie Curie were impressive in scope, her career is blemished by her failure to determine the mechanism of radioactivity.
(D) The commitment of Marie Curie and other physicists of her time to the physicists' model of the atom prevented them from conducting fruitful investigations into radioactivity.
(E) Although today's theories have shown it to be inconclusive, Marie Curie's research into the sources and nature of radioactivity helped refute the chemists' model of the atom.

9. The passage suggests that the author would be most likely to agree with which one of the following statements about the contemporary critics of Curie's studies of radioactivity?

   (A) The critics fail to take into account the obstacles Curie faced in dealing with the scientific community of her time.
   (B) The critics do not appreciate that the eventual development of quantum mechanics depended on Curie's conjecture that radiating substances can lose atoms.
   (C) The critics are unaware of the differing conceptions of the atom held by physicists and chemists.
   (D) The critics fail to appreciate the importance of the historical context in which Curie's scientific conclusions were reached.
   (E) The critics do not comprehend the intricate reasoning that Curie used in discovering polonium and radium.

10. The passage implies which one of the following with regard to the time at which Curie began studying radioactivity?

    (A) Pitchblende was not known by scientists to contain any radioactive element besides uranium.
    (B) Radioactivity was suspected by scientists to arise from the overall structure of pitchblende rather than from particular elements in it.
    (C) Physicists and chemists had developed rival theories regarding the cause of radiation.
    (D) Research was not being conducted in connection with the question of whether or not matter is composed of atoms.
    (E) The majority of physicists believed uranium to be the sole source of radioactivity.

11. The author's primary purpose in the passage is to

    (A) summarize some aspects of one scientist's work and defend it against recent criticism
    (B) describe a scientific dispute and argue for the correctness of an earlier theory
    (C) outline a currently accepted scientific theory and analyze the evidence that led to its acceptance
    (D) explain the mechanism by which a natural phenomenon occurs and summarize the debate that gave rise to this explanation
    (E) discover the antecedents of a scientific theory and argue that the theory is not a genuine advance over its forerunners

12. The primary function of the first paragraph of the passage is to

    (A) narrate the progress of turn-of-the-century studies of radioactivity
    (B) present a context for the conflict between physicists and chemists
    (C) provide the factual background for an evaluation of Curie's work
    (D) outline the structure of the author's central argument
    (E) identify the error in Curie's work that undermines its usefulness

13. Which one of the following most accurately expresses the meaning of the word "mechanism" as used by the author in the last sentence of the first paragraph?

    (A) the physical process that underlies a phenomenon
    (B) the experimental apparatus in which a phenomenon arises
    (C) the procedure scientists use to bring about the occurrence of a phenomenon
    (D) the isotopes of an element needed to produce a phenomenon
    (E) the scientific theory describing a phenomenon

Passage #13: December 2002 Questions 17-23

With the approach of the twentieth century, the classical wave theory of radiation—a widely accepted theory in physics—began to encounter obstacles. This theory held that all electromagnetic radiation—the
(5) entire spectrum from gamma and X rays to radio frequencies, including heat and light—exists in the form of waves. One fundamental assumption of wave theory was that as the length of a wave of radiation shortens, its energy increases smoothly—like a volume
(10) dial on a radio that adjusts smoothly to any setting— and that any conceivable energy value could thus occur in nature.

The major challenge to wave theory was the behavior of thermal radiation, the radiation emitted by
(15) an object due to the object's temperature, commonly called "blackbody" radiation because experiments aimed at measuring it require objects, such as black velvet or soot, with little or no reflective capability. Physicists can monitor the radiation coming from a
(20) blackbody object and be confident that they are observing its thermal radiation and not simply reflected radiation that has originated elsewhere. Employing the principles of wave theory, physicists originally predicted that blackbody objects radiated much more at
(25) short wavelengths, such as ultraviolet, than at long wavelengths. However, physicists using advanced experimental techniques near the turn of the century did not find the predicted amount of radiation at short wavelengths—in fact, they found almost none, a result
(30) that became known among wave theorists as the "ultraviolet catastrophe."

Max Planck, a classical physicist who had made important contributions to wave theory, developed a hypothesis about atomic processes taking place in a
(35) blackbody object that broke with wave theory and accounted for the observed patterns of blackbody radiation. Planck discarded the assumption of radiation's smooth energy continuum and took the then bizarre position that these atomic processes could only
(40) involve discrete energies that jump between certain units of value—like a volume dial that "clicks" between incremental settings—and he thereby obtained numbers that perfectly fit the earlier experimental result. This directly opposed wave theory's picture of
(45) atomic processes, and the physics community was at first quite critical of Planck's hypothesis, in part because he presented it without physical explanation.

Soon thereafter, however, Albert Einstein and other physicists provided theoretical justification for
(50) Planck's hypothesis. They found that upon being hit with part of the radiation spectrum, metal surfaces give off energy at values that are discontinuous. Further, they noted a threshold along the spectrum beyond which no energy is emitted by the metal. Einstein
(55) theorized, and later found evidence to confirm, that radiation is composed of particles, now called photons, which can be emitted only in discrete units and at certain wavelengths, in accordance with Planck's speculations. So in just a few years, what was
(60) considered a catastrophe generated a new vision in physics that led to theories still in place today.

17. Which one of the following most accurately states the main point of the passage?

(A) If classical wave theorists had never focused on blackbody radiation, Planck's insights would not have developed and the stage would not have been set for Einstein.
(B) Classical wave theory, an incorrect formulation of the nature of radiation, was corrected by Planck and other physicists after Planck performed experiments that demonstrated that radiation exists as particles.
(C) Planck's new model of radiation, though numerically consistent with observed data, was slow to win the support of the scientific community, which was critical of his ideas.
(D) Prompted by new experimental findings, Planck discarded an assumption of classical wave theory and proposed a picture of radiation that matched experimental results and was further supported by theoretical justification.
(E) At the turn of the century, Planck and Einstein revolutionized studies in radiation by modifying classical wave theory in response to experimental results that suggested the energy of radiation is less at short wavelengths than at long ones.

18. Which one of the following does the author use to illustrate the difference between continuous energies and discrete energies?

(A) radio waves
(B) black velvet or soot
(C) microscopic particles
(D) metal surfaces
(E) radio volume dials

19. Which one of the following can most clearly be inferred from the description of blackbody objects in the second paragraph?

(A) Radiation reflected by and radiation emitted by an object are difficult to distinguish from one another.
(B) Any object in a dark room is a nearly ideal blackbody object.
(C) All blackbody objects of comparable size give off radiation at approximately the same wavelengths regardless of the objects' temperatures.
(D) Any blackbody object whose temperature is difficult to manipulate would be of little use in an experiment.
(E) Thermal radiation cannot originate from a blackbody object.

20. The author's attitude toward Planck's development of a new hypothesis about atomic processes can most aptly be described as

    (A) strong admiration for the intuitive leap that led to a restored confidence in wave theory's picture of atomic processes
    (B) mild surprise at the bizarre position Planck took regarding atomic processes
    (C) reasoned skepticism of Planck's lack of scientific justification for his hypothesis
    (D) legitimate concern that the hypothesis would have been abandoned without the further studies of Einstein and others
    (E) scholarly interest in a step that led to a more accurate picture of atomic processes

21. The passage provides information that answers each of the following questions EXCEPT:

    (A) What did Planck's hypothesis about atomic processes try to account for?
    (B) What led to the scientific community's acceptance of Planck's ideas?
    (C) Roughly when did the blackbody radiation experiments take place?
    (D) What contributions did Planck make to classical wave theory?
    (E) What type of experiment led Einstein to formulate a theory regarding the composition of radiation?

22. The primary function of the first two paragraphs of the passage is to

    (A) describe the process by which one theory's assumption was dismantled by a competing theory
    (B) introduce a central assumption of a scientific theory and the experimental evidence that led to the overthrowing of that theory
    (C) explain two competing theories that are based on the same experimental evidence
    (D) describe the process of retesting a theory in light of ambiguous experimental results
    (E) provide the basis for an argument intended to dismiss a new theory

23. The passage is primarily concerned with

    (A) discussing the value of speculation in a scientific discipline
    (B) summarizing the reasons for the rejection of an established theory by the scientific community
    (C) describing the role that experimental research plays in a scientific discipline
    (D) examining a critical stage in the evolution of theories concerning the nature of a physical phenomenon
    (E) comparing the various assumptions that lie at the foundation of a scientific discipline

Passage #14: June 2003 Questions 13-19

According to the theory of gravitation, every particle of matter in the universe attracts every other particle with a force that increases as either the mass of the particles increases, or their proximity to one
(5) another increases, or both. Gravitation is believed to shape the structures of stars, galaxies, and the entire universe. But for decades cosmologists (scientists who study the universe) have attempted to account for the finding that at least 90 percent of the universe seems
(10) to be missing: that the total amount of observable matter—stars, dust, and miscellaneous debris—does not contain enough mass to explain why the universe is organized in the shape of galaxies and clusters of galaxies. To account for this discrepancy, cosmologists
(15) hypothesize that something else, which they call "dark matter," provides the gravitational force necessary to make the huge structures cohere.

What is dark matter? Numerous exotic entities have been postulated, but among the more attractive
(20) candidates—because they are known actually to exist— are neutrinos, elementary particles created as a by-product of nuclear fusion, radioactive decay, or catastrophic collisions between other particles. Neutrinos, which come in three types, are by far the
(25) most numerous kind of particle in the universe; however, they have long been assumed to have no mass. If so, that would disqualify them as dark matter. Without mass, matter cannot exert gravitational force; without such force, it cannot induce other matter to
(30) cohere.

But new evidence suggests that a neutrino does have mass. This evidence came by way of research findings supporting the existence of a long-theorized but never observed phenomenon called oscillation,
(35) whereby each of the three neutrino types can change into one of the others as it travels through space. Researchers held that the transformation is possible only if neutrinos also have mass. They obtained experimental confirmation of the theory by generating
(40) one neutrino type and then finding evidence that it had oscillated into the predicted neutrino type. In the process, they were able to estimate the mass of a neutrino at from 0.5 to 5 electron volts.

While slight, even the lowest estimate would yield
(45) a lot of mass given that neutrinos are so numerous, especially considering that neutrinos were previously assumed to have no mass. Still, even at the highest estimate, neutrinos could only account for about 20 percent of the universe's "missing" mass.
(50) Nevertheless, that is enough to alter our picture of the universe even if it does not account for all of dark matter. In fact, some cosmologists claim that this new evidence offers the best theoretical solution yet to the dark matter problem. If the evidence holds up, these
(55) cosmologists believe, it may add to our understanding of the role elementary particles play in holding the universe together.

13. Which one of the following most accurately expresses the main idea of the passage?

(A) Although cosmologists believe that the universe is shaped by gravitation, the total amount of observable matter in the universe is greatly insufficient to account for the gravitation that would be required to cause the universe to be organized into galaxies.
(B) Given their inability to account for more than 20 percent of the universe's "missing" mass, scientists are beginning to speculate that our current understanding of gravity is significantly mistaken.
(C) Indirect evidence suggesting that neutrinos have mass may allow neutrinos to account for up to 20 percent of dark matter, a finding that could someday be extended to a complete solution of the dark matter problem.
(D) After much speculation, researchers have discovered that neutrinos oscillate from one type into another as they travel through space, a phenomenon that proves that neutrinos have mass.
(E) Although it has been established that neutrinos have mass, such mass does not support the speculation of cosmologists that neutrinos constitute a portion of the universe's "missing" mass.

14. Which one of the following titles most completely and accurately expresses the contents of the passage?

(A) "The Existence of Dark Matter: Arguments For and Against"
(B) "Neutrinos and the Dark Matter Problem: A Partial Solution?"
(C) "Too Little, Too Late: Why Neutrinos Do Not Constitute Dark Matter"
(D) "The Role of Gravity: How Dark Matter Shapes Stars"
(E) "The Implications of Oscillation: Do Neutrinos Really Have Mass?"

15. Based on the passage, the author most likely holds which one of the following views?

    (A) Observable matter constitutes at least 90 percent of the mass of the universe.
    (B) Current theories are incapable of identifying the force that causes all particles in the universe to attract one another.
    (C) The key to the problem of dark matter is determining the exact mass of a neutrino.
    (D) It is unlikely that any force other than gravitation will be required to account for the organization of the universe into galaxies.
    (E) Neutrinos probably account for most of the universe's "missing" mass.

16. As described in the last paragraph of the passage, the cosmologists' approach to solving the dark matter problem is most analogous to which one of the following?

    (A) A child seeking information about how to play chess consults a family member and so learns of a book that will instruct her in the game.
    (B) A child seeking to earn money by delivering papers is unable to earn enough money for a bicycle and so decides to buy a skateboard instead.
    (C) A child hoping to get a dog for his birthday is initially disappointed when his parents bring home a cat but eventually learns to love the animal.
    (D) A child seeking money to attend a movie is given some of the money by one of his siblings and so decides to go to each of his other siblings to ask for additional money.
    (E) A child enjoys playing sports with the neighborhood children but her parents insist that she cannot participate until she has completed her household chores.

17. The author's attitude toward oscillation can most accurately be characterized as being

    (A) satisfied that it occurs and that it suggests that neutrinos have mass
    (B) hopeful that it will be useful in discovering other forms of dark matter
    (C) concerned that it is often misinterpreted to mean that neutrinos account for all of dark matter
    (D) skeptical that it occurs until further research can be done
    (E) convinced that it cannot occur outside an experimental setting

18. Which one of the following phrases could replace the word "cohere" at line 30 without substantively altering the author's meaning?

    (A) exert gravitational force
    (B) form galactic structures
    (C) oscillate into another type of matter
    (D) become significantly more massive
    (E) fuse to produce new particles

19. The passage states each of the following EXCEPT:

    (A) There are more neutrinos in the universe than there are non-neutrinos.
    (B) Observable matter cannot exert enough gravitational force to account for the present structure of the universe.
    (C) Scientific experiments support the theory of neutrino oscillation.
    (D) Neutrinos likely cannot account for all of the universe's "missing" mass.
    (E) Dark matter may account for a large portion of the universe's gravitational force.

CHAPTER FIVE: HARD SCIENCE

HUMANITIES

Humanities Passages

Passage #1: December 1996 Questions 1-8 148
Passage #2: June 1997 Questions 17-21 150
Passage #3: October 1997 Questions 1-5 152
Passage #4: October 1997 Questions 14-18 154
Passage #5: December 1997 Questions 21-27 156
Passage #6: June 1998 Questions 8-13 158
Passage #7: September 1998 Questions 1-5 160
Passage #8: June 1999 Questions 14-21 162
Passage #9: June 1999 Questions 22-26 164
Passage #10: October 1999 Questions 1-7 166
Passage #11: December 1999 Questions 7-14 168
Passage #12: June 2000 Questions 21-28 170
Passage #13: December 2000 Questions 1-7 172
Passage #14: June 2001 Questions 1-6 174
Passage #15: June 2001 Questions 7-12 176
Passage #16: June 2001 Questions 19-26 178
Passage #17: December 2001 Questions 1-6 180
Passage #18: December 2001 Questions 7-14 182
Passage #19: October 2002 Questions 21-27 184
Passage #20: June 2003 Questions 1-5 186

Passage #1: December 1996 Questions 1-8

Musicologists concerned with the "London Pianoforte school," the group of composers, pedagogues, pianists, publishers, and builders who contributed to the development of the piano in
(5) London at the turn of the nineteenth century, have long encountered a formidable obstacle in the general unavailability of music of this "school" in modern scholarly editions. Indeed, much of this repertory has more or less vanished from our
(10) historical consciousness. Granted, the sonatas and *Gradus ad Parnassum* of Muzio Clementi and the nocturnes of John Field have remained familiar enough (though more often than not in editions lacking scholarly rigor), but the work of other
(15) leading representatives, like Johann Baptist Cramer and Jan Ladislav Dussek, has eluded serious attempts at revival.

Nicholas Temperley's ambitious new anthology decisively overcomes this deficiency. What
(20) underscores the intrinsic value of Temperley's editions is that the anthology reproduces nearly all of the original music in facsimile. Making available this cross section of English musical life—some 800 works by 49 composers—should encourage
(25) new critical perspectives about how piano music evolved in England, an issue of considerable relevance to our understanding of how piano music developed on the European continent, and of how, finally, the instrument was transformed from the
(30) fortepiano to what we know today as the piano.

To be sure, the concept of the London Pianoforte school itself calls for review. "School" may well be too strong a word for what was arguably a group unified not so much by stylistic
(35) principles or aesthetic creed as by the geographical circumstance that they worked at various times in London and produced pianos and piano music for English pianos and English markets. Indeed, Temperley concedes that their "variety may be so
(40) great as to cast doubt on the notion of a 'school.'" The notion of a school was first propounded by Alexander Ringer, who argued that laws of artistic survival forced the young, progressive Beethoven to turn outside Austria for creative models, and that he
(45) found inspiration in a group of pianists connected with Clementi in London. Ringer's proposed London Pianoforte school did suggest a circumscribed and fairly unified group—for want of a better term, a school—of musicians whose
(50) influence was felt primarily in the decades just before and after 1800. After all, Beethoven did respond to the advances of the Broadwood piano— its reinforced frame, extended compass, triple stringing, and pedals, for example—and it is
(55) reasonable to suppose that London pianists who composed music for such an instrument during the critical phase of its development exercised no small degree of influence on Continental musicians. Nevertheless, perhaps the most sensible approach
(60) to this issue is to define the school by the period (c. 1766-1873) during which it flourished, as Temperley has done in the anthology.

1. Which one of the following most accurately states the author's main point?

    (A) Temperley has recently called into question the designation of a group of composers, pedagogues, pianists, publishers, and builders as the London Pianoforte school.
    (B) Temperley's anthology of the music of the London Pianoforte school contributes significantly to an understanding of an influential period in the history of music.
    (C) The music of the London Pianoforte school has been revived by the publication of Temperley's new anthology.
    (D) Primary sources for musical manuscripts provide the most reliable basis for musicological research.
    (E) The development of the modern piano in England influenced composers and other musicians throughout Europe.

2. It can be inferred that which one of the following is true of the piano music of the London Pianoforte school?

    (A) The nocturnes of John Field typify the London Pianoforte school style.
    (B) The *Gradus ad Parnassum* of Muzio Clementi is the best-known work of these composers.
    (C) No original scores for this music are extant.
    (D) Prior to Temperley's edition, no attempts to issue new editions of this music had been made.
    (E) In modern times much of the music of this school has been little known even to musicians.

3. The author mentions the sonatas of Muzio Clementi and the nocturnes of John Field as examples of which one of the following?

   (A) works by composers of the London Pianoforte school that have been preserved in rigorous scholarly editions
   (B) works that are no longer remembered by most people
   (C) works acclaimed by the leaders of the London Pianoforte school
   (D) works by composers of the London Pianoforte school that are relatively well known
   (E) works by composers of the London Pianoforte school that have been revived by Temperley in his anthology

4. Which one of the following, if true, would most clearly undermine a portion of Ringer's argument as the argument is described in the passage?

   (A) Musicians in Austria composed innovative music for the Broadwood piano as soon as the instrument became available.
   (B) Clementi and his followers produced most of their compositions between 1790 and 1810.
   (C) The influence of Continental musicians is apparent in some of the works of Beethoven.
   (D) The pianist-composers of the London Pianoforte school shared many of the same stylistic principles.
   (E) Most composers of the London Pianoforte school were born on the Continent and were drawn to London by the work of Clementi and his followers.

5. It can be inferred that the author uses the word "advances" (line 52) to refer to

   (A) enticements offered musicians by instrument manufacturers
   (B) improvements in the structure of a particular instrument
   (C) innovations in the forms of music produced for a particular instrument
   (D) stylistic elaborations made possible by changes in a particular instrument
   (E) changes in musicians' opinions about a particular instrument

6. It can be inferred from the passage as a whole that the author's purpose in the third paragraph is primarily to

   (A) cast doubt on the usefulness of Temperley's study of the London Pianoforte school
   (B) introduce a discussion of the coherency of the London Pianoforte school
   (C) summarize Ringer's argument about the London Pianoforte school
   (D) emphasize the complex nature of the musicological elements shared by members of the London Pianoforte school
   (E) identify the unique contributions made to music by the London Pianoforte school

7. The author of the passage is primarily concerned with

   (A) explaining the influence of the development of the pianoforte on the music of Beethoven
   (B) describing Temperley's view of the contrast between the development of piano music in England and the development of piano music elsewhere in Europe
   (C) presenting Temperley's evaluation of the impact of changes in piano construction on styles and forms of music composed in the era of the London Pianoforte school
   (D) considering an alternative theory to that proposed by Ringer concerning the London Pianoforte school
   (E) discussing the contribution of Temperley's anthology to what is known of the history of the London Pianoforte school

8. It can be inferred that Temperley's anthology treats the London Pianoforte school as

   (A) a group of pianist-composers who shared certain stylistic principles and artistic creeds
   (B) a group of people who contributed to the development of piano music between 1766 and 1873
   (C) a group of composers who influenced the music of Beethoven in the decades just before and just after 1800
   (D) a series of compositions for the pianoforte published in the decades just before and just after 1800
   (E) a series of compositions that had a significant influence on the music of the Continent in the eighteenth and nineteenth centuries

CHAPTER SIX: HUMANITIES

Passage #2: June 1997 Questions 17-21

Many people complain about corporations, but there are also those whose criticism goes further and who hold corporations morally to blame for many of the problems in Western society. Their
(5) criticism not reserved solely for fraudulent or illegal business activities, but extends to the basic corporate practice of making decisions based on what will maximize profits without regard to whether such decisions will contribute to the public
(10) good. Others, mainly economists, have responded that this criticism is flawed because it inappropriately applies ethical principles to economic relationships.

It is only by extension that we attribute the
(15) quality of morality to corporations, for corporations are not persons. Corporate responsibility is an aggregation of the responsibilities of those persons employed by the corporation when they act in and on behalf of the corporation. Some corporations are
(20) owner operated, but in many corporations and in most larger ones there is a syndicate of owners to whom the chief executive officer, or CEO, who runs the corporation is said to have a fiduciary obligation.

(25) The economists argue that a CEO's sole responsibility is to the owners, whose primary interest, except in charitable institutions, is the protection of their profits. CEOs are bound, as a condition of their employment, to seek a profit for
(30) the owners. But suppose a noncharitable organization is owner operated, or, for some other reason, its CEO is not obligated to maximize profits. The economists' view is that even if such a CEO's purpose is to look to the public good and
(35) nothing else, the CEO should still work to maximize profits, because that will turn out best for the public anyway.

But the economists' position does not hold up under careful scrutiny. For one thing, although there
(40) are, no doubt, strong underlying dynamics in national and international economies that tend to make the pursuit of corporate interest contribute to the public good, there is no guarantee, either theoretically or in practice, that a given CEO will
(45) benefit the public by maximizing corporate profit. It is absurd to deny the possibility, say, of a paper mill legally maximizing its profits over a five-year period by decimating a forest for its wood or polluting a lake with its industrial waste.
(50) Furthermore, while obligations such as those of corporate CEOs to corporate owners are binding in a business or legal sense, they are not morally paramount. The CEO could make a case to the owners that certain profitable courses of action
(55) should not be taken because they are likely to detract from the public good. The economic consequences that may befall the CEO for doing so, such as penalty or dismissal, ultimately do not excuse the individual from the responsibility for
(60) acting morally.

17. Which one of the following most accurately states the main point of the passage?

    (A) Although CEOs may be legally obligated to maximize their corporations' profits, this obligation does not free them from the moral responsibility of considering the implications of the corporations' actions for the public good.
    (B) Although morality is not easily ascribed to nonhuman entities, corporations can be said to have an obligation to act morally in the sense that they are made up of individuals who must act morally.
    (C) Although economists argue that maximizing a corporation's profits is likely to turn out best for the public, a CEO's true obligation is still to seek a profit for the corporation's owners.
    (D) Although some people criticize corporations for making unethical decisions, economists argue that such criticisms are unfounded because ethical considerations cannot be applied to economics.
    (E) Although critics of corporations argue that CEOs ought to consider the public good when making financial decisions, the results of such decisions in fact always benefit the public.

18. The discussion of the paper mill in lines 46-49 is intended primarily to

    (A) offer an actual case of unethical corporate behavior
    (B) refute the contention that maximization of profits necessarily benefits the public
    (C) illustrate that ethical restrictions on corporations would be difficult to enforce
    (D) demonstrate that corporations are responsible for many social ills
    (E) deny that corporations are capable of acting morally

19. With which one of the following would the economists mentioned in the passage be most likely to agree?

    (A) Even CEOs of charitable organizations are obligated to maximize profits.
    (B) CEOs of owner-operated noncharitable corporations should make decisions based primarily on maximizing profits.
    (C) Owner-operated noncharitable corporations are less likely to be profitable than other corporations.
    (D) It is highly unlikely that the actions of any particular CEO will benefit the public.
    (E) CEOs should attempt to maximize profits unless such attempts result in harm to the environment.

20. The conception of morality that underlies the author's argument in the passage is best expressed by which one of the following principles?

    (A) What makes actions morally right is their contribution to the public good.
    (B) An action is morally right if it carries the risk of personal penalty.
    (C) Actions are morally right if they are not fraudulent or illegal.
    (D) It is morally wrong to try to maximize one's personal benefit.
    (E) Actions are not morally wrong unless they harm others.

21. The primary purpose of the passage is to

    (A) illustrate a paradox
    (B) argue for legal reform
    (C) refute a claim
    (D) explain a decision
    (E) define a concept

Passage #3: October 1997 Questions 1-5

It has recently been discovered that many attributions of paintings to the seventeenth-century Dutch artist Rembrandt may be false. The contested paintings are not minor works, whose removal from
(5) the Rembrandt corpus would leave it relatively unaffected: they are at its very center. In her recent book, Svetlana Alpers uses these cases of disputed attribution as a point of departure for her provocative discussion of the radical distinctiveness
(10) of Rembrandt's approach to painting.
Alpers argues that Rembrandt exercised an unprecedentedly firm control over his art, his students, and the distribution of his works. Despite Gary Schwartz's brilliant documentation of
(15) Rembrandt's complicated relations with a wide circle of patrons, Alpers takes the view that Rembrandt refused to submit to the prevailing patronage system. He preferred, she claims, to sell his works on the open market and to play the
(20) entrepreneur. At a time when Dutch artists were organizing into professional brotherhoods and academies, Rembrandt stood apart. In fact, Alpers' portrait of Rembrandt shows virtually every aspect of his art pervaded by economic motives. Indeed, so
(25) complete was Rembrandt's involvement with the market, she argues, that he even presented himself as a commodity, viewing his studio's products as extensions of himself, sent out into the world to earn money. Alpers asserts that Rembrandt's
(30) enterprise is found not just in his paintings, but in his refusal to limit his enterprise to those paintings he actually painted. He marketed Rembrandt.
Although there may be some truth in the view that Rembrandt was an entrepreneur who made
(35) some aesthetic decisions on the basis of what he knew the market wanted, Alpers' emphasis on economic factors sacrifices discussion of the aesthetic qualities that make Rembrandt's work unique. For example, Alpers asserts that Rembrandt
(40) deliberately left his works unfinished so as to get more money for their revision and completion. She implies that Rembrandt actually wished the Council of Amsterdam to refuse the great *Claudius Civilis*, which they had commissioned for their new town
(45) hall, and she argues that "he must have calculated that he would be able to get more money by retouching [the] painting." Certainly the picture is painted with very broad strokes, but there is no evidence that it was deliberately left unfinished. The
(50) fact is that the look of a work like *Claudius Civilis* must also be understood as the consequence of Rembrandt's powerful and profound meditations on painting itself. Alpers makes no mention of the pictorial dialectic that can be discerned between,
(55) say, the lessons Rembrandt absorbed from the Haarlem school of painters and the styles of his native Leiden. The trouble is that while Rembrandt's artistic enterprise may indeed not be reducible to the works he himself painted, it is not
(60) reducible to marketing practices either.

1. Which one of the following best summarizes the main conclusion of the author of the passage?

    (A) Rembrandt differed from other artists of his time both in his aesthetic techniques and in his desire to meet the demands of the marketplace.
    (B) The aesthetic qualities of Rembrandt's work cannot be understood without consideration of how economic motives pervaded decisions he made about his art.
    (C) Rembrandt was one of the first artists to develop the notion of a work of art as a commodity that could be sold in an open marketplace.
    (D) Rembrandt's artistic achievement cannot be understood solely in terms of decisions he made on the basis of what would sell in the marketplace.
    (E) Rembrandt was an entrepreneur whose artistic enterprise was not limited to the paintings he actually painted himself.

2. According to the passage, Alpers and Schwartz disagree about which one of the following?

    (A) the degree of control Rembrandt exercised over the production of his art
    (B) the role that Rembrandt played in organizing professional brotherhoods and academies
    (C) the kinds of relationships Rembrandt had with his students
    (D) the degree of Rembrandt's involvement in the patronage system
    (E) the role of the patronage system in seventeenth-century Holland

3. In the third paragraph, the author of the passage discusses aesthetic influences on Rembrandt's work most probably in order to

   (A) suggest that many critics have neglected to study the influence of the Haarlem school of painters on Rembrandt's work
   (B) suggest that *Claudius Civilis* is similar in style to many paintings from the seventeenth century
   (C) suggest that Rembrandt's style was not affected by the aesthetic influences that Alpers points out
   (D) argue that Rembrandt's style can best be understood as a result of the influences of his native Leiden
   (E) indicate that Alpers has not taken into account some important aspects of Rembrandt's work

4. Which one of the following, if true, would provide the most support for Alpers' argument about *Claudius Civilis*?

   (A) Rembrandt was constantly revising his prints and paintings because he was never fully satisfied with stylistic aspects of his earlier drafts.
   (B) The works of many seventeenth-century Dutch artists were painted with broad strokes and had an unfinished look.
   (C) Many of Rembrandt's contemporaries eschewed the patronage system and sold their works on the open market.
   (D) Artists were frequently able to raise the price of a painting if the buyer wanted the work revised in some way.
   (E) Rembrandt did not allow his students to work on paintings that were commissioned by public officials.

5. It can be inferred that the author of the passage and Alpers would be most likely to agree on which one of the following?

   (A) Rembrandt made certain aesthetic decisions on the basis of what he understood about the demands of the marketplace.
   (B) The Rembrandt corpus will not be affected if attributions of paintings to Rembrandt are found to be false.
   (C) Stylistic aspects of Rembrandt's painting can be better explained in economic terms than in historical or aesthetic terms.
   (D) Certain aesthetic aspects of Rembrandt's art are the result of his experimentation with different painting techniques.
   (E) Most of Rembrandt's best-known works were painted by his students, but were sold under Rembrandt's name.

Passage #4: October 1997 Questions 14-18

The debate over the environmental crisis is not new; anxiety about industry's impact on the environment has existed for over a century. What is new is the extreme polarization of views. Mounting
(5) evidence of humanity's capacity to damage the environment irreversibly coupled with suspicions that government, industry, and even science might be impotent to prevent environmental destruction have provoked accusatory polemics on the part of
(10) environmentalists. In turn, these polemics have elicited a corresponding backlash from industry. The sad effect of this polarization is that it is now even more difficult for industry than it was a hundred years ago to respond appropriately to
(15) impact analyses that demand action.

Unlike today's adversaries, earlier ecological reformers shared with advocates of industrial growth a confidence in timely corrective action. George P. Marsh's pioneering conservation tract
(20) *Man and Nature* (1864) elicited wide acclaim without embittered denials. *Man and Nature* castigated Earth's despoilers for heedless greed, declaring that humanity "has brought the face of the Earth to a desolation almost as complete as that of
(25) the Moon." But no entrepreneur or industrialist sought to refute Marsh's accusations, to defend the gutting of forests or the slaughter of wildlife as economically essential, or to dismiss his ecological warnings as hysterical. To the contrary, they
(30) generally agreed with him.

Why? Marsh and his followers took environmental improvement and economic progress as givers; they disputed not the desirability of conquering nature but the bungling way in which
(35) the conquest was carried out. Blame was not personalized; Marsh denounced general greed rather than particular entrepreneurs, and the media did not hound malefactors. Further, corrective measures seemed to entail no sacrifice, to demand no
(40) draconian remedies. Self-interest underwrote most prescribed reforms. Marsh's emphasis on future stewardship was then a widely accepted ideal (if not practice). His ecological admonitions were in keeping with the Enlightenment premise that
(45) humanity's mission was to subdue and transform nature.

Not until the 1960s did a gloomier perspective gain popular ground. Frederic Clements' equilibrium model of ecology, developed in the
(50) 1930s, seemed consistent with mounting environmental disasters. In this view, nature was most fruitful when least altered. Left undisturbed, flora and fauna gradually attained maximum diversity and stability. Despoliation thwarted the
(55) culmination or shortened the duration of this beneficent climax; technology did not improve nature but destroyed it.

The equilibrium model became an ecological mystique: environmental interference was now
(60) taboo, wilderness adored. Nature as unfinished fabric perfected by human ingenuity gave way to the image of nature debased and endangered by technology. In contrast to the Enlightenment vision of nature, according to which rational managers
(65) construct an ever more improved environment, twentieth-century reformers' vision of nature calls for a reduction of human interference in order to restore environmental stability.

14. Which one of the following most accurately states the main idea of the passage?

(A) Mounting evidence of humanity's capacity to damage the environment should motivate action to prevent further damage.
(B) The ecological mystique identified with Frederic Clements has become a religious conviction among ecological reformers.
(C) George P. Marsh's ideas about conservation and stewardship have heavily influenced the present debate over the environment.
(D) The views of ecologists and industrial growth advocates concerning the environment have only recently become polarized.
(E) General greed, rather than particular individuals or industries, should be blamed for the environmental crisis.

15. The author refers to the equilibrium model of ecology as an "ecological mystique" (lines 58-59) most likely in order to do which one of the following?

    (A) underscore the fervor with which twentieth-century reformers adhere to the equilibrium model
    (B) point out that the equilibrium model of ecology has recently been supported by empirical scientific research
    (C) express appreciation for how plants and animals attain maximum diversity and stability when left alone
    (D) indicate that the ideas of twentieth-century ecological reformers are often so theoretical as to be difficult to understand
    (E) indicate how widespread support is for the equilibrium model of ecology in the scientific community

16. Which one of the following practices is most clearly an application of Frederic Clements' equilibrium model of ecology?

    (A) introducing a species into an environment to which it is not native to help control the spread of another species that no longer has any natural predators
    (B) developing incentives for industries to take corrective measures to protect the environment
    (C) using scientific methods to increase the stability of plants and animals in areas where species are in danger of becoming extinct
    (D) using technology to develop plant and animal resources but balancing that development with stringent restrictions on technology
    (E) setting areas of land aside to be maintained as wilderness from which the use or extraction of natural resources is prohibited

17. The passage suggests that George P. Marsh and today's ecological reformers would be most likely to agree with which one of the following statements?

    (A) Regulating industries in order to protect the environment does not conflict with the self-interest of those industries.
    (B) Solving the environmental crisis does not require drastic and costly remedies.
    (C) Human despoliation of the Earth has caused widespread environmental damage.
    (D) Environmental improvement and economic progress are equally important goals.
    (E) Rather than blaming specific industries, general greed should be denounced as the cause of environmental destruction.

18. The passage is primarily concerned with which one of the following?

    (A) providing examples of possible solutions to a current crisis
    (B) explaining how conflicting viewpoints in a current debate are equally valid
    (C) determining which of two conflicting viewpoints in a current debate is more persuasive
    (D) outlining the background and development of conflicting viewpoints in a current debate
    (E) demonstrating weaknesses in the arguments made by one side in a current debate

Passage #5: December 1997 Questions 21-27

A fake can be defined as an artwork intended to deceive. The motives of its creator are decisive, and the merit of the object itself is a separate issue. The question mark in the title of Mark Jones's *Fake?*
(5) *The Art of Deception* reveals the study's broader concerns. Indeed, it might equally be entitled *Original?*, and the text begins by noting a variety of possibilities somewhere between the two extremes. These include works by an artist's followers in the
(10) style of the master, deliberate archaism, copying for pedagogical purposes, and the production of commercial facsimiles

The greater part of *Fake?* is devoted to a chronological survey suggesting that faking feeds
(15) on the many different motives people have for collecting art, and that, on the whole, the faking of art flourishes whenever art collecting flourishes. In imperial Rome there was a widespread interest in collecting earlier Greek art, and therefore in faking
(20) it. No doubt many of the sculptures now exhibited as "Roman copies" were originally passed off as Greek. In medieval Europe, because art was celebrated more for its devotional uses than for its provenance or the ingenuity of its creators, the
(25) faking of art was virtually nonexistent. The modern age of faking began in the Italian Renaissance, with two linked developments: a passionate identification with the world of antiquity and a growing sense of individual artistic identity. A patron of the young
(30) Michelangelo prevailed upon the artist to make his sculpture *Sleeping Cupid* look as though it had been buried in the earth so that "it will be taken for antique, and you will sell it much better." Within a few years, however, beginning with his first
(35) masterpiece, the Bacchus, Michelangelo had shown his contemporaries that great art can assimilate and transcend what came before, resulting in a wholly original work. Soon his genius made him the object of imitators.
(40) *Fake?* also reminds us that in certain cultures authenticity is a foreign concept. This is true of much African art, where the authenticity of an object is considered by collectors to depend on its function. As an illustration, the study compares two
(45) versions of a *chi wara* mask made by the Bambara people of Mali. One has pegs allowing it to be attached to a cap for its intended ceremonial purpose. The second, otherwise identical, lacks the pegs and is a replica made for sale. African carving
(50) is notoriously difficult to date, but even if the ritual mask is recent, made perhaps to replace a damaged predecessor, and the replica much older, only the ritual mask should be seen as authentic, for it is tied to the form's original function. That, at least, is the
(55) consensus of the so-called experts. One wonders whether the Bambaran artists would agree.

21. The passage can best be described as doing which one of the following?

    (A) reconciling varied points of view
    (B) chronicling the evolution of a phenomenon
    (C) exploring a complex question
    (D) advocating a new approach
    (E) rejecting an inadequate explanation

22. Which one of the following best expresses the author's main point?

    (A) The faking of art has occurred throughout history and in virtually every culture.
    (B) Whether a work of art is fake or not is less important than whether it has artistic merit.
    (C) It is possible to show that a work of art is fake, but the authenticity of a work cannot be proved conclusively.
    (D) A variety of circumstances make it difficult to determine whether a work of art can appropriately be called a fake.
    (E) Without an international market to support it, the faking of art would cease.

23. According to the passage, an artwork can be definitively classified as a fake if the person who created it

    (A) consciously adopted the artistic style of an influential mentor
    (B) deliberately imitated a famous work of art as a learning exercise
    (C) wanted other people to be fooled by its appearance
    (D) made multiple, identical copies of the work available for sale
    (E) made the work resemble the art of an earlier era

24. The author provides at least one example of each of the following EXCEPT:

    (A) categories of art that are neither wholly fake nor wholly original
    (B) cultures in which the faking of art flourished
    (C) qualities that art collectors have prized in their acquisitions
    (D) cultures in which the categories "fake" and "original" do not apply
    (E) contemporary artists whose works have inspired fakes

25. The author implies which one of the following about the artistic merits of fakes?

    (A) Because of the circumstances of its production, a fake cannot be said to have true artistic merit.
    (B) A fake can be said to have artistic merit only if the attempted deception is successful.
    (C) A fake may or may not have artistic merit in its own right, regardless of the circumstances of its production.
    (D) Whether a fake has artistic merit depends on whether its creator is accomplished as an artist.
    (E) The artistic merit of a fake depends on the merit of the original work that inspired the fake.

26. By the standard described in the last paragraph of the passage, which one of the following would be considered authentic?

    (A) an ancient Roman copy of an ancient Greek sculpture
    (B) a painting begun by a Renaissance master and finished by his assistants after his death
    (C) a print of a painting signed by the artist who painted the original
    (D) a faithful replica of a ceremonial crown that preserves all the details of, and is indistinguishable from, the original
    (E) a modern reconstruction of a medieval altarpiece designed to serve its traditional role in a service of worship

27. Which one of the following best describes how the last paragraph functions in the context of the passage?

    (A) It offers a tentative answer to a question posed by the author in the opening paragraph.
    (B) It summarizes an account provided in detail in the preceding paragraph.
    (C) It provides additional support for an argument advanced by the author in the preceding paragraph.
    (D) It examines another facet of a distinction developed in the preceding paragraphs.
    (E) It affirms the general principle enunciated at the beginning of the passage.

Passage #6: June 1998 Questions 8-13

While a new surge of critical interest in the ancient Greek poems conventionally ascribed to Homer has taken place in the last twenty years or so, it was nonspecialists rather than professional scholars who
(5) studied the poetic aspects of the *Iliad* and the *Odyssey* between, roughly, 1935 and 1970. During these years, while such nonacademic intellectuals as Simone Weil and Erich Auerbach were trying to define the qualities that made these epic accounts of the Trojan War and its
(10) aftermath great poetry, the questions that occupied the specialists were directed elsewhere: "Did the Trojan War really happen?" "Does the bard preserve Indo-European folk memories?" "How did the poems get written down?" Something was driving scholars away
(15) from the actual works to peripheral issues. Scholars produced books about archaeology, about gift-exchange in ancient societies, about the development of oral poetry, about virtually anything except the *Iliad* and the *Odyssey* themselves as unique reflections or
(20) distillations of life itself—as, in short, great poetry. The observations of the English poet Alexander Pope seemed as applicable in 1970 as they had been when he wrote them in 1715: according to Pope, the remarks of critics "are rather Philosophical, Historical,
(25) Geographical . . . or rather anything than Critical and Poetical."

Ironically, the modern manifestation of this "nonpoetical" emphasis can be traced to the profoundly influential work of Milman Parry, who attempted to
(30) demonstrate in detail how the Homeric poems, believed to have been recorded nearly three thousand years ago, were the products of a long and highly developed tradition of oral poetry about the Trojan War. Parry proposed that this tradition built up its
(35) diction and its content by a process of constant accumulation and refinement over many generations of storytellers. But after Parry's death in 1935, his legacy was taken up by scholars who, unlike Parry, forsook intensive analysis of the poetry itself and focused
(40) instead on only one element of Parry's work: the creative limitations and possibilities of oral composition, concentrating on fixed elements and inflexibilities, focusing on the things that oral poetry allegedly can and cannot do. The dryness of this kind
(45) of study drove many of the more inventive scholars away from the poems into the rapidly developing field of Homer's archaeological and historical background.

Appropriately, Milman Parry's son Adam was among those scholars responsible for a renewed
(50) interest in Homer's poetry as literary art. Building on his father's work, the younger Parry argued that the Homeric poems exist both within and against a tradition. The *Iliad* and the *Odyssey* were, Adam Parry thought, the beneficiaries of an inherited store of
(55) diction, scenes, and concepts, and at the same time highly individual works that surpassed these conventions. Adam Parry helped prepare the ground for the recent Homeric revival by affirming his father's belief in a strong inherited tradition, but also by
(60) emphasizing Homer's unique contributions within that tradition.

8. Which one of the following best states the main idea of the passage?

   (A) The Homeric poems are most fruitfully studied as records of the time and place in which they were written.
   (B) The Homeric poems are the products of a highly developed and complicated tradition of oral poetry.
   (C) The Homeric poems are currently enjoying a resurgence of critical interest after an age of scholarship largely devoted to the poems' nonpoetic elements.
   (D) The Homeric poems are currently enjoying a resurgence of scholarly interest after an age during which most studies were authored by nonacademic writers.
   (E) Before Milman Parry published his pioneering work in the early twentieth century, it was difficult to assign a date or an author to the Homeric poems.

9. According to the passage, the work of Simone Weil and Erich Auerbach on Homer was primarily concerned with which one of the following?

   (A) considerations of why criticism of Homer had moved to peripheral issues
   (B) analyses of the poetry itself in terms of its literary qualities
   (C) studies in the history and nature of oral poetry
   (D) analyses of the already ancient epic tradition inherited by Homer
   (E) critiques of the highly technical analyses of academic critics

10. The passage suggests which one of the following about scholarship on Homer that has appeared since 1970?

    (A) It has dealt extensively with the Homeric poems as literary art.
    (B) It is more incisive than the work of the Parrys.
    (C) It has rejected as irrelevant the scholarship produced by specialists between 1935 and 1970.
    (D) It has ignored the work of Simone Weil and Erich Auerbach.
    (E) It has attempted to confirm that the *Iliad* and the *Odyssey* were written by Homer.

11. The author of the passage most probably quotes Alexander Pope (lines 24-26) in order to

    (A) indicate that the Homeric poems have generally received poor treatment at the hands of English critics
    (B) prove that poets as well as critics have emphasized elements peripheral to the poems
    (C) illustrate that the nonpoetical emphasis also existed in an earlier century
    (D) emphasize the problems inherent in rendering classical Greek poetry into modern English
    (E) argue that poets and literary critics have seldom agreed about the interpretation of poetry

12. According to the passage, which one of the following is true of Milman Parry's immediate successors in the field of Homeric studies?

    (A) They reconciled Homer's poetry with archaeological and historical concerns.
    (B) They acknowledged the tradition of oral poetry, but focused on the uniqueness of Homer's poetry within the tradition.
    (C) They occupied themselves with the question of what qualities made for great poetry.
    (D) They emphasized the boundaries of oral poetry.
    (E) They called for a revival of Homer's popularity.

13. Which one of the following best describes the organization of the passage?

    (A) A situation is identified and its origins are examined.
    (B) A series of hypotheses is reviewed and one is advocated.
    (C) The works of two influential scholars are summarized.
    (D) Several issues contributing to a current debate are summarized.
    (E) Three possible solutions to a long-standing problem are posed.

Passage #7: September 1998 Questions 1-5

Opponents of compulsory national service claim that such a program is not in keeping with the liberal principles upon which Western democracies are founded. This reasoning is reminiscent of the argument
(5) that a tax on one's income is undemocratic because it violates one's right to property. Such conceptions of the liberal state fail to take into account the intricate character of the social agreement that undergirds our liberties. It is only in the context of a community that
(10) the notion of individual rights has any application; individual rights are meant to define the limits of people's actions with respect to other people. Implicit in such a context is the concept of shared sacrifice. Were no taxes paid, there could be no law enforcement,
(15) and the enforcement of law is of benefit to everyone in society. Thus, each of us must bear a share of the burden to ensure that the community is protected.

The responsibility to defend one's nation against outside aggression is surely no less than the
(20) responsibility to help pay for law enforcement within the nation. Therefore, the state is certainly within its rights to compel citizens to perform national service when it is needed for the benefit of society.

It might be objected that the cases of taxation and
(25) national service are not analogous: While taxation must be coerced, the military is quite able to find recruits without resorting to conscription. Furthermore, proponents of national service do not limit its scope to only those duties absolutely necessary to the defense of
(30) the nation. Therefore, it may be contended, compulsory national service oversteps the acceptable boundaries of governmental interference in the lives of its citizens.

By responding thus, the opponent of national service has already allowed that it is a right of
(35) government to demand service when it is needed. But what is the true scope of the term "need"? If it is granted, say, that present tax policies are legitimate intrusions on the right to property, then it must also be granted that need involves more than just what is
(40) necessary for a sound national defense. Even the most conservative of politicians admits that tax money is rightly spent on programs that, while not necessary for the survival of the state, are nevertheless of great benefit to society. Can the opponent of national service
(45) truly claim that activities of the military such as quelling civil disorders, rebuilding dams and bridges, or assisting the victims of natural disasters—all extraneous to the defense of society against outside aggression—do not provide a similar benefit to the
(50) nation? Upon reflection, opponents of national service must concede that such a broadened conception of what is necessary is in keeping with the ideas of shared sacrifice and community benefit that are essential to the functioning of a liberal democratic state.

1. Which one of the following most accurately describes the author's attitude toward the relationship between citizenship and individual rights in a democracy?

    (A) confidence that individual rights are citizens' most important guarantees of personal freedom
    (B) satisfaction at how individual rights have protected citizens from unwarranted government intrusion
    (C) alarm that so many citizens use individual rights as an excuse to take advantage of one another
    (D) concern that individual rights represent citizens' only defense against government interference
    (E) dissatisfaction at how some citizens cite individual rights as a way of avoiding certain obligations to their government

2. The author indicates that all politicians agree about the

   (A) legitimacy of funding certain programs that serve the national good
   (B) use of the military to prevent domestic disorders
   (C) similarity of conscription and compulsory taxation
   (D) importance of broadening the definition of necessity
   (E) compatibility of compulsion with democratic principles

3. Which one of the following most accurately characterizes what the author means by the term "social agreement" (line 8)?

   (A) an agreement among members of a community that the scope of their individual liberties is limited somewhat by their obligations to one another
   (B) an agreement among members of a community that they will not act in ways that infringe upon each other's pursuit of individual liberty
   (C) an agreement among members of a community that they will petition the government for redress when government actions limit their rights
   (D) an agreement between citizens and their government detailing which government actions do or do not infringe upon citizens' personal freedoms
   (E) an agreement between citizens and their government stating that the government has the right to suspend individual liberties whenever it sees fit

4. According to the author, national service and taxation are analogous in the sense that both

   (A) do not require that citizens be compelled to help bring them about
   (B) are at odds with the notion of individual rights in a democracy
   (C) require different degrees of sacrifice from different citizens
   (D) allow the government to overstep its boundaries and interfere in the lives of citizens
   (E) serve ends beyond those related to the basic survival of the state

5. Based on the information in the passage, which one of the following would most likely be found objectionable by those who oppose compulsory national service?

   (A) the use of tax revenues to prevent the theft of national secrets by foreign agents
   (B) the use of tax revenues to fund relief efforts for victims of natural disasters in other nations
   (C) the use of tax revenues to support the upkeep of the nation's standing army
   (D) the use of tax revenues to fund programs for the maintenance of domestic dams and bridges
   (E) the use of tax revenues to aid citizens who are victims of natural disasters

Passage #8: June 1999 Questions 14-21

Recently, a new school of economics called steady-state economics has seriously challenged neoclassical economics, the reigning school in Western economic decision making. According to the neoclassical model,
(5) an economy is a closed system involving only the circular flow of exchange value between producers and consumers. Therefore, no noneconomic constraints impinge upon the economy and growth has no limits. Indeed, some neoclassical economists argue that
(10) growth itself is crucial, because, they claim, the solutions to problems often associated with growth (income inequities, for example) can be found only in the capital that further growth creates.

Steady-state economists believe the neoclassical
(15) model to be unrealistic and hold that the economy is dependent on nature. Resources, they argue, enter the economy as raw material and exit as consumed products or waste; the greater the resources, the greater the size of the economy. According to these
(20) economists, nature's limited capacity to regenerate raw material and absorb waste suggests that there is an optimal size for the economy, and that growth beyond this ideal point would increase the cost to the environment at a faster rate than the benefit to
(25) producers and consumers, generating cycles that impoverish rather than enrich. Steady-state economists thus believe that the concept of an ever growing economy is dangerous, and that the only alternative is to maintain a state in which the economy remains in
(30) equilibrium with nature. Neoclassical economists, on the other hand, consider nature to be just one element of the economy rather than an outside constraint, believing that natural resources, if depleted, can be replaced with other elements—i.e., human-made
(35) resources—that will allow the economy to continue with its process of unlimited growth.

Some steady-state economists, pointing to the widening disparity between indices of actual growth (which simply count the total monetary value of goods
(40) and services) and the index of environmentally sustainable growth (which is based on personal consumption, factoring in depletion of raw materials and production costs), believe that Western economies have already exceeded their optimal size. In response
(45) to the warnings from neoclassical economists that checking economic growth only leads to economic stagnation, they argue that there are alternatives to growth that still accomplish what is required of any economy: the satisfaction of human wants. One of
(50) these alternatives is conservation. Conservation—for example, increasing the efficiency of resource use through means such as recycling—differs from growth in that it is qualitative, not quantitative, requiring improvement in resource management rather than an
(55) increase in the amount of resources. One measure of the success of a steady-state economy would be the degree to which it could implement alternatives to growth, such as conservation, without sacrificing the ability to satisfy the wants of producers and consumers.

14. Which one of the following most completely and accurately expresses the main point of the passage?

(A) Neoclassical economists, who, unlike steady-state economists, hold that economic growth is not subject to outside constraints, believe that nature is just one element of the economy and that if natural resources in Western economies are depleted they can be replaced with human-made resources.
(B) Some neoclassical economists, who, unlike steady-state economists, hold that growth is crucial to the health of economies, believe that the solutions to certain problems in Western economies can thus be found in the additional capital generated by unlimited growth.
(C) Some steady-state economists, who, unlike neoclassical economists, hold that unlimited growth is neither possible nor desirable, believe that Western economies should limit economic growth by adopting conservation strategies, even if such strategies lead temporarily to economic stagnation.
(D) Some steady-state economists, who, unlike neoclassical economists, hold that the optimal sizes of economies are limited by the availability of natural resources, believe that Western economies should limit economic growth and that, with alternatives like conservation, satisfaction of human wants need not be sacrificed.
(E) Steady-state and neoclassical economists, who both hold that economies involve the circular flow of exchange value between producers and consumers, nevertheless differ over the most effective way of guaranteeing that a steady increase in this exchange value continues unimpeded in Western economies.

15. Based on the passage, neoclassical economists would likely hold that steady-state economists are wrong to believe each of the following EXCEPT:

(A) The environment's ability to yield raw material is limited.
(B) Natural resources are an external constraint on economies.
(C) The concept of unlimited economic growth is dangerous.
(D) Western economies have exceeded their optimal size.
(E) Economies have certain optimal sizes.

16. According to the passage, steady-state economists believe that unlimited economic growth is dangerous because it

   (A) may deplete natural resources faster than other natural resources are discovered to replace them
   (B) may convert natural resources into products faster than more efficient resource use can compensate for
   (C) may proliferate goods and services faster than it generates new markets for them
   (D) may create income inequities faster than it creates the capital needed to redress them
   (E) may increase the cost to the environment faster than it increases benefits to producers and consumers

17. A steady-state economist would be LEAST likely to endorse which one of the following as a means of helping a steady-state economy reduce growth without compromising its ability to satisfy human wants?

   (A) a manufacturer's commitment to recycle its product packaging
   (B) a manufacturer's decision to use a less expensive fuel in its production process
   (C) a manufacturer's implementation of a quality control process to reduce the output of defective products
   (D) a manufacturer's conversion from one type of production process to another with greater fuel efficiency
   (E) a manufacturer's reduction of output in order to eliminate an overproduction problem

18. Based on the passage, a steady-state economist is most likely to claim that a successful economy is one that satisfies which one of the following principles?

   (A) A successful economy uses human-made resources in addition to natural resources.
   (B) A successful economy satisfies human wants faster than it creates new ones.
   (C) A successful economy maintains an equilibrium with nature while still satisfying human wants.
   (D) A successful economy implements every possible means to prevent growth.
   (E) A successful economy satisfies the wants of producers and consumers by using resources to spur growth.

19. In the view of steady-state economists, which one of the following is a noneconomic constraint as referred to in line 7?

   (A) the total amount of human wants
   (B) the index of environmentally sustainable growth
   (C) the capacity of nature to absorb waste
   (D) the problems associated with economic growth
   (E) the possibility of economic stagnation

20. Which one of the following most accurately describes what the last paragraph does in the passage?

   (A) It contradicts the ways in which the two economic schools interpret certain data and gives a criterion for judging between them based on the basic goals of an economy.
   (B) It gives an example that illustrates the weakness of the new economic school and recommends an economic policy based on the basic goals of the prevailing economic school.
   (C) It introduces an objection to the new economic school and argues that the policies of the new economic school would be less successful than growth-oriented economic policies at achieving the basic goal an economy must meet.
   (D) It notes an objection to implementing the policies of the new economic school and identifies an additional policy that can help avoid that objection and still meet the goal an economy must meet.
   (E) It contrasts the policy of the prevailing economic school with the recommendation mentioned earlier of the new economic school and shows that they are based on differing views on the basic goal an economy must meet.

21. The passage suggests which one of the following about neoclassical economists?

   (A) They assume that natural resources are infinitely available.
   (B) They assume that human-made resources are infinitely available.
   (C) They assume that availability of resources places an upper limit on growth.
   (D) They assume that efficient management of resources is necessary to growth.
   (E) They assume that human-made resources are preferable to natural resources.

Passage #9: June 1999 Questions 22-26

As one of the most pervasive and influential popular arts, the movies feed into and off of the rest of the culture in various ways. In the United States, the star system of the mid-1920s—in which actors were
(5) placed under exclusive contract to particular Hollywood film studios—was a consequence of studios' discovery that the public was interested in actors' private lives, and that information about actors could be used to promote their films. Public relations
(10) agents fed the information to gossip columnists, whetting the public's appetite for the films—which, audiences usually discovered, had the additional virtue of being created by talented writers, directors, and producers devoted to the art of storytelling. The
(15) important feature of this relationship was not the benefit to Hollywood, but rather to the press; in what amounted to a form of cultural cross-fertilization, the press saw that they could profit from studios' promotion of new films.
(20) Today this arrangement has mushroomed into an intricately interdependent mass-media entertainment industry. The faith by which this industry sustains itself is the belief that there is always something worth promoting. A vast portion of the mass media—
(25) television and radio interviews, magazine articles, even product advertisements—now does most of the work for Hollywood studios attempting to promote their movies. It does so not out of altruism but because it makes for good business: If you produce a talk show
(30) or edit a newspaper, and other media are generating public curiosity about a studio's forthcoming film, it would be unwise for you not to broadcast or publish something about the film, too, because the audience for your story is already guaranteed.
(35) The problem with this industry is that it has begun to affect the creation of films as well as their promotion. Choices of subject matter and actors are made more and more frequently by studio executives rather than by producers, writers, or directors. This
(40) problem is often referred to simply as an obsession with turning a profit, but Hollywood movies have almost always been produced to appeal to the largest possible audience. The new danger is that, increasingly, profit comes only from exciting an
(45) audience's curiosity about a movie instead of satisfying its desire to have an engaging experience watching the film. When movies can pull people into theaters instantly on the strength of media publicity rather than relying on the more gradual process of word of mouth
(50) among satisfied moviegoers, then the intimate relationship with the audience—on which the vitality of all popular art depends—is lost. But studios are making more money than ever by using this formula, and for this reason it appears that films whose appeal is
(55) due not merely to their publicity value but to their ability to affect audiences emotionally will become increasingly rare in the U.S. film industry.

22. The passage suggests that the author would be most likely to agree with which one of the following statements?

(A) The Hollywood films of the mid-1920s were in general more engaging to watch than are Hollywood films produced today.
(B) The writers, producers, and directors in Hollywood in the mid-1920s were more talented than are their counterparts today.
(C) The Hollywood film studios of the mid-1920s had a greater level of dependence on the mass-media industry than do Hollywood studios today.
(D) The publicity generated for Hollywood films in the mid-1920s was more interesting than is the publicity generated for these films today.
(E) The star system of the mid-1920s accounts for most of the difference in quality between the Hollywood films of that period and Hollywood films today.

23. According to the author, the danger of mass-media promotion of films is that it

(A) discourages the work of filmmakers who attempt to draw the largest possible audiences to their films
(B) discourages the critical review of the content of films that have been heavily promoted
(C) encourages the production of films that excite an audience's curiosity but that do not provide satisfying experiences
(D) encourages decisions to make the content of films parallel the private lives of the actors that appear in them
(E) encourages cynicism among potential audience members about the merits of the films publicized

24. The phrase "cultural cross-fertilization" (line 17) is used in the passage to refer to which one of the following?

(A) competition among different segments of the U.S. mass media
(B) the interrelationship of Hollywood movies with other types of popular art
(C) Hollywood film studios' discovery that the press could be used to communicate with the public
(D) the press's mutually beneficial relationship with Hollywood film studios
(E) interactions between public relations agents and the press

25. Which one of the following most accurately describes the organization of the passage?

    (A) description of the origins of a particular aspect of a popular art; discussion of the present state of this aspect; analysis of a problem associated with this aspect; introduction of a possible solution to the problem
    (B) description of the origins of a particular aspect of a popular art; discussion of the present state of this aspect; analysis of a problem associated with this aspect; suggestion of a likely consequence of the problem
    (C) description of the origins of a particular aspect of a popular art; analysis of a problem associated with this aspect; introduction of a possible solution to the problem; suggestion of a likely consequence of the solution
    (D) summary of the history of a particular aspect of a popular art; discussion of a problem that accompanied the growth of this aspect; suggestion of a likely consequence of the problem; appraisal of the importance of avoiding this consequence
    (E) summary of the history of a particular aspect of a popular art; analysis of factors that contributed to the growth of this aspect; discussion of a problem that accompanied the growth of this aspect; appeal for assistance in solving the problem

26. The author's position in lines 35-47 would be most weakened if which one of the following were true?

    (A) Many Hollywood studio executives do consider a film's ability to satisfy moviegoers emotionally.
    (B) Many Hollywood studio executives achieved their positions as a result of demonstrating talent at writing, producing, or directing films that satisfy audiences emotionally.
    (C) Most writers, producers, and directors in Hollywood continue to have a say in decisions about the casting and content of films despite the influence of studio executives.
    (D) The decisions made by most Hollywood studio executives to improve a film's chances of earning a profit also add to its ability to satisfy moviegoers emotionally.
    (E) Often the U.S. mass media play an indirect role in influencing the content of the films that Hollywood studios make by whetting the public's appetite for certain performers or subjects.

Passage #10: October 1999 Questions 1-7

For some years before the outbreak of World War I, a number of painters in different European countries developed works of art that some have described as prophetic: paintings that by challenging
(5) viewers' habitual ways of perceiving the world of the present are thus said to anticipate a future world that would be very different. The artistic styles that they brought into being varied widely, but all these styles had in common a very important break with traditions
(10) of representational art that stretched back to the Renaissance.

So fundamental is this break with tradition that it is not surprising to discover that these artists—among them Picasso and Braque in France, Kandinsky in
(15) Germany, and Malevich in Russia—are often credited with having anticipated not just subsequent developments in the arts, but also the political and social disruptions and upheavals of the modern world that came into being during and after the war. One art
(20) critic even goes so far as to claim that it is the very prophetic power of these artworks, and not their break with traditional artistic techniques, that constitutes their chief interest and value.

No one will deny that an artist may, just as much as
(25) a writer or a politician, speculate about the future and then try to express a vision of that future through making use of a particular style or choice of imagery; speculation about the possibility of war in Europe was certainly widespread during the early years of the
(30) twentieth century. But the forward-looking quality attributed to these artists should instead be credited to their exceptional aesthetic innovations rather than to any power to make clever guesses about political or social trends. For example, the clear impression we get
(35) of Picasso and Braque, the joint founders of cubism, from their contemporaries as well as from later statements made by the artists themselves, is that they were primarily concerned with problems of representation and form and with efforts to create a far
(40) more "real" reality than the one that was accessible only to the eye. The reformation of society was of no interest to them as artists.

It is also important to remember that not all decisive changes in art are quickly followed by
(45) dramatic events in the world outside art. The case of Delacroix, the nineteenth-century French painter, is revealing. His stylistic innovations startled his contemporaries—and still retain that power over modern viewers—but most art historians have decided
(50) that Delacroix adjusted himself to new social conditions that were already coming into being as a result of political upheavals that had occurred in 1830, as opposed to other artists who supposedly told of changes still to come.

1. Which one of the following most accurately states the main idea of the passage?

(A) Although they flourished independently, the pre-World War I European painters who developed new ways of looking at the world shared a common desire to break with the traditions of representational art.

(B) The work of the pre-World War I European painters who developed new ways of looking at the world cannot be said to have intentionally predicted social changes but only to have anticipated new directions in artistic perception and expression.

(C) The work of the pre-World War I European painters who developed new ways of looking at the world was important for its ability to predict social changes and its anticipation of new directions in artistic expression.

(D) Art critics who believe that the work of some pre-World War I European painters foretold imminent social changes are mistaken because art is incapable of expressing a vision of the future.

(E) Art critics who believe that the work of some pre-World War I European painters foretold imminent social changes are mistaken because the social upheavals that followed World War I were impossible to predict.

2. The art critic mentioned in lines 19-20 would be most likely to agree with which one of the following statements?

   (A) The supposed innovations of Picasso, Braque, Kandinsky, and Malevich were based on stylistic discoveries that had been made in the Renaissance but went unexplored for centuries.
   (B) The work of Picasso, Braque, Kandinsky, and Malevich possessed prophetic power because these artists employed the traditional techniques of representational art with unusual skill.
   (C) The importance of the work of Picasso, Braque, Kandinsky, and Malevich is due largely to the fact that the work was stylistically ahead of its time.
   (D) The prophecies embodied in the work of Picasso, Braque, Kandinsky, and Malevich were shrewd predictions based on insights into the European political situation.
   (E) The artistic styles brought into being by Picasso, Braque, Kandinsky, and Malevich, while stylistically innovative, were of little significance to the history of post-World War I.

3. According to the passage, the statements of Picasso and Braque indicate that

   (A) they had a long-standing interest in politics
   (B) they worked actively to bring about social change
   (C) their formal innovations were actually the result of chance
   (D) their work was a deliberate attempt to transcend visual reality
   (E) the formal aspects of their work were of little interest to them

4. The author presents the example of Delacroix in order to illustrate which one of the following claims?

   (A) Social or political changes usually lead to important artistic innovations.
   (B) Artistic innovations do not necessarily anticipate social or political upheavals.
   (C) Some European painters have used art to predict social or political changes.
   (D) Important stylistic innovations are best achieved by abandoning past traditions.
   (E) Innovative artists can adapt themselves to social or political changes.

5. Which one of the following most accurately describes the contents of the passage?

   (A) The author describes an artistic phenomenon; introduces one interpretation of this phenomenon; proposes an alternative interpretation and then supports this alternative by criticizing the original interpretation.
   (B) The author describes an artistic phenomenon; identifies the causes of that phenomenon; illustrates some of the consequences of the phenomenon and then speculates about the significance of these consequences.
   (C) The author describes an artistic phenomenon; articulates the traditional interpretation of this phenomenon; identifies two common criticisms of this view and then dismisses each of these criticisms by appeal to an example.
   (D) The author describes an artistic phenomenon; presents two competing interpretations of the phenomenon; dismisses both interpretations by appeal to an example and then introduces an alternative interpretation.
   (E) The author describes an artistic phenomenon; identifies the causes of the phenomenon; presents an argument for the importance of the phenomenon and then advocates an attempt to recreate the phenomenon.

6. According to the author, the work of the pre-World War I painters described in the passage contains an example of each of the following EXCEPT:

   (A) an interest in issues of representation and form
   (B) a stylistic break with traditional art
   (C) the introduction of new artistic techniques
   (D) the ability to anticipate later artists
   (E) the power to predict social changes

7. Which one of the following characteristics of the painters discussed in the second paragraph does the author of the passage appear to value most highly?

   (A) their insights into pre-World War I politics
   (B) the visionary nature of their social views
   (C) their mastery of the techniques of representational art
   (D) their ability to adjust to changing social conditions
   (E) their stylistic and aesthetic accomplishments

Passage #11: December 1999 Questions 7-14

Tragic dramas written in Greece during the fifth century B.C. engender considerable scholarly debate over the relative influence of individual autonomy and the power of the gods on the drama's action. One early
(5) scholar, B. Snell, argues that Aeschylus, for example, develops in his tragedies a concept of the autonomy of the individual. In these dramas, the protagonists invariably confront a situation that paralyzes them, so that their prior notions about how to behave or think
(10) are dissolved. Faced with a decision on which their fate depends, they must reexamine their deepest motives, and then act with determination. They are given only two alternatives, each with grave consequences, and they make their decision only after a tortured internal
(15) debate. According to Snell, this decision is "free" and "personal" and such personal autonomy constitutes the central theme in Aeschylean drama, as if the plays were devised to isolate an abstract model of human action. Drawing psychological conclusions from this
(20) interpretation, another scholar, Z. Barbu, suggests that "[Aeschylean] drama is proof of the emergence within ancient Greek civilization of the individual as a free agent."

To A. Rivier, Snell's emphasis on the decision
(25) made by the protagonist, with its implicit notions of autonomy and responsibility, misrepresents the role of the superhuman forces at work, forces that give the dramas their truly tragic dimension. These forces are not only external to the protagonist; they are also
(30) experienced by the protagonist as an internal compulsion, subjecting him or her to constraint even in what are claimed to be his or her "choices." Hence all that the deliberation does is to make the protagonist aware of the impasse, rather than motivating one
(35) choice over another. It is finally a necessity imposed by the deities that generates the decision, so that at a particular moment in the drama necessity dictates a path. Thus, the protagonist does not so much "choose" between two possibilities as "recognize" that there is
(40) only one real option.

A. Lesky, in his discussion of Aeschylus' play *Agamemnon,* disputes both views. Agamemnon, ruler of Argos, must decide whether to brutally sacrifice his own daughter. A message from the deity Artemis has
(45) told him that only the sacrifice will bring a wind to blow his ships to an important battle. Agamemnon is indeed constrained by a divine necessity. But he also deeply desires a victorious battle: "If this sacrifice will loose the winds, it is permitted to desire it fervently,"
(50) he says. The violence of his passion suggests that Agamemnon chooses a path—chosen by the gods for their own reasons—on the basis of desires that must be condemned by us, because they are his own. In Lesky's view, tragic action is bound by the constant tension
(55) between a self and superhuman forces.

7. Based on the information presented in the passage, which one of the following statements best represents Lesky's view of Agamemnon?

(A) Agamemnon's motivations are identical to those of the gods.
(B) The nature of Agamemnon's character solely determines the course of the tragedy.
(C) Agamemnon's decision-making is influenced by his military ambitions.
(D) Agamemnon is concerned only with pleasing the deity Artemis.
(E) Agamemnon is especially tragic because of his political position.

8. Which one of the following paraphrases most accurately restates the quotation from Agamemnon found in lines 48-49 of the passage?

(A) If the goddess has ordained that the only way I can evade battle is by performing this sacrifice, then it is perfectly appropriate for me to deeply desire this sacrifice.
(B) If the goddess has ordained that the only way I can get a wind to move my ships to battle is by performing this sacrifice, then it is perfectly appropriate for me to deeply desire victory in battle.
(C) If the goddess has ordained that the only way I can get a wind to move my ships to battle is by performing this sacrifice, then it is perfectly appropriate for me to deeply desire this sacrifice.
(D) As I alone have determined that only this sacrifice will give me victory in battle, I will perform it, without reservations.
(E) As I have determined that only deeply desiring victory in battle will guarantee the success of the sacrifice, I will perform it, as ordained by the goddess.

9. Which one of the following statements best expresses Rivier's view, as presented in the passage, of what makes a drama tragic?

(A) The tragic protagonist is deluded by the gods into thinking he or she is free.
(B) The tragic protagonist struggles for a heroism that belongs to the gods.
(C) The tragic protagonist wrongly seeks to take responsibility for his or her actions.
(D) The tragic protagonist cannot make a decision that is free of divine compulsion.
(E) The tragic protagonist is punished for evading his or her responsibilities.

10. It can be inferred from the passage that the central difference between the interpretations of Lesky and Rivier is over which one of the following points?

    (A) whether or not the tragic protagonist is aware of the consequences of his or her actions
    (B) whether or not the tragic protagonist acknowledges the role of the deities in his or her life
    (C) whether or not the tragic protagonist's own desires have relevance to the outcome of the drama
    (D) whether or not the actions of the deities are relevant to the moral evaluation of the character's action
    (E) whether or not the desires of the tragic protagonist are more ethical than those of the deities

11. Which one of the following summaries of the plot of a Greek tragedy best illustrates the view attributed to Rivier in the passage?

    (A) Although she knows that she will be punished for violating the law of her city, a tragic figure bravely decides to bury her dead brother over the objections of local authorities.
    (B) Because of her love for her dead brother, a tragic figure, although aware that she will be punished for violating the law of her city, accedes to the gods' request that she bury his body.
    (C) After much careful thought, a tragic figure decides to disobey the dictates of the gods and murder her unfaithful husband.
    (D) A tragic figure, defying a curse placed on his family by the gods, leads his city into a battle that he realizes will prove futile.
    (E) After much careful thought, a tragic figure realizes that he has no alternative but to follow the course chosen by the gods and murder his father.

12. The quotation in lines 21-23 suggests that Barbu assumes which one of the following about Aeschylean drama?

    (A) Aeschylean drama helped to initiate a new understanding of the person in ancient Greek society.
    (B) Aeschylean drama introduced new ways of understanding the role of the individual in ancient Greek society.
    (C) Aeschylean drama is the original source of the understanding of human motivation most familiar to the modern Western world.
    (D) Aeschylean drama accurately reflects the way personal autonomy was perceived in ancient Greek society.
    (E) Aeschylean drama embodies the notion of freedom most familiar to the modern Western world.

13. All of the following statements describe Snell's view of Aeschylus' tragic protagonists, as it is presented in the passage, EXCEPT:

    (A) They are required to choose a course of action with grave consequences.
    (B) Their final choices restore harmony with supernatural forces.
    (C) They cannot rely on their customary notions of appropriate behavior.
    (D) They are compelled to confront their true motives.
    (E) They are aware of the available choices.

14. The primary purpose of the passage is to

    (A) argue against one particular interpretation of Greek tragedy
    (B) establish that there are a variety of themes in Greek tragedy
    (C) present aspects of an ongoing scholarly debate about Greek tragedy
    (D) point out the relative merits of different scholarly interpretations of Greek tragedy
    (E) suggest the relevance of Greek tragedy to the philosophical debate over human motivation

Passage #12: June 2000 Questions 21-28

Some philosophers find the traditional, subjective approach to studying the mind outdated and ineffectual. For them, the attempt to describe the sensation of pain or anger, for example, or the
(5) awareness that one is aware, has been surpassed by advances in fields such as psychology, neuroscience, and cognitive science. Scientists, they claim, do not concern themselves with how a phenomenon feels from the inside; instead of investigating private evidence
(10) perceivable only to a particular individual, scientists pursue hard data—such as the study of how nerves transmit impulses to the brain—which is externally observable and can be described without reference to any particular point of view. With respect to features of
(15) the universe such as those investigated by chemistry, biology, and physics, this objective approach has been remarkably successful in yielding knowledge. Why, these philosophers ask, should we suppose the mind to be any different?

(20) But philosophers loyal to subjectivity are not persuaded by appeals to science when such appeals conflict with the data gathered by introspection. Knowledge, they argue, relies on the data of experience, which includes subjective experience. Why
(25) should philosophy ally itself with scientists who would reduce the sources of knowledge to only those data that can be discerned objectively?

On the face of it, it seems unlikely that these two approaches to studying the mind could be reconciled.
(30) Because philosophy, unlike science, does not progress inexorably toward a single truth, disputes concerning the nature of the mind are bound to continue. But what is particularly distressing about the present debate is that genuine communication between the two sides is
(35) virtually impossible. For reasoned discourse to occur, there must be shared assumptions or beliefs. Starting from radically divergent perspectives, subjectivists and objectivists lack a common context in which to consider evidence presented from each other's
(40) perspectives.

The situation may be likened to a debate between adherents of different religions about the creation of the universe. While each religion may be confident that its cosmology is firmly grounded in its respective
(45) sacred text, there is little hope that conflicts between their competing cosmologies could be resolved by recourse to the texts alone. Only further investigation into the authority of the texts themselves would be sufficient.

(50) What would be required to resolve the debate between the philosophers of mind, then, is an investigation into the authority of their differing perspectives. How rational is it to take scientific description as the ideal way to understand the nature of
(55) consciousness? Conversely, how useful is it to rely solely on introspection for one's knowledge about the workings of the mind? Are there alternative ways of gaining such knowledge? In this debate, epistemology—the study of knowledge—may itself
(60) lead to the discovery of new forms of knowledge about how the mind works.

21. Which one of the following most accurately summarizes the main point of the passage?

(A) In order to gain new knowledge of the workings of the mind, subjectivists must take into consideration not only the private evidence of introspection but also the more objective evidence obtainable from disciplines such as psychology, neuroscience, and cognitive science.

(B) In rejecting the traditional, subjective approach to studying the mind, objectivists have made further progress virtually impossible because their approach rests on a conception of evidence that is fundamentally incompatible with that employed by subjectivists.

(C) Because the subjectivist and objectivist approaches rest on diametrically opposed assumptions about the kinds of evidence to be used when studying the mind, the only way to resolve the dispute is to compare the two approaches' success in obtaining knowledge.

(D) Although subjectivists and objectivists appear to employ fundamentally irreconcilable approaches to the study of the mind, a common ground for debate may be found if both sides are willing to examine the authority of the evidence on which their competing theories depend.

(E) While the success of disciplines such as chemistry, biology, and physics appears to support the objectivist approach to studying the mind, the objectivist approach has failed to show that the data of introspection should not qualify as evidence.

22. Which one of the following most likely reflects the author's belief about the current impasse between subjectivists and objectivists?

(A) It cannot be overcome because of the radically different conceptions of evidence favored by each of the two sides.

(B) It is resolvable only if the two sides can find common ground from which to assess their competing conceptions of evidence.

(C) It is unavoidable unless both sides recognize that an accurate understanding of the mind requires both types of evidence.

(D) It is based on an easily correctable misunderstanding between the two sides about the nature of evidence.

(E) It will prevent further progress until alternate ways of gaining knowledge about the mind are discovered.

23. The author's primary purpose in writing the passage is to

   (A) suggest that there might be valid aspects to both the subjective and the objective approaches to studying the mind
   (B) advocate a possible solution to the impasse undermining debate between subjectivists and objectivists
   (C) criticize subjectivist philosophers for failing to adopt a more scientific methodology
   (D) defend the subjective approach to studying the mind against the charges leveled against it by objectivists
   (E) evaluate the legitimacy of differing conceptions of evidence advocated by subjectivists and objectivists

24. According to the passage, subjectivists advance which one of the following claims to support their charge that objectivism is faulty?

   (A) Objectivism rests on evidence that conflicts with the data of introspection.
   (B) Objectivism restricts the kinds of experience from which philosophers may draw knowledge.
   (C) Objectivism relies on data that can be described and interpreted only by scientific specialists.
   (D) Objectivism provides no context in which to view scientific data as relevant to philosophical questions.
   (E) Objectivism concerns itself with questions that have not traditionally been part of philosophical inquiry.

25. The author discusses the work of scientists in lines 7-14 primarily to

   (A) contrast the traditional approach to studying the mind with the approach advocated by objectivists
   (B) argue that the attempt to describe the sensation of pain should be done without reference to any particular point of view
   (C) explain why scientists should not concern themselves with describing how a phenomenon feels from the inside
   (D) criticize subjectivists for thinking there is little to be gained from studying the mind scientifically
   (E) clarify why the objectivists' approach has been successful in disciplines such as chemistry, biology, and physics

26. The author characterizes certain philosophers as "loyal to subjectivity" (line 20) for each of the following reasons EXCEPT:

   (A) These philosophers believe scientists should adopt the subjective approach when studying phenomena such as how nerves transmit impulses to the brain.
   (B) These philosophers favor subjective evidence about the mind over objective evidence about the mind when the two conflict.
   (C) These philosophers maintain that subjective experience is essential to the study of the mind.
   (D) These philosophers hold that objective evidence is only a part of the full range of experience.
   (E) These philosophers employ evidence that is available only to a particular individual.

27. Based on the passage, which one of the following is most clearly an instance of the objectivist approach to studying the mind?

   (A) collecting accounts of dreams given by subjects upon waking in order to better understand the nature of the subconscious
   (B) interviewing subjects during extremes of hot and cold weather in order to investigate a connection between weather and mood
   (C) recording subjects' evaluation of the stress they experienced while lecturing in order to determine how stress affects facility at public speaking
   (D) analyzing the amount of a certain chemical in subjects' bloodstreams in order to investigate a proposed link between the chemical and aggressive behavior
   (E) asking subjects to speak their thoughts aloud as they attempt to learn a new skill in order to test the relationship between mental understanding and physical performance

28. Which one of the following is most closely analogous to the debate described in the hypothetical example given by the author in the fourth paragraph?

   (A) a debate among investigators attempting to determine a criminal's identity when conflicting physical evidence is found at the crime scene
   (B) a debate among jurors attempting to determine which of two conflicting eyewitness accounts of an event is to be believed
   (C) a debate between two archaeologists about the meaning of certain written symbols when no evidence exists to verify either's claim
   (D) a debate between two museum curators about the value of a painting that shows clear signs of both genuineness and forgery
   (E) a debate between two historians who draw conflicting conclusions about the same event based on different types of historical data

Passage #13: December 2000 Questions 1-7

Many political economists believe that the soundest indicator of the economic health of a nation is the nation's gross national product (GNP) per capita—a figure reached by dividing the total value of the goods
(5) produced yearly in a nation by its population and taken to be a measure of the welfare of the nation's residents. But there are many factors affecting residents' welfare that are not captured by per capita GNP; human indicators, while sometimes more difficult to calculate
(10) or document, provide sounder measures of a nation's progress than does the indicator championed by these economists. These human indicators include nutrition and life expectancy; birth weight and level of infant mortality; ratio of population level to availability of
(15) resources; employment opportunities; and the ability of governments to provide services such as education, clean water, medicine, public transportation, and mass communication for their residents.

The economists defend their use of per capita GNP
(20) as the sole measure of a nation's economic health by claiming that improvements in per capita GNP eventually stimulate improvements in human indicators. But, in actuality, this often fails to occur. Even in nations where economic stimulation has
(25) brought about substantial improvements in per capita GNP, economic health as measured by human indicators does not always reach a level commensurate with the per capita GNP. Nations that have achieved a relatively high per capita GNP, for example, sometimes
(30) experience levels of infant survival, literacy, nutrition, and life expectancy no greater than levels in nations where per capita GNP is relatively low. In addition, because per capita GNP is an averaged figure, it often presents a distorted picture of the wealth of a nation;
(35) for example, in a relatively sparsely populated nation where a small percentage of residents receives most of the economic benefits of production while the majority receives very little benefit, per capita GNP may nevertheless be high. The welfare of a nation's
(40) residents is a matter not merely of total economic benefit, but also of the distribution of economic benefits across the entire society. Measuring a nation's economic health only by total wealth frequently obscures a lack of distribution of wealth across the
(45) society as a whole.

In light of the potential for such imbalances in distribution of economic benefits, some nations have begun to realize that their domestic economic efforts are better directed away from attempting to raise per
(50) capita GNP and instead toward ensuring that the conditions measured by human indicators are salutary. They recognize that unless a shift in focus away from using material wealth as the sole indicator of economic success is effected, the well-being of the nation may be
(55) endangered, and that nations that do well according to human indicators may thrive even if their per capita GNP remains stable or lags behind that of other nations.

1. Which one of the following titles most accurately expresses the main point of the passage?

    (A) "The Shifting Meaning of Per Capita GNP: A Historical Perspective"
    (B) "A Defense of Per Capita GNP: An Economist's Rejoinder"
    (C) "The Preferability of Human Indicators as Measures of National Economic Health"
    (D) "Total Wealth vs. Distribution of Wealth as a Measure of Economic Health"
    (E) "A New Method of Calculating Per Capita GNP to Measure National Economic Health"

2. The term "welfare" is used in the first paragraph to refer most specifically to which one of the following?

    (A) the overall quality of life for individuals in a nation
    (B) the services provided to individuals by a government
    (C) the material wealth owned by individuals in a nation
    (D) the extent to which the distribution of wealth among individuals in a nation is balanced
    (E) government efforts to redistribute wealth across society as a whole

3. The passage provides specific information about each of the following EXCEPT:

    (A) how per capita GNP is calculated
    (B) what many political economists believe to be an accurate measure of a nation's economic health
    (C) how nations with a relatively low per capita GNP can sometimes be economically healthier than nations whose per capita GNP is higher
    (D) why human indicators may not provide the same picture of a nation's economic health that per capita GNP does
    (E) how nations can adjust their domestic economic efforts to bring about substantial improvements in per capita GNP

4. Which one of the following scenarios, if true, would most clearly be a counterexample to the views expressed in the last paragraph of the passage?

(A) The decision by a nation with a low level of economic health as measured by human indicators to focus on increasing the levels of human indicators results in slower growth in its per capita GNP.
(B) The decision by a nation with a low level of economic health as measured by human indicators to focus on increasing domestic production of goods results in significant improvements in the levels of human indicators.
(C) The decision by a nation with a low level of economic health as measured by human indicators to focus on increasing the levels of human indicators results in increased growth in per capita GNP.
(D) The decision by a nation with a low per capita GNP to focus on improving its level of economic health as measured by human indicators fails to bring about an increase in per capita GNP.
(E) The decision by a nation with a low per capita GNP to focus on increasing domestic production of goods fails to improve its economic health as measured by human indicators.

5. The primary function of the last paragraph of the passage is to

(A) offer a synthesis of the opposing positions outlined in the first two paragraphs
(B) expose the inadequacies of both positions outlined in the first two paragraphs
(C) summarize the argument made in the first two paragraphs
(D) correct a weakness in the political economists' position as outlined in the second paragraph
(E) suggest policy implications of the argument made in the first two paragraphs

6. Based on the passage, the political economists discussed in the passage would be most likely to agree with which one of the following statements?

(A) A change in a nation's per capita GNP predicts a similar future change in the state of human indicators in that nation.
(B) The level of human indicators in a nation is irrelevant to the welfare of the individuals in that nation.
(C) A high per capita GNP in a nation usually indicates that the wealth in the nation is not distributed across the society as a whole.
(D) The welfare of a nation's residents is irrelevant to the economic health of the nation.
(E) The use of indicators other than material wealth to measure economic well-being would benefit a nation.

7. In the passage, the author's primary concern is to

(A) delineate a new method of directing domestic economic efforts
(B) point out the weaknesses in one standard for measuring a nation's welfare
(C) explain the fact that some nations have both a high per capita GNP and a low quality of life for its citizens
(D) demonstrate that unequal distribution of wealth is an inevitable result of a high per capita GNP
(E) argue that political economists alone should be responsible for economic policy decisions

Passage #14: June 2001 Questions 1-6

Most authoritarian rulers who undertake democratic reforms do so not out of any intrinsic commitment or conversion to democratic ideals, but rather because they foresee or recognize that certain
(5) changes and mobilizations in civil society make it impossible for them to hold on indefinitely to absolute power.

Three major types of changes can contribute to a society's no longer condoning the continuation of
(10) authoritarian rule. First, the values and norms in the society alter over time, reducing citizens' tolerance for repression and concentration of power and thus stimulating their demands for freedom. In some Latin American countries during the 1970s and 1980s, for
(15) example, this change in values came about partly as a result of the experience of repression, which brought in its wake a resurgence of democratic values. As people come to place more value on political freedom and civil liberties they also become more inclined to speak
(20) out, protest, and organize for democracy, frequently beginning with the denunciation of human rights abuses.

In addition to changing norms and values, the alignment of economic interests in a society can shift.
(25) As one scholar notes, an important turning point in the transition to democracy comes when privileged people in society—landowners, industrialists, merchants, bankers—who had been part of a regime's support base come to the conclusion that the authoritarian regime is
(30) dispensable and that its continuation might damage their long-term interests. Such a large-scale shift in the economic interests of these elites was crucial in bringing about the transition to democracy in the Philippines and has also begun occurring incrementally
(35) in other authoritarian nations.

A third change derives from the expanding resources, autonomy, and self-confidence of various segments of society and of newly formed organizations both formal and informal. Students march in the streets
(40) demanding change; workers paralyze key industries; lawyers refuse to cooperate any longer in legal charades; alternative sources of information pierce and then shatter the veil of secrecy and disinformation; informal networks of production and exchange emerge
(45) that circumvent the state's resources and control. This profound development can radically alter the balance of power in a country, as an authoritarian regime that could once easily dominate and control its citizens is placed on the defensive.

(50) Authoritarian rule tends in the long run to generate all three types of changes. Ironically, all three types can be accelerated by the authoritarian regime's initial success at producing economic growth and maintaining social order—success that, by creating a period of
(55) stability, gives citizens the opportunity to reflect on the circumstances in which they live. The more astute or calculating of authoritarian rulers will recognize this and realize that their only hope of retaining some power in the future is to match these democratic social
(60) changes with democratic political changes.

1. Which one of the following most accurately expresses the main point of the passage?

   (A) Authoritarian rulers tend to undertake democratic reforms only after it becomes clear that the nation's economic and social power bases will slow economic growth and disrupt social order until such reforms are instituted.
   (B) Authoritarian regimes tend to ensure their own destruction by allowing opposition groups to build support among the wealthy whose economic interests are easily led away from support for the regime.
   (C) Authoritarian policies tend in the long run to alienate the economic power base in a nation once it becomes clear that the regime's initial success at generating economic growth and stability will be short lived.
   (D) Authoritarian principles tend in the long run to be untenable because they demand from the nation a degree of economic and social stability that is impossible to maintain in the absence of democratic institutions.
   (E) Authoritarian rulers who institute democratic reforms are compelled to do so because authoritarian rule tends to bring about various changes in society that eventually necessitate corresponding political changes.

2. The author's attitude toward authoritarian regimes is most accurately described as which one of the following?

   (A) uncertainty whether the changes in authoritarian regimes represent genuine progress or merely superficial changes
   (B) puzzlement about the motives of authoritarian rulers given their tendency to bring about their own demise
   (C) confidence that most authoritarian regimes will eventually be replaced by a more democratic form of government
   (D) insistence that authoritarian rule constitutes an intrinsically unjust form of government
   (E) concern that authoritarian rulers will discover ways to retain power without instituting democratic reforms

3. Which one of the following titles most completely summarizes the content of the passage?

   (A) "Avenues for Change: The Case for Dissent in Authoritarian Regimes"
   (B) "Human Rights Abuses under Authoritarian Regimes: A Case Study"
   (C) "Democratic Coalitions under Authoritarian Regimes: Strategies and Solutions"
   (D) "Why Authoritarian Regimes Compromise: An Examination of Societal Forces"
   (E) "Growing Pains: Economic Instability in Countries on the Brink of Democracy"

4. Which one of the following most accurately describes the organization of the passage?

   (A) A political phenomenon is linked to a general set of causes; this set is divided into categories and the relative importance of each category is assessed; the possibility of alternate causes is considered and rejected.
   (B) A political phenomenon is linked to a general set of causes; this set is divided into categories and an explication of each category is presented; the causal relationship is elaborated upon and reaffirmed.
   (C) A political phenomenon is identified; the possible causes of the phenomenon are described and placed into categories; one possible cause is preferred over the others and reasons are given for the preference.
   (D) A political phenomenon is identified; similarities between this phenomenon and three similar phenomena are presented; the similarities among the phenomena are restated in general terms and argued for.
   (E) A political phenomenon is identified; differences between this phenomenon and three similar phenomena are presented; the differences among the phenomena are restated in general terms and argued for.

5. It can most reasonably be inferred from the passage that

   (A) many authoritarian rulers would eventually institute democratic reform even if not pressured to do so
   (B) citizen dissatisfaction in authoritarian regimes is highest when authoritarian rule is first imposed
   (C) popular support for authoritarian regimes is lowest when economic conditions are weak
   (D) absolute power in an authoritarian society cannot be maintained indefinitely if the society does not condone the regime
   (E) citizens view human rights abuses as the only objectionable aspect of authoritarian regimes

6. Given the information in the passage, authoritarian rulers who institute democratic reforms decide to do so on the basis of which one of the following principles?

   (A) Rulers should act in ways that allow occasional curbs on their power if the health of the nation requires it.
   (B) Rulers should act in ways that offer the greatest amount of personal freedoms to citizens.
   (C) Rulers should act in ways that speed the transition from authoritarian rule to democracy.
   (D) Rulers should act in ways that ensure the long-term health of the nation's economy.
   (E) Rulers should act in ways that maximize their long-term political power.

Passage #15: June 2001 Questions 7-12

The term "blues" is conventionally used to refer to a state of sadness or melancholy, but to conclude from this that the musical genre of the same name is merely an expression of unrelieved sorrow is to miss its deeper
(5) meaning. Despite its frequent focus on such themes as suffering and self-pity, and despite the censure that it has sometimes received from church communities, the blues, understood more fully, actually has much in common with the traditional religious music known as
(10) spirituals. Each genre, in its own way, aims to bring about what could be called a spiritual transformation: spirituals produce a religious experience and the blues elicits an analogous response. In fact the blues has even been characterized as a form of "secular spiritual." The
(15) implication of this apparently contradictory terminology is clear: the blues shares an essential aspect of spirituals. Indeed, the blues and spirituals may well arise from a common reservoir of experience, tapping into an aesthetic that underlies many aspects of
(20) African American culture.

Critics have noted that African American folk tradition, in its earliest manifestations, does not sharply differentiate reality into sacred and secular strains or into irreconcilable dichotomies between good and evil,
(25) misery and joy. This is consistent with the apparently dual aspect of the blues and spirituals. Spirituals, like the blues, often express longing or sorrow, but these plaintive tones are indicative of neither genre's full scope: both aim at transforming their participants'
(30) spirits to elation and exaltation. In this regard, both musical forms may be linked to traditional African American culture in North America and to its ancestral cultures in West Africa, in whose traditional religions worshippers play an active role in invoking the
(35) divine—in creating the psychological conditions that are conducive to religious experience. These conditions are often referred to as "ecstasy," which is to be understood here with its etymological connotation of standing out from oneself, or rather from one's
(40) background psychological state and from one's centered concept of self.

Working in this tradition, blues songs serve to transcend negative experiences by invoking the negative so that it can be transformed through the
(45) virtuosity and ecstatic mastery of the performer. This process produces a double-edged irony that is often evident in blues lyrics themselves; consider, for example the lines "If the blues was money, I'd be a millionaire," in which the singer reconfigures the
(50) experience of sorrow into a paradoxical asset through a kind of boasting bravado. One critic has observed that the impulse behind the blues is the desire to keep painful experiences alive in the performer and audience not just for their own sake, but also in order to coax
(55) from these experiences a lyricism that is both tragic and comic.

7. Based on the passage, with which one of the following statements would the author be most likely to agree?

(A) The emphasis on spiritual transcendence takes the blues out of the realm of folk art and into the realm of organized religion.
(B) Little of the transcendent aspect of the blues is retained in its more modern, electronically amplified, urban forms.
(C) Other forms of African American folk art rely heavily on uses of irony similar to those observed in the blues.
(D) The distinctive musical structure of blues songs is the primary means of producing tensions between sadness and transcendence.
(E) The blues may be of psychological benefit to its listeners.

8. Each of the following is indicated by the passage as a shared aspect of the blues and spirituals EXCEPT:

(A) expressions of sorrow or longing
(B) a striving to bring about a kind of spiritual transformation
(C) a possible link to ancestral West African cultures
(D) the goal of producing exalted emotions
(E) the use of traditional religious terminology in their lyrics

9. Which one of the following most accurately expresses what the author intends "a common reservoir of experience" (line 18) to refer to?

   (A) a set of experiences that members of differing cultures frequently undergo and that similarly affects the music of those cultures
   (B) a set of ordinary experiences that underlies the development of all musical forms
   (C) a set of experiences that contributed to the development of both the blues and spirituals
   (D) a set of musically relevant experiences that serves to differentiate reality into irreconcilable dichotomies
   (E) a set of experiences arising from the folk music of a community and belonging to the community at large

10. The primary purpose of the second paragraph is to

    (A) uncover the shared origin of both the blues and spirituals
    (B) examine the process by which ecstasy is produced
    (C) identify the musical precursors of the blues
    (D) explore the sacred and secular strains of the blues
    (E) trace the early development of African American folk tradition

11. The reference to "standing out from oneself" in line 39 primarily serves to

    (A) distinguish the standard from the nonstandard, and thus incorrect, use of a word
    (B) specify a particular sense of a word that the author intends the word to convey
    (C) point out a word that incorrectly characterizes experiences arising from blues performance
    (D) identify a way in which religious participation differs from blues performance
    (E) indicate the intensity that a good blues artist brings to a performance

12. Which one of the following is most closely analogous to the author's account of the connections among the blues, spirituals, and certain West African religious practices?

    (A) Two species of cacti, which are largely dissimilar, have very similar flowers; this has been proven to be due to the one's evolution from a third species, whose flowers are nonetheless quite different from theirs.
    (B) Two species of ferns, which are closely similar in most respects, have a subtly different arrangement of stem structures; nevertheless, they may well be related to a third, older species, which has yet a different arrangement of stem structures.
    (C) Two types of trees, which botanists have long believed to be unrelated, should be reclassified in light of the essential similarities of their flower structures and their recently discovered relationship to another species, from which they both evolved.
    (D) Two species of grass, which may have some subtle similarities, are both very similar to a third species, and thus it can be inferred that the third species evolved from one of the two species.
    (E) Two species of shrubs, which seem superficially unalike, have a significantly similar leaf structure; this may be due to their relation to a third, older species, which is similar to both of them.

Passage #16: June 2001 Questions 19-26

When women are persecuted on account of their gender, they are likely to be eligible for asylum. Persecution is the linchpin of the definition of a refugee set out in the *United Nations Convention Relating to*
(5) *the Status of Refugees*. In this document, a refugee is defined as any person facing persecution "for reasons of race, religion, nationality, membership of a particular social group, or political opinion." While persecution on the basis of gender is not explicitly
(10) listed, this omission does not preclude victims of gender-based persecution from qualifying as refugees, nor does it reflect an intention that such persons be excluded from international protection. Rather, women persecuted on account of gender are eligible for asylum
(15) under the category of "social group." The history of the inclusion of the social-group category in the definition of a refugee indicates that this category was intended to cover groups, such as women facing gender-based persecution, who are otherwise not covered by the
(20) definition's specific categories.

The original definition of refugee, which came from the constitution of the International Refugee Organization, did not include social group. However, the above-mentioned *United Nations Convention* added
(25) the category in order to provide a "safety net" for asylum-seekers who should qualify for refugee status but who fail to fall neatly into one of the enumerated categories. The drafters of the *Convention* intentionally left the precise boundaries of the social-group category
(30) undefined to ensure that the category would retain the flexibility necessary to address unanticipated situations.

A broad interpretation of social group is supported by the *Handbook on Procedures and Criteria for*
(35) *Determining Refugee Status* (1979) published by the office of the United Nations High Commissioner for Refugees (UNHCR). The *Handbook* describes a social group as persons of similar background, habits, or social status. This expansive interpretation of the
(40) category is resonant with the intentions of the *Convention* drafters—a malleable category created for future asylum determinations. Since many women fleeing gender-based persecution share a common background and social status, they should fall within
(45) the *Handbook's* definition of a social group. Furthermore, a 1985 UNHCR Executive Committee report counseled member states to use the social-group category to classify women asylum-seekers "who face harsh or inhuman treatment due to their having
(50) transgressed the social mores of the society in which they live."

Such a pronouncement is particularly significant. A position taken by an organization such as the UNHCR is likely to exert a strong influence on the international
(55) community. In particular, the UNHCR's position is likely to have an impact on the interpretation of national asylum laws, since the terms and definitions used in many national laws have been developed under the international consensus that UNHCR represents.

19. According to the passage, which one of the following is true about both the *United Nations Convention* and the UNHCR *Handbook*?

(A) Both documents are likely to exert a strong influence on improving the status of women in countries that are members of the United Nations.
(B) Both documents explicitly support granting refugee status to women fleeing gender-based persecution.
(C) Both documents recommend using the social-group category to classify women refugees seeking asylum from persecution.
(D) Both documents suggest that the social-group category can be applied to a wide variety of asylum-seekers.
(E) Both documents describe a social group as persons who share a similar background and hold a similar status in society.

20. The passage suggests that which one of the following is true about the drafters of the *United Nations Convention*?

(A) They wanted to ensure that the United Nations would be consulted as new reasons for seeking refugee status arose.
(B) They followed the precedent set by the International Refugee Organization concerning the status of refugees seeking asylum from gender-based persecution.
(C) They recognized that it would be difficult to list every possible reason why a person might seek refuge from persecution in the *Convention's* definition of a refugee.
(D) They did not consider persecution on the basis of gender to be as valid a reason for seeking asylum as persecution on the basis of race, nationality, or religion.
(E) They did not list gender as a category in the *Convention's* definition of a refugee because gender-based persecution was not a significant problem at the time the *Convention* was drafted.

21. Which one of the following asylum-seekers would be most likely to qualify for refugee status under the social-group category as it is described in the passage?

    (A) a woman who is unable to earn enough money to support her family because she comes from a poor country
    (B) a woman who has limited opportunities to improve her socioeconomic status because of racial discrimination in her country
    (C) a woman who is unable to obtain an education because she is a member of a particular religious group
    (D) a woman who faces persecution because she rejects the accepted norm in her country concerning arranged marriages
    (E) a woman who faces persecution because she opposes her government's harsh treatment of political prisoners

22. The author describes the definition of social group in the UNHCR *Handbook* as

    (A) specific but flexible
    (B) obscure but substantive
    (C) exhaustive and impartial
    (D) general and adaptable
    (E) comprehensive and exemplary

23. The author of the passage would most likely agree with which one of the following statements about the definition of a refugee in the constitution of the International Refugee Organization?

    (A) It failed to include some asylum-seekers who should have been considered eligible for refugee status.
    (B) It provided a strong basis to support the claim that women seeking asylum from gender-based persecution should be eligible for asylum.
    (C) It reflected an awareness that some groups of refugees seeking asylum do not easily fall into specific categories.
    (D) It established that a person's social-group membership may be as significant a cause of persecution as a person's race, religion, or nationality.
    (E) It prevented individual nations from refusing asylum to persons who were clearly eligible for such status on the basis of the definition.

24. The author describes persecution as the "linchpin of the definition of a refugee" (line 3) in order to indicate that

    (A) international acceptance of the definition was dependent on reaching consensus about what constituted persecution
    (B) international concern about the number of people fleeing persecution was the primary force behind the creation of the definition
    (C) persecution is a controversial term and it was difficult to reach international agreement about its exact meaning
    (D) persecution is the primary reason why people are forced to leave their home countries and seek asylum elsewhere
    (E) persecution is the central factor in determining whether a person is eligible for refugee status

25. The passage suggests that which one of the following is most likely to be true of the relationship between UNHCR documents concerning refugees and many nations' asylum laws?

    (A) The terms and definitions in the United Nations documents are frequently interpreted more narrowly than are similar terms and definitions in many national asylum laws.
    (B) Many of the specific terms and definitions in the United Nations documents represent a compilation of terms and definitions that were first used in national asylum laws.
    (C) A new interpretation of a term or definition in one of the United Nations documents is likely to influence the interpretation of a similar term or definition in a national asylum law.
    (D) A change in the wording of a specific definition in one of the United Nations documents must also be reflected in any similar terms or definitions contained in national asylum laws.
    (E) The terms and definitions used in many national asylum laws are in direct opposition to the terms and definitions used in the United Nations documents.

26. The primary purpose of the passage is to

    (A) trace the development of the definition of an important term
    (B) interpret the historical circumstances leading to the development of two documents
    (C) resolve two apparently contradictory interpretations of a legal document
    (D) suggest an alternative solution to a much-disputed problem
    (E) argue against the current definition of a specific term

Passage #17: December 2001 Questions 1-6

Traditionally, members of a community such as a town or neighborhood share a common location and a sense of necessary interdependence that includes, for example, mutual respect and emotional support. But as
(5) modern societies grow more technological and sometimes more alienating, people tend to spend less time in the kinds of interactions that their communities require in order to thrive. Meanwhile, technology has made it possible for individuals to interact via personal
(10) computer with others who are geographically distant. Advocates claim that these computer conferences, in which large numbers of participants communicate by typing comments that are immediately read by other participants and responding immediately to those
(15) comments they read, function as communities that can substitute for traditional interactions with neighbors.

What are the characteristics that advocates claim allow computer conferences to function as communities? For one, participants often share
(20) common interests or concerns; conferences are frequently organized around specific topics such as music or parenting. Second, because these conferences are conversations, participants have adopted certain conventions in recognition of the importance of
(25) respecting each others' sensibilities. Abbreviations are used to convey commonly expressed sentiments of courtesy such as "pardon me for cutting in" ("pmfci") or "in my humble opinion" ("imho"). Because a humorous tone can be difficult to communicate in
(30) writing, participants will often end an intentionally humorous comment with a set of characters that, when looked at sideways, resembles a smiling or winking face. Typing messages entirely in capital letters is avoided, because its tendency to demand the attention
(35) of a reader's eye is considered the computer equivalent of shouting. These conventions, advocates claim, constitute a form of etiquette, and with this etiquette as a foundation, people often form genuine, trusting relationships, even offering advice and support during
(40) personal crises such as illness or the loss of a loved one.

But while it is true that conferences can be both respectful and supportive, they nonetheless fall short of communities. For example, conferences discriminate
(45) along educational and economic lines because participation requires a basic knowledge of computers and the ability to afford access to conferences. Further, while advocates claim that a shared interest makes computer conferences similar to traditional
(50) communities—insofar as the shared interest is analogous to a traditional community's shared location—this analogy simply does not work. Conference participants are a self-selecting group; they are drawn together by their shared interest in the topic
(55) of the conference. Actual communities, on the other hand, are "nonintentional": the people who inhabit towns or neighborhoods are thus more likely to exhibit genuine diversity—of age, career, or personal interests—than are conference participants. It might be
(60) easier to find common ground in a computer conference than in today's communities, but in so doing it would be unfortunate if conference participants cut themselves off further from valuable interactions in their own towns or neighborhoods.

1. Which one of the following most accurately expresses the central idea of the passage?

   (A) Because computer conferences attract participants who share common interests and rely on a number of mutually acceptable conventions for communicating with one another, such conferences can substitute effectively for certain interactions that have become rarer within actual communities.
   (B) Since increased participation in computer conferences threatens to replace actual communities, members of actual communities are returning to the traditional interactions that distinguish towns or neighborhoods.
   (C) Because participants in computer conferences are geographically separated and communicate only by typing, their interactions cannot be as mutually respectful and supportive as are the kinds of interactions that have become rarer within actual communities.
   (D) Although computer conferences offer some of the same benefits that actual communities do, the significant lack of diversity among conference participants makes such conferences unlike actual communities.
   (E) Even if access to computer technology is broad enough to attract a more diverse group of people to participate in computer conferences, such conferences will not be acceptable substitutes for actual communities.

2. Based on the passage, the author would be LEAST likely to consider which one of the following a community?

   (A) a group of soldiers who serve together in the same battalion and who come from a variety of geographic regions
   (B) a group of university students who belong to the same campus political organization and who come from several different socioeconomic backgrounds
   (C) a group of doctors who work at a number of different hospitals and who meet at a convention to discuss issues relevant to their profession
   (D) a group of teachers who work interdependently in the same school with the same students and who live in a variety of cities and neighborhoods
   (E) a group of worshipers who attend and support the same religious institution and who represent a high degree of economic and cultural diversity

3. The author's statement that "conferences can be both respectful and supportive" (lines 42-43) serves primarily to

   (A) counter the claim that computer conferences may discriminate along educational or economic lines
   (B) introduce the argument that the conventions of computer conferences constitute a form of social etiquette
   (C) counter the claim that computer conferences cannot be thought of as communities
   (D) suggest that not all participants in computer conferences may be equally respectful of one another
   (E) acknowledge that computer conferences can involve interactions that are similar to those in an actual community

4. Given the information in the passage, the author can most reasonably be said to use which one of the following principles to refute the advocates' claim that computer conferences can function as communities (line 15)?

   (A) A group is a community only if its members are mutually respectful and supportive of one another.
   (B) A group is a community only if its members adopt conventions intended to help them respect each other's sensibilities.
   (C) A group is a community only if its members inhabit the same geographic location.
   (D) A group is a community only if its members come from the same educational or economic background.
   (E) A group is a community only if its members feel a sense of interdependence despite different economic and educational backgrounds.

5. What is the primary function of the second paragraph of the passage?

   (A) to add detail to the discussion in the first paragraph of why computer conferences originated
   (B) to give evidence challenging the argument of the advocates discussed in the first paragraph
   (C) to develop the claim of the advocates discussed in the first paragraph
   (D) to introduce an objection that will be answered in the third paragraph
   (E) to anticipate the characterization of computer conferences given in the third paragraph

6. Which one of the following, if true, would most weaken one of the author's arguments in the last paragraph?

   (A) Participants in computer conferences are generally more accepting of diversity than is the population at large.
   (B) Computer technology is rapidly becoming more affordable and accessible to people from a variety of backgrounds.
   (C) Participants in computer conferences often apply the same degree of respect and support they receive from one another to interactions in their own actual communities.
   (D) Participants in computer conferences often feel more comfortable interacting on the computer because they are free to interact without revealing their identities.
   (E) The conventions used to facilitate communication in computer conferences are generally more successful than those used in actual communities.

Passage #18: December 2001 Questions 7-14

In *Intellectual Culture in Elizabethan and Jacobean England*, J. W. Binns asserts that the drama of Shakespeare, the verse of Marlowe, and the prose of Sidney—all of whom wrote in English—do not alone
(5) represent the high culture of Renaissance (roughly sixteenth- and seventeenth-century) England. Latin, the language of ancient Rome, continued during this period to be the dominant form of expression for English intellectuals, and works of law, theology, and science
(10) written in Latin were, according to Binns, among the highest achievements of the Renaissance. However, because many academic specializations do not overlap, many texts central to an interpretation of early modern English culture have gone unexamined. Even the most
(15) learned students of Renaissance Latin generally confine themselves to humanistic and literary writings in Latin. According to Binns, these language specialists edit and analyze poems and orations, but leave works of theology and science, law and medicine—the very
(20) works that revolutionized Western thought—to "specialists" in those fields, historians of science, for example, who lack philological training. The intellectual historian can find ample guidance when reading the Latin poetry of Milton, but little or none
(25) when confronting the more alien and difficult terminology, syntax, and content of the scientist Newton.

Intellectual historians of Renaissance England, by contrast with Latin language specialists, have surveyed
(30) in great detail the historical, cosmological, and theological battles of the day, but too often they have done so on the basis of texts written in or translated into English. Binns argues that these scholars treat the English-language writings of Renaissance England as
(35) an autonomous and coherent whole, underestimating the influence on English writers of their counterparts on the European Continent. In so doing they ignore the fact that English intellectuals were educated in schools and universities where they spoke and wrote Latin, and
(40) inhabited as adults an intellectual world in which what happened abroad and was recorded in Latin was of great importance. Writers traditionally considered characteristically English and modern were steeped in Latin literature and in the esoteric concerns of late
(45) Renaissance humanism (the rediscovery and study of ancient Latin and Greek texts), and many Latin works by Continental humanists that were not translated at the time into any modern language became the bases of classic English works of literature and scholarship.
(50) These limitations are understandable. No modern classicist is trained to deal with the range of problems posed by a difficult piece of late Renaissance science; few students of English intellectual history are trained to read the sort of Latin in which such works were
(55) written. Yet the result of each side's inability to cross boundaries has been that each presents a distorted reading of the intellectual culture of Renaissance England.

7. Which one of the following best states the main idea of the passage?

(A) Analyses of the scientific, theological, and legal writings of the Renaissance have proved to be more important to an understanding of the period than have studies of humanistic and literary works.
(B) The English works of such Renaissance writers as Shakespeare, Marlowe, and Sidney have been overemphasized at the expense of these writers' more intellectually challenging Latin works.
(C) Though traditionally recognized as the language of the educated classes of the Renaissance, Latin has until recently been studied primarily in connection with ancient Roman texts.
(D) Many Latin texts by English Renaissance writers, though analyzed in depth by literary critics and philologists, have been all but ignored by historians of science and theology.
(E) Many Latin texts by English Renaissance writers, though important to an analysis of the period, have been insufficiently understood for reasons related to academic specialization.

8. The passage contains support for which one of the following statements concerning those scholars who analyze works written in Latin during the Renaissance?

(A) These scholars tend to lack training both in language and in intellectual history, and thus base their interpretations of Renaissance culture on works translated into English.
(B) These scholars tend to lack the combination of training in both language and intellectual history that is necessary for a proper study of important and neglected Latin texts.
(C) Specialists in such literary forms as poems and orations too frequently lack training in the Latin language that was written and studied during the Renaissance.
(D) Language specialists have surveyed in too great detail important works of law and medicine, and thus have not provided a coherent interpretation of early modern English culture.
(E) Scholars who analyze important Latin works by such writers as Marlowe, Shakespeare, and Sidney too often lack the historical knowledge of Latin necessary for a proper interpretation of early modern English culture.

9. Which one of the following statements concerning the relationship between English and Continental writers of the Renaissance era can be inferred from the passage?

    (A) Continental writers wrote in Latin more frequently than did English writers, and thus rendered some of the most important Continental works inaccessible to English readers.
    (B) Continental writers, more intellectually advanced than their English counterparts, were on the whole responsible for familiarizing English audiences with Latin language and literature.
    (C) English and Continental writers communicated their intellectual concerns, which were for the most part different, by way of works written in Latin.
    (D) The intellectual ties between English and Continental writers were stronger than has been acknowledged by many scholars and were founded on a mutual knowledge of Latin.
    (E) The intellectual ties between English and Continental writers have been overemphasized in modern scholarship due to a lack of dialogue between language specialists and intellectual historians.

10. The author of the passage most likely cites Shakespeare, Marlowe, and Sidney in the first paragraph as examples of writers whose

    (A) nonfiction works are less well known than their imaginative works
    (B) works have unfairly been credited with revolutionizing Western thought
    (C) works have been treated as an autonomous and coherent whole
    (D) works have traditionally been seen as representing the high culture of Renaissance England
    (E) Latin writings have, according to Binns, been overlooked

11. Binns would be most likely to agree with which one of the following statements concerning the English language writings of Renaissance England traditionally studied by intellectual historians?

    (A) These writings have unfortunately been undervalued by Latin-language specialists because of their nonliterary subject matter.
    (B) These writings, according to Latin-language specialists, had very little influence on the intellectual upheavals associated with the Renaissance.
    (C) These writings, as analyzed by intellectual historians, have formed the basis of a superficially coherent reading of the intellectual culture that produced them.
    (D) These writings have been compared unfavorably by intellectual historians with Continental works of the same period.
    (E) These writings need to be studied separately, according to intellectual historians, from Latin-language writings of the same period.

12. The information in the passage suggests which one of the following concerning late-Renaissance scientific works written in Latin?

    (A) These works are easier for modern scholars to analyze than are theological works of the same era.
    (B) These works have seldom been translated into English and thus remain inscrutable to modern scholars, despite the availability of illuminating commentaries.
    (C) These works are difficult for modern scholars to analyze both because of the concepts they develop and the language in which they are written.
    (D) These works constituted the core of an English university education during the Renaissance.
    (E) These works were written mostly by Continental writers and reached English intellectuals only in English translation.

13. The author of the passage mentions the poet Milton and the scientist Newton primarily in order to

    (A) illustrate the range of difficulty in Renaissance Latin writing, from relatively straightforward to very difficult
    (B) illustrate the differing scholarly attitudes toward Renaissance writers who wrote in Latin and those who wrote in English
    (C) illustrate the fact that the concerns of English writers of the Renaissance differed from the concerns of their Continental counterparts
    (D) contrast a writer of the Renaissance whose merit has long been recognized with one whose literary worth has only recently begun to be appreciated
    (E) contrast a writer whose Latin writings have been the subject of illuminating scholarship with one whose Latin writings have been neglected by philologists

14. The author of the passage is primarily concerned with presenting which one of the following?

    (A) an enumeration of new approaches
    (B) contrasting views of disparate theories
    (C) a summary of intellectual disputes
    (D) a discussion of a significant deficiency
    (E) a correction of an author's misconceptions

Passage #19: October 2002 Questions 21-27

One of the greatest challenges facing medical students today, apart from absorbing volumes of technical information and learning habits of scientific thought, is that of remaining empathetic to the needs of
(5) patients in the face of all this rigorous training. Requiring students to immerse themselves completely in medical coursework risks disconnecting them from the personal and ethical aspects of doctoring, and such strictly scientific thinking is insufficient for grappling
(10) with modern ethical dilemmas. For these reasons, aspiring physicians need to develop new ways of thinking about and interacting with patients. Training in ethics that takes narrative literature as its primary subject is one method of accomplishing this.

(15) Although training in ethics is currently provided by medical schools, this training relies heavily on an abstract, philosophical view of ethics. Although the conceptual clarity provided by a traditional ethics course can be valuable, theorizing about ethics
(20) contributes little to the understanding of everyday human experience or to preparing medical students for the multifarious ethical dilemmas they will face as physicians. A true foundation in ethics must be predicated on an understanding of human behavior that
(25) reflects a wide array of relationships and readily adapts to various perspectives, for this is what is required to develop empathy. Ethics courses drawing on narrative literature can better help students prepare for ethical dilemmas precisely because such literature attaches its
(30) readers so forcefully to the concrete and varied world of human events.

The act of reading narrative literature is uniquely suited to the development of what might be called flexible ethical thinking. To grasp the development of
(35) characters, to tangle with heightening moral crises, and to engage oneself with the story not as one's own but nevertheless as something recognizable and worthy of attention, readers must use their moral imagination. Giving oneself over to the ethical conflicts in a story
(40) requires the abandonment of strictly absolute, inviolate sets of moral principles. Reading literature also demands that the reader adopt another person's point of view—that of the narrator or a character in a story— and thus requires the ability to depart from one's
(45) personal ethical stance and examine moral issues from new perspectives.

It does not follow that readers, including medical professionals, must relinquish all moral principles, as is the case with situational ethics, in which decisions
(50) about ethical choices are made on the basis of intuition and are entirely relative to the circumstances in which they arise. Such an extremely relativistic stance would have as little benefit for the patient or physician as would a dogmatically absolutist one. Fortunately, the
(55) incorporation of narrative literature into the study of ethics, while serving as a corrective to the latter stance, need not lead to the former. But it can give us something that is lacking in the traditional philosophical study of ethics—namely, a deeper
(60) understanding of human nature that can serve as a foundation for ethical reasoning and allow greater flexibility in the application of moral principles.

21. Which one of the following most accurately states the main point of the passage?

(A) Training in ethics that incorporates narrative literature would better cultivate flexible ethical thinking and increase medical students' capacity for empathetic patient care as compared with the traditional approach of medical schools to such training.
(B) Traditional abstract ethical training, because it is too heavily focused on theoretical reasoning, tends to decrease or impair the medical student's sensitivity to modern ethical dilemmas.
(C) Only a properly designed curriculum that balances situational, abstract, and narrative approaches to ethics will adequately prepare the medical student for complex ethical confrontations involving actual patients.
(D) Narrative-based instruction in ethics is becoming increasingly popular in medical schools because it requires students to develop a capacity for empathy by examining complex moral issues from a variety of perspectives.
(E) The study of narrative literature in medical schools would nurture moral intuition, enabling the future doctor to make ethical decisions without appeal to general principles.

22. Which one of the following most accurately represents the author's use of the term "moral imagination" in line 38?

(A) a sense of curiosity, aroused by reading, that leads one to follow actively the development of problems involving the characters depicted in narratives
(B) a faculty of seeking out and recognizing the ethical controversies involved in human relationships and identifying oneself with one side or another in such controversies
(C) a capacity to understand the complexities of various ethical dilemmas and to fashion creative and innovative solutions to them
(D) an ability to understand personal aspects of ethically significant situations even if one is not a direct participant and to empathize with those involved in them
(E) an ability to act upon ethical principles different from one's own for the sake of variety

23. It can be inferred from the passage that the author would most likely agree with which one of the following statements?

    (A) The heavy load of technical coursework in today's medical schools often keeps them from giving adequate emphasis to courses in medical ethics.
    (B) Students learn more about ethics through the use of fiction than through the use of nonfictional readings.
    (C) The traditional method of ethical training in medical schools should be supplemented or replaced by more direct practical experience with real-life patients in ethically difficult situations.
    (D) The failings of an abstract, philosophical training in ethics can be remedied only by replacing it with a purely narrative-based approach.
    (E) Neither scientific training nor traditional philosophical ethics adequately prepares doctors to deal with the emotional dimension of patients' needs.

24. Which one of the following is most likely the author's overall purpose in the passage?

    (A) to advise medical schools on how to implement a narrative-based approach to ethics in their curricula
    (B) to argue that the current methods of ethics education are counterproductive to the formation of empathetic doctor-patient relationships
    (C) to argue that the ethical content of narrative literature foreshadows the pitfalls of situational ethics
    (D) to propose an approach to ethical training in medical school that will preserve the human dimension of medicine
    (E) to demonstrate the value of a well-designed ethics education for medical students

25. The passage ascribes each of the following characteristics to the use of narrative literature in ethical education EXCEPT:

    (A) It tends to avoid the extreme relativism of situational ethics.
    (B) It connects students to varied types of human events.
    (C) It can help lead medical students to develop new ways of dealing with patients.
    (D) It requires students to examine moral issues from new perspectives.
    (E) It can help insulate future doctors from the shock of the ethical dilemmas they will confront.

26. With regard to ethical dilemmas, the passage explicitly states each of the following EXCEPT:

    (A) Doctors face a variety of such dilemmas.
    (B) Purely scientific thinking is inadequate for dealing with modern ethical dilemmas.
    (C) Such dilemmas are more prevalent today as a result of scientific and technological advances in medicine.
    (D) Theorizing about ethics does little to prepare students to face such dilemmas.
    (E) Narrative literature can help make medical students ready to face such dilemmas.

27. The author's attitude regarding the traditional method of teaching ethics in medical school can most accurately be described as

    (A) unqualified disapproval of the method and disapproval of all of its effects
    (B) reserved judgment regarding the method and disapproval of all of its effects
    (C) partial disapproval of the method and clinical indifference toward its effects
    (D) partial approval of the method and disapproval of all of its effects
    (E) partial disapproval of the method and approval of some of its effects

Passage #20: June 2003 Questions 1-5

Social scientists have traditionally defined multipolar international systems as consisting of three or more nations, each of roughly equal military and economic strength. Theoretically, the members of such
(5) systems create shifting, temporary alliances in response to changing circumstances in the international environment. Such systems are, thus, fluid and flexible. Frequent, small confrontations are one attribute of multipolar systems and are usually the result of less
(10) powerful members grouping together to counter threats from larger, more aggressive members seeking hegemony. Yet the constant and inevitable counterbalancing typical of such systems usually results in stability. The best-known example of a
(15) multipolar system is the Concert of Europe, which coincided with general peace on that continent lasting roughly 100 years beginning around 1815.

Bipolar systems, on the other hand, involve two major members of roughly equal military and
(20) economic strength vying for power and advantage. Other members of lesser strength tend to coalesce around one or the other pole. Such systems tend to be rigid and fixed, in part due to the existence of only one axis of power. Zero-sum political and military
(25) maneuverings, in which a gain for one side results in an equivalent loss for the other, are a salient feature of bipolar systems. Overall superiority is sought by both major members, which can lead to frequent confrontations, debilitating armed conflict, and,
(30) eventually, to the capitulation of one or the other side. Athens and Sparta of ancient Greece had a bipolar relationship, as did the United States and the USSR during the Cold War.

However, the shift in the geopolitical landscape
(35) following the end of the Cold War calls for a reassessment of the assumptions underlying these two theoretical concepts. The emerging but still vague multipolar system in Europe today brings with it the unsettling prospect of new conflicts and shifting
(40) alliances that may lead to a diminution, rather than an enhancement, of security. The frequent, small confrontations that are thought to have kept the Concert of Europe in a state of equilibrium would today, as nations arm themselves with modern
(45) weapons, create instability that could destroy the system. And the larger number of members and shifting alliance patterns peculiar to multipolar systems would create a bewildering tangle of conflicts.

This reassessment may also lead us to look at the
(50) Cold War in a new light. In 1914 smaller members of the multipolar system in Europe brought the larger members into a war that engulfed the continent. The aftermath—a crippled system in which certain members were dismantled, punished, or voluntarily
(55) withdrew—created the conditions that led to World War II. In contrast, the principal attributes of bipolar systems-two major members with only one possible axis of conflict locked in a rigid yet usually stable struggle for power-may have created the necessary
(60) parameters for general peace in the second half of the twentieth century.

1. Which one of the following most accurately expresses the main point of the passage?

   (A) Peace can be maintained in Europe only if a new bipolar system emerges to replace Cold War alliances.
   (B) All kinds of international systems discussed by social scientists carry within themselves the seeds of their own collapse and ultimately endanger international order.
   (C) The current European geopolitical landscape is a multipolar system that strongly resembles the Concert of Europe which existed through most of the nineteenth century.
   (D) Multipolarity fostered the conditions that led to World War II and is incompatible with a stable, modern Europe.
   (E) The characterization of multipolar systems as stable and bipolar systems as open to debilitating conflict needs to be reconsidered in light of the realities of post-Cold War Europe.

2. Which one of the following statements most accurately describes the function of the final paragraph?

   (A) The weaknesses of both types of systems are discussed in the context of twentieth-century European history.
   (B) A prediction is made regarding European security based on the attributes of both types of systems.
   (C) A new argument is introduced in favor of European countries embracing a new bipolar system.
   (D) Twentieth-century European history is used to expand on the argument in the previous paragraph.
   (E) The typical characteristics of the major members of a bipolar system are reviewed.

3. The author's reference to the possibility that confrontations may lead to capitulation (lines 27-30) serves primarily to

   (A) indicate that bipolar systems can have certain unstable characteristics
   (B) illustrate how multipolar systems can transform themselves into bipolar systems
   (C) contrast the aggressive nature of bipolar members with the more rational behavior of their multipolar counterparts
   (D) indicate the anarchic nature of international relations
   (E) suggest that military and economic strength shifts in bipolar as frequently as in multipolar systems

4. With respect to the Cold War, the author's attitude can most accurately be described as

   (A) fearful that European geopolitics may bring about a similar bipolar system
   (B) surprised that it did not end with a major war
   (C) convinced that it provides an important example of bipolarity maintaining peace
   (D) regretful that the major European countries were so ambivalent about it
   (E) confident it will mark only a brief hiatus between long periods of European multipolarity

5. Which one of the following statements concerning the Concert of Europe (lines 14-17) can most reasonably be inferred from the passage?

   (A) Each of the many small confrontations that occurred under the Concert of Europe threatened the integrity of the system.
   (B) It provided the highest level of security possible for Europe in the late nineteenth century.
   (C) All the factors contributing to stability during the late nineteenth century continue to contribute to European security.
   (D) Equilibrium in the system was maintained as members grouped together to counterbalance mutual threats.
   (E) It was more stable than most multipolar systems because its smaller members reacted promptly to aggression by its larger members.

Answer Key

Chapter 2: Diversity

Diversity I: Affirming Underrepresented Groups

Passage #1: June 1997 Questions 1-8—page 20

1. C	(GR, MP)	8-12	"Kahlo was......cultural identity."
2. B	(GR, Must, AP)	4-12	"Suggesting much......cultural identity."
3. A	(CR, Must)	21-23	"Mexican nationalism......labor disputes"
4. B	(SR, Must)	26-29	"Kahlo's form......pre-Columbian society"
5. C	(GR, Must X)		Incorrect answer choices are eliminated as follows:
		34	"skeletons"
		51	"Aztec sculpture"
		52	"skull"
		34	"bleeding hearts"
6. E	(SR, Must, O)	All	
7. C	(CR, Must, SP)	58-60	"she favored......cultural identity."
8. D	(GR, MP)	5-12	"many of......cultural identity."

Passage #2: December 1997 Questions 7-13—page 22

7. D	(GR, MP)	8-11	"the union......several levels."
8. C	(CR, Must)	5-7	"who upon......the workers."
9. B	(CR, Cannot)		Incorrect answer choices are eliminated as follows:
		22-23	"In addition......Korean Americans,"
		40-41	"support received......American unionists."
		15-17	"mobilized many......campaign before,"
		12-14	"it served......political ideologies."
10. A	(GR, Must, AP)	55-58	"ethnic communities......ethnic identity."
11. C	(SR, Must, P)	28-34	"These immigrants......from China."
12. B	(GR, Must, P)	8-11	"the union......several levels."
13. C	(SR, Must, P)	43-47	"The issues......workers' rights."

Passage #3: June 1998 Questions 14-21—page 24

14. C	(GR, MP)	51-58	"Tribalism…outside influences."
15. A	(SR, P)	47-48	"Cultural borrowing…old news."
16. A	(GR, Must, AP)	20-22	"…these sociologists…individual tribes."
17. E	(SR, Must, O)	All	
18. E	(CR, Must, AP)	27-29	"Obviously, a more complex…can account for."
19. C	(GR, Must, AP)	55-58	"Intertribal activities…outside influences."
20. B	(CR, Must)	17-20	"Indeed, the rapid diffusion…has been increasing."
21. C	(GR, Must, P)	33-40	"Like other…native American groups."

Passage #4: September 1998 Questions 22-27—page 26

22. C	(GR, MP)	9-12	"…whatever gains…were undermined…rights."
23. E	(SR, P)	45-47	"Staves…England."
24. B	(GR, P)	5-12	"Historians…contractual rights."
25. A	(CR, Must)	55-57	"Staves does not…married women."
26. C	(CR, Must)	41-44	"Staves shows…about property."
27. D	(SR, Must, SP)	5-8	"Historians…in 1660

Passage #5: December 1998 Questions 8-14—page 28

8. E	(GR, MP)	48-59	"Hopi personal names do several…names."
9. B	(SR, P)	44-47	"The condensed…tiny imagist poems."
10. E	(CR, Must)	7-10	"Claude Levi-Strauss's …very influential."
11. D	(SR, Must, P)	19-29	"Throughout life…representative animal."
12. A	(CR, Must, AP/SP)	53-59	"This view of Hopi…names."
13. D	(CR, Must, X)	\multicolumn{2}{l}{Incorrect answer choices are eliminated as follows:}
		52	"…they can be understood as oral texts…"
		44-47	"The condensed image… poems."
		52-53	"they can be understood…aesthetic delight."
		30-32	"More often… not apparent…literal translation."
14. D	(GR, Must, P)	53-59	"This view of Hopi names is thus opposed…names."

Passage #6: October 1999 Questions 8-15—page 30

8. D	(GR, MP)	7-11	"In some communities…self-teaching."
9. A	(CR, Must)	12-17	"Before any…linguistic structures."
10. A	(SR, Must, SP)	57-58	"…but they concede…oral form."
11. C	(CR, Cannot)	All	
12. C	(GR, Must, O)	All	
13. B	(SR, Must—X, SP)	38-39	"Northern Utes decided not to standardize…"
14. A	(CR, Must, AP)	23-35	"Certain obstacles… ever fully satisfied."
15. B	(GR, Must, PR)	All	

Passage #7: December 1999 Questions 22-27—page 32

22. A	(GR, MP)	All	
23. B	(GR, Must, AP)	1-7	"While…eighteenth century."
24. D	(CR, Parallel)	44-55	"In other words…African Americans."
25. C	(GR, Must, O)	All	
26. B	(CR, Must)	34-37	"…tenant system…only cotton as payment."
27. C	(GR, Must, P)	All	

Passage #8: June 2000 Questions 6-12—page 34

6. C	(GR, MP)	All	
7. D	(CR, Must)	5-11	"Some legal scholars…success in *Brown*."
8. B	(CR, Must, P)	50-53	"Marshall presented…discrimination."
9. B	(GR, Must, SP)	5-11	"Some legal scholars…success in *Brown*."
10. B	(CR, Must)	23-27	"A second, more…legally unsound."
11. A	(SR, Must, O)	All	
12. C	(GR, Must, P)	5-11	"…the cases he presented…in *Brown*."

Passage #9: June 2000 Questions 13-20—page 36

13. C	(GR, Must, P)	All	
14. A	(GR, Must, AP)	All	
15. E	(CR, Must)	12-15	"Haraway's most…(nature/history)."
16. D	(CR, Must, SP)	7-11	"Primatology is a…and culture."
17. A	(SR, Must)	28-31	"…she insists…partial realities."
18. A	(SR, Must)	28-39	"Haraway does…historians of science."
19. E	(CR, Must)	28-39	"Haraway does…historians of science."
20. C	(SR, Must, P)	45-50	"Despite…difficult to set aside."

Passage #10: October 2000 Questions 14-19—page 38

14. D	(GR, MP)	6-14	"Limiting their…word's root meaning."
15. A	(CR, Must, AP)	6-14	"Limiting their…word's root meaning."
16. E	(SR, Must, P)	2-4	"…as-told-to life histories…collaborators."
17. C	(SR, Must, O)	All	
18. A	(SR, Must, P)	8-13	"In addition…concept of an autobiography."
19. B	(GR, Must, SP)	15-18	"The idea of self was…and the cosmos."

Passage #11: December 2000 Questions 8-14—page 40

8. A	(SR, Must, AP)	26-27	"But the relationship...is more complex."
9. D	(CR, Must)	41-42	"…she does not…stable home with family."
10. E	(SR, Must, SP)	23-27	"Some critics…typical slave narrative."
11. A	(SR, Strengthen)	23-27	"Some critics…typical slave narrative."
12. C	(SR, Must)	48-55	"Her narrative thus…conventional perspectives."
13. B	(GR, Must, AP)	25-28	"…one critic…two genres is more complex."
14. C	(GR, Must, AP)	50-55	"Jacobs…shedding conventional perspectives."

Passage #12: October 2001 Questions 1-6—page 42

1. C	(GR, MP)	All	
2. D	(CR, Must)	7-8	"…only members of…able to write easily."
3. D	(SR, Must, P)	40-50	"…instances of social activism…in court."
4. A	(CR, Must)	11-15	"Those written by royalists…their work."
5. C	(SR, Must, SP)	16-21	"Because the memoirs…of the past."
6. A	(SR, Must)	28-31	"Are there internal…writer's character?"

Passage #13: October 2001 Questions 7-14—page 44

7. B	(GR, MP)	All	
8. C	(CR, Must)	8-14	"Be presenting scene…resourceful artist."
9. A	(SR, Must)	26-34	"Through his depiction…composition."
10. B	(GR, Must, SP)	34-40	"Another important…social processes."
11. D	(CR, Must)	45-48	"Bearden sought…photography."
12. A	(GR, Must, X)	Incorrect answer choices are eliminated as follows:	
		1-14	"By presenting…to the resourceful artist."
		1-34	"During the Great Depression…composition."
		1-14	"By presenting…to the resourceful artist."
		1-40	"Another important…social processes."
13. D	(CR, Must, X)	Incorrect answer choices eliminated as follows:	
		26-29	"Through his depiction…human suffering."
		29-34	"His human figures…artistic composition."
		29-34	"His human figures…artistic composition."
		30-31	"…placed in...familiar urban settings."
14. A	(CR, Must, AP)	1-7	"The paintings of Romare…experience."

ANSWER KEY AND LINE REFERENCE NOTES

Passage #14: June 2002 Questions 14-21—page 46

14. A	(GR, Must, AP)	29-37	"Models for…African American culture."
15. A	(CR, Must)	8-13	"For this thematic…state of affairs"
16. E	(SR, Must, P)	23-28	"Such a view…own perspectives."
17. E	(SR, Must, O)	29-41	"Models for…European writers."
18. C	(CR, Must)	32-33	"Jazz has never closed…other musical forms."
19. C	(CR, Must, SP)	23-28	"Such a view…own perspectives."
20. D	(GR, Must, P)	All	
21. B	(GR, Must, X)	\multicolumn{2}{l}{Incorrect answer choices eliminated as follows:}
		29-32	"Models for…celebration of jazz."
		20-28	"He responded…their own perspectives."
		47-52	"Ellison's exploration…the protagonist."
		33-37	"…some jazz musicians have…culture."

Passage #15: October 2002 Questions 1-8—page 48

1. C	(GR, MP)	All	
2. A	(CR, Cannot)	\multicolumn{2}{l}{Incorrect answer choices eliminated as follows:}
		1-34	"Much of the mature…by burning."
		1-37	"In North America…sun-loving foods."
		1-31	"Burning also…ecological development."
		1-28	"Controlled burning…meadows and glades."
3. E	(CR, Must)	44-46	"An example is the…rain forests."
4. B	(CR, Must)	44-50	"An example is…even prehuman."
5. D	(GR, Must, AP)	35-42	"In North America…maintained it."
6. A	(CR, Must, X)	\multicolumn{2}{l}{Incorrect answer choices eliminated as follows:}
		1-34	"other evidence shows…burning."
		31-34	"Much of the mature…by burning."
		18-20	"One group…settlements were greatest."
		27-28	"Controlled burning…meadows and glades."
7. D	(SR, Must)	50-57	"Today, the Nicaraguan… hardwoods."
8. A	(GR, Must, P)	1-6	"The myth persists…of Europeans."

Passage #16: December 2002 Questions 1-8—page 50

1. B	(GR, MP)	1-7	"The contemporary…Mexican Revolution."
2. D	(SR, Must, P)	34-39	"…they developed their own…people."
3. C	(CR, Must, AP)	48-49	"This stylistic…demands of a new medium."
4. D	(GR, Must, SP)	33-37	"Moreover, while…brilliant color."
5. C	(CR, Must)	7-10	"This government…richness and possibility."
6. A	(SR, Strengthen)	33-37	"Moreover, while…brilliant color."
7. E	(CR, Must)	56-57	"…their works…different vantage points."
8. E	(SR, Must, P)	21-24	"But while…official government art."

Passage #17: June 2003 Questions 6-12—page 52

6. B	(SR, Must, P)	19-29	"Latin American…experimental ways."
7. A	(CR, Parallel)	39-54	"…Latin American…cultures began."
8. C	(CR, Weaken)	27-29	"Spanish poets…experimental ways."
9. D	(GR, Must, X)	\multicolumn{2}{l}{Incorrect answer choices eliminated as follows:}
		42-44	"For example, the first…Mexican."
		27-29	"Spanish poets…experimental ways."
		25-26	"By contrast, when these…reluctance."
		39-54	"…Latin American…cultures began."
10. B	(CR, Must)	34-38	"Because no…past to romanticize."
11. D	(CR, Must, AP)	30-33	"The most distinctive…distant past."
12. C	(GR, Must)	27-29	"Spanish poets…experimental ways."

Diversity II: Undermining Overrepresented Groups

Passage #1: December 2002 Questions 9-16—page 54

9. D	(GR, Must, MP)	All	
10. A	(CR, Must, SP)	46-49	"Bettelheim interprets...to indulge."
11. C	(GR, Must, AP)	49-52	"Fortunately, these...psychoanalytic literature."
12. E	(GR, Must)	52-58	"The need...playful pleasure."
13. D	(CR, Must)	39-43	"Once we...and expectations."
14. E	(CR, Must)	46-52	"Bettelheim interprets...psychoanalytic literature."
15. D	(CR, Must, SP)	32-36	"What makes...unruly children."
16. B	(GR, Cannot, SP)	32-39	"What makes...through reinterpretation."

Diversity III: Mixed Group Passages

Passage #1: December 1996 Questions 22-27—page 56

22. C	(GR, MP)	All	
23. B	(CR, Must, SP)	20-24	"Because of concerns...proficiency."
24. B	(GR, Must, AP)	51-67	"Tollefson ably...nature of the programs."
25. A	(CR, Must)	56-62	"He recommends...public assistance."
26. A	(SR, Must, O)	1-14	"Most studies...educational programs."
27. B	(SR, Must, P)	63-67	"Unfortunately, though...of the programs."

Passage #2: October 1997 Questions 19-26—page 58

19. C	(GR, Must, MP)	9-12	"Fugita and......such scholarship."
20. E	(CR, Must)	26-31	"their data......layered identities."
21. C	(SR, Parallel)	4-7	"earlier historians......national character."
22. D	(CR, Must)	1-4	"the focus......its preservation."
23. B	(SR, Must, P)	35-48	"Because of......family ties."
24. C	(SR, Must, AP)	57-59	"However, it......distinct phenomenon."
25. A	(SR, Must)	51-59	"Like historians......distinct phenomenon."
26. B	(GR, Must, SP)	53-57	"Fugita and......States culture."

Passage #3: September 1998 Questions 6-13—page 60

6. E	(GR, MP)	All	
7. B	(CR, Must, P)	31-38	"While these earlier...artisanship."
8. B	(SR, Must)	44-47	"In his later...fragmentary evidence."
9. D	(CR, Must)	22-24	"Porter proved...African ancestry."
10. D	(CR, Must)	52-56	"At his death...not exhausted."
11. C	(CR, Parallel)	34-43	"Porter's book...various African peoples."
12. A	(CR, Must)	34-37	"Porter's book...African artisanship."
13. E	(CR, Must)	52-56	"At his death...not exhausted."

Passage #4: October 2000 Questions 8-13—page 62

8. E	(GR, MP)	44-61	"The methods of...can be achieved."
9. B	(CR, Must, SP)	15-18	"Critics of this first...perspective."
10. C	(GR, Must, O)	All	
11. B	(SR, Must, P)	5-13	"The most modest...majority culture."
12. D	(SR, Must, SP)	29-31	"The values of...taken on its own terms."
13. A	(SR, Weaken)	54-61	"To insist on trying...can be achieved."

Chapter 3: Law Related Passages

Law Passages

Passage #1: December 1996 Questions 9-16—page 66

9. A	(GR, Must, MP)		All	
			12-17	"Since the......of law."
10. B	(GR, Must X)		Incorrect answer choices are eliminated as follows:	
			46	"political acts"
			46-47	"attempts to......efficient rules,"
			48	"artistic performances."
			54	"act of 'translation,' "
11. B	(CR, Must)		33-37	"it is......or gender."
12. D	(CR, Must)		28-30	"Drawing on......and history,"
			38-40	"White began......traditional questions,"
13. E	(CR, Must)		14-17	"This novelty......of law."
14. D	(CR, Must, SP)		49-51	"each judicial......ethical value."
15. C	(SR, Must, P)		53-54	"opinion-writing......as 'translators.' "
			57-59	"A judge......new one,"
16. A	(GR, Must, P)		All	

Passage #2: June 1997 Questions 9-16—page 68

9. C	(GR, MP)		All	
			34-44	"The societal......legal narratives."
10. A	(SR, Must)		10-16	"This procedure......other accounts."
11. A	(SR, Must)		45-47	"Objectivist legal......narrowest sense."
			13-20	"Objectivism holds......thought happened."
12. D	(CR, Must, SP)		41-44	"Legal scholars......legal narratives."
			47-53	"These legal......legal language."
13. D	(CR, Must, AP)		57-64	"Such alternative......emotional empathy."
14. B	(CR, Must, SP)		59-64	"the engaging......emotional empathy."
15. B	(CR, Must)		53-56	"The compelling......from power."
16. A	(SR, Parallel)		20-22	"The serious......objective observer."

Passage #3: October 1997 Questions 6-13—page 70

6. C	(GR, Must, MP)		All	
			6-13	"Although medieval......thirteenth-century England."
7. E	(SR, Must, AP)		5-6	"Examination…overly simplistic."
			10-13	"women's control......thirteenth-century England."
8. B	(SR, Must)		59-64	"widows could......multiple counties."
9. C	(SR, Must, P)		13-22	"Since land......making wills."
			23-43	"Although feudal......these lands."
10. E	(CR, Must)		44-49	"Since many......her son"
11. D	(CR, Must)		57-58	"Many married......at war;"
12. A	(SR, Must, P)		27-34	"In addition......bridal dowry;"
13. B	(GR, Must, P)		All	

Passage #4: June 1998 Questions 1-7—page 72

1. D	(GR, MP)	All	
2. B	(CR, Must)	27-30	"Government officials…government business."
3. A	(GR, Must, O)	All	
4. D	(CR, Must, AP)	8-11	"In fact, the question…electronic age."
5. B	(CR, Must, AP)	53-57	"The only solution…its convenience."
6. C	(GR, Cannot)	18-23	"Some hold…destruction is forbidden."
7. D	(GR, Must, P)	All	

Passage #5: December 1998 Questions 1-7—page 74

1. E	(GR, MP)	1-13	"The expansion of mass…public interest."
2. A	(CR, Must, SP)	21-26	"Nor, they claim…power to execute.'"
3. B	(SR, Must, P)	27-42	"The remedy for partiality…accordingly."
4. C	(GR, Must, AP)	51-58	"But if a jury…opinionated people."
5. C	(CR, Must)	55-58	"Impartiality does not…opinionated people."
6. B	(GR, Must)	49-58	"It merely recognizes…opinionated people."
7. E	(GR, Must, P)	43-55	"These criticisms have been…mass media."

Passage #6: June 1999 Questions 1-5—page 76

1. C	(GR, MP)	All	
2. E	(CR, Must)	26-29	"The Mashpee's 1976…federal approval."
3. E	(CR, Must, AP)	52-56	"Similar claims have…legal decisions."
4. D	(CR, Must)	43-56	"The Mashpee marshaled…legal decisions."
5. B	(GR, Must, P)	1-15	"Some Native American…sometimes at variance."

Passage #7: October 1999 Questions 22-27—page 78

22. D	(CR, Must, AP)	1-7	"Until about…serious deficiency."
23. D	(SR, Must, O)	1-28	"Until about…attempted by few."
24. D	(SR, Must)	15-28	"But these sources…by few."
25. A	(CR, Must)	9-15	"…how the…write about medieval law."
26. C	(SR, Must)	32-41	"there are over…in the first place."
27. A	(CR, Must, AP)	39-41	"the fact is that few…in the first place."

Passage #8: December 1999 Questions 15-21—page 80

15. E	(GR,MP)	1-7	"Philosopher Denise…legal theory."
16. B	(SR, Must, P)	44-50	"Meyerson claims…rules of the game."
17. D	(GR, Must, P)	All	
18. E	(SR, Must, SP)	50-56	"A CLS scholar might…rules of the game."
19. A	(SR, Must)	34-38	"The acknowledgement…be reasonable."
20. A	(SR, Must, O)	39-56	"Last, Meyerson…rules of the game."
21. C	(CR, Must, SP)	8-15	"According to Meyerson…or irrational."

Passage #9: October 2000 Questions 1-7—page 82

1. D	(GR, MP)	42-51	"The lawyer's obligation…facts of the case."
2. E	(SR, Must, AP)	23-28	"For this reason…their innocence."
3. A	(GR, Must, E)	46-51	"The fact that every client…facts of the case."
4. C	(SR, Must, SP)	15-19	"…the lawyer's role is…represent themselves."
5. B	(SR, Method)	28-31	"Guilty defendants…insincere representation."
		7-11	"They argue that lawyers…before the court."
6. A	(CR, Must, AP)	26-28	"But by the same principle…their innocence."
7. B	(GR, Must, P)	42-51	"The lawyer's obligation…facts of the case."

ANSWER KEY AND LINE REFERENCE NOTES

Passage #10: December 2000 Questions 23-28—page 84

23. B	(GR, MP)	51-59	"Despite concerns…to a presumption."
24. B	(SR, Must, AP)	24-26	"Reform was frustrated…precedent."
25. A	(SR, Must, P)	45-50	"Further, in granting…children?"
26. B	(GR, Must)	4-10	"Among common-law…their innocence."
27. A	(GR, Must, P)	All	
28. D	(SR, Must, SP)	37-39	"Bentham argued…ignorance to knowledge."

Passage #11: October 2001 Questions 21-26—page 86

21. B	(GR, MP)	All	
22. D	(SR, Must, P)	12-26	"Legal Positivism…the absence thereof."
23. A	(CR, Must, AP)	49-53	"Once we realize…the original authors."
24. E	(CR, Must)	30-39	"The theory he proposes…consensus."
25. E	(GR, Must, SP)	12-34	"Legal positivism…legal positivism."
26. D	(GR, Must, SP)	14-16	"The meaning of the law…of a word."

Passage #12: June 2002 Questions 1-7—page 88

1. E	(GR, MP)	All	
2. D	(CR, Must, AP)	39-54	"Requiring unanimity…be undermined."
3. A	(SR, Must)	33-38	"Hung juries…to an unjust verdict."
4. C	(SR, Must, E)	39-54	"Requiring unanimity…be undermined."
5. A	(SR, Must)	12-17	"Critics of the unanimity…a retrial."
6. C	(CR, Must)	51-54	"…if even one…be undermined."
7. D	(GR, Must, AP)	33-38	"Hung juries…to an unjust verdict."

Passage #13: October 2002 Questions 9-14—page 90

9. D	(GR, MP)	All	
10. A	(SR, Must, P)	20-27	"Not all arguments…the same thing."
11. E	(CR, Weaken)	46-51	"But the critics…throw out the decision."
12. B	(GR, Cannot)	42-45	"The analogous legal…institutional authority."
13. D	(CR, Must, P)	30-41	"For example, if…distinctions in the past."
14. C	(CR, Must, AP)	42-57	"The analogous…predominantly institutional."

Passage #14: June 2003 Questions 20-27—page 92

20. B	(GR, MP)	All	
21. E	(CR, Must)	11-17	"Alarmingly, the beliefs…already interacted."
22. A	(CR, Must)	27-32	"…experimental evidence…in those details."
23. D	(SR, Parallel)	52-59	"But what is tangential…the perpetrator."
24. E	(GR, Must)	45-48	"The farther removed…original memories."
25. A	(SR, Must)	18-44	"Recent studies…saw no stop sign."
26. E	(CR, Must, AP)	11-17	"Alarmingly, the beliefs…already interacted."
27. D	(GR, Must)	45-48	"The farther removed…original memories."

Law-Regulation Passages

Passage #1: December 2001 Questions 21-26—page 94

21. D	(GR, MP)	All	
22. C	(SR, Must, P)	10-19	"That is to say…bill of rights."
23. D	(CR, Must, AP)	53-57	"If a rights-based culture…of justice."
24. C	(CR, Must)	10-15	"That is…counteract their rulings."
25. E	(SR, Must, O)	44-57	"South Africa must…cause of justice."
26. A	(SR, Must, SP)	34-43	"But some scholars warn…of its citizens."

Passage #2: December 2002 Questions 24-28—page 96

24. B	(GR, Must, MP)	All	
25. A	(CR, Must, SP)	All	
26. B	(SR, Must, P)	14-17	"Copyright experts…digitalization."
27. C	(GR, Must X)	All	The line references that eliminate each incorrect answer choice are as follows:
			(A): 44-48 "laws against…process."
			(B): 23-25 "Current law…material form."
			(D): 44-48 "laws against…process."
			(E): 51-53 "current copyright…research."
28. A	(SR, Must, SP)	34-36	"copyright holders…reproduction."
		51-53	"current copyright…research."

Chapter 4: Social Science Passages

Passage #1: June 1997 Questions 22-26—page 100

22. D	(GR, Must, MP)	14-16	"At the……refers to."
23. A	(CR, Strengthen)	19-26	"The debate……and inexact."
24. B	(CR, Must)	3-5	"mathematics is……of signs,"
25. B	(SR, Must, P)	27-28	"Lately the……wider acceptance."
		35-36	"Certainly this……the sciences."
26. A	(SR, Must, SP)	23-25	"whether the……agreed-upon conventions,"

Passage #2: December 1997 Questions 1-6—page 102

1. B	(GR, MP)	All	
2. A	(CR, Must, P)	57-64	"Subjects who……technological risks."
3. C	(CR, Must)	45-47	"If they……the messages."
4. D	(SR, Must)	8-12	"they can……or injury."
5. E	(SR, Must, AP)	41-50	"Risk communication……or misinterpreted."
6. B	(CR, Must)	12-15	"Because some……by experts."

Passage #3: December 1997 Questions 14-20—page 104

14. D	(GR, MP)	All	
15. B	(CR, Must, AP)	2-7	"These scholars……legal problems."
16. E	(CR, Must)	11-15	"Their studies……analysis' technique"
17. A	(SR, Must,P)	All	
18. A	(CR, Parallel)	19-23	"Although the……such evidence."
19. D	(CR/SR, Must)	51-59	"other scholars……to prevail."
20. A	(GR, Must, O)	All	

Passage #4: June 1998 Questions 22-26—page 106

22. D	(GR, MP)	All	
23. A	(CR, Must, SP)	4-6	"…nineteenth century…to be lost."
24. E	(GR, Must, X)	Incorrect answer choices eliminated as follows:	
		34-41	"The ultimate difficulty…to satisfy."
		6-10	"To address possible…interdependent."
		11-33	"Organicism depended on…unchanged."
		15-22	"In an entity…characteristic of the entity."
25. B	(CR, Must, SP)	42-56	"Organicists' criticism…replacement for it."
26. B	(CR, Must, Pr)	34-41	"The ultimate difficulty…to satisfy."

Passage #5: December 1998 Questions 22-26—page 108

22. B	(CR, Must, SP)	48-52	"The fairy tail is therapeutic…in their lives."
23. C	(CR, Must)	42-45	"By telling the child…approval of the stories."
24. C	(SR, Must)	23-25	"…in those stories...so nothing is incredible."
25. A	(CR, Must, SP)	48-52	"The fairy tail is therapeutic…in their lives."
26. E	(GR, Must, AP)	All	

Passage #6: June 2000 Questions 1-5—page 110

1. D	(CR, Must)	42-49	"Such recycling…inadequate to the task."
2. D	(CR, Must, AP)	50-57	"However, if industrialized…pollution."
3. D	(SR, Must, AP)	42-45	"Such recycling still…typical today."
4. C	(CR, Must, X)	Incorrect answer choices eliminated as follows:	
		24	"…wastes and pollution are minimized…"
		42-45	"Such recycling…levels than are typical today."
		22-23	"In such a system the …is optimized."
		39-42	"…tailoring the production…or a related one."
5. D	(SR, Must)	35-39	"A chunk of steel could…and some plastics."

Passage #7: June 2002 Questions 22-26—page 112

22. A	(CR, Must, AP)	17-24	"Previously, the notion…taking the risk."
23. C	(SR, Must, P)	17-35	"Previously…to win more than $300."
24. B	(GR, Must, AP)	41-49	"Such observations are…of the lost assets."
25. D	(GR, Must)	All	
26. C	(GR, Must, AP)	47-56	"This type of motivation…recapturing them."

Passage #8: October 2002 Questions 15-20—page 114

15. D	(GR, MP)	All	
16. E	(SR, Must, E)	45-54	"In order to capture…for the individual."
17. B	(CR, Must, X)	Incorrect answer choices eliminated as follows:	
		21-22	"… 'contingencies' –social…degrees of control."
		26	"…and accidental circumstances."
		21-22	"…social phenomena…varying degrees of control."
		27-30	"The ways in which…able to perform."
18. A	(CR, Parallel)	45-54	"In order to capture…for the individual."
19. E	(SR, Must, P)	1-13	"In explaining the foundations…structuring."
20. C	(CR, Cannot)	22-30	"Contingencies include…able to perform."

Chapter 5: Hard Science Passages

Passage #1: December 1996 Questions 17-21—page 118

17. D	(GR, Must, MP)	1-8	"Since the......been promulgated."
		38-41	"If the......actuality exist."
18. B	(SR, Must, P)	24-37	"Opponents of......the mantle."
19. A	(SR, Must, SP)	24-25	"Opponents of......the mantle,"
20. B	(SR, Parallel)	41-47	"One company......organic compounds,"
21. C	(CR, Must X)	45-58	"Siljan Ring......the granite."

Passage #2: September 1998 Questions 14-21—page 120

14. D	(GR, Must, P)	All	
15. E	(SR, Must)	49-52	"PCB poisoning is…diseased animals."
16. A	(SR, Parallel)	22-42	"The research…not entirely plausible."
17. A	(SR, Must, O)	41-60	"For several reasons…synthetic pollutants."
18. E	(CR, Must, AP)	41-47	"For several…October red tide bloom."
19. E	(CR, Must)	52-56	"An alternative…laden with pollutants."
20. C	(SR, Must, P)	42-45	"First, bottlenose…has been noted there."
21. D	(CR, Must)	32-37	"The emaciated…exacerbated their condition."
		56-60	"Although brevetoxin…synthetic pollutants."

Passage #3: December 1998 Questions 15-21—page 122

15. B	(GR, MP)	All	
16. B	(CR, Must)	1-5	"Homing pigeons…and fly home."
17. A	(SR, Must)	5-7	"Aside from reading…investigation"
18. C	(SR, Must)	16-33	"The first alternative…at the same time."
19. B	(SR, Must, P)	8-11	"The birds might…such as honeybees."
20. D	(CR, Weaken)	36-42	"Papi has posited…direction of home."
21. C	(CR, Must, SP/AP)	34-37	"The other alternative…olfactory."

Passage #4: June 1999 Questions 6-13—page 124

6. D	(GR, MP)	All	
7. E	(CR, Parallel)	13-31	"The volcano-climate…on temperature."
8. D	(CR, Must, X)	Incorrect answer choices eliminated as follows:	
		24-26	"…but it can also mimic…beginning to fade."
		23-24	"Such warming can mask…an eruption…"
		18-22	"In the process they…warms the atmosphere."
		27-37	"Once El Nino effects…opposite hemisphere."
9. D	(SR, Must, AP)	29-37	"Contrary to what earlier…hemisphere."
10. A	(CR, Must)	41-56	"For example…into a year without a summer."
11. C	(GR, Must, AP)	27-31	"Once El Nino effects…effect on temperature."
12. C	(CR, Cannot)	32-37	"And major, dust-splitting…hemisphere."
13. C	(SR, Must, P)	38-56	"Other researchers…without a summer."

ANSWER KEY

Passage #5: October 1999 Questions 16-21—page 126

16. B	(GR, Must, P)	All		
17. B	(GR, MP)	All		
18. E	(CR, Must)	22-24	"…stimulation with a fine…to the motor cortex."
19. C	(CR, Parallel)	29-56	"Scheich's neurophysiological…electric fields."
20. C	(CR, Must)	45-50	"The platypus, sensitive to…as if it were food."
21. B	(GR, Must, O)	All		

Passage #6: December 1999 Questions 1-6—page 128

1. C	(GR, MP)	All	
2. D	(SR, Must, P)	27-43	"One reason for…congregated foraging."
3. D	(CR, Parallel)	37-40	"Okapis never eat one…sample other leaves."
4. E	(CR, Must, SP)	55-58	"Zoologists theorize that okapis…expanded."
5. E	(GR, Must, X)	Incorrect answer choices eliminated as follows:	
		27 – 29	"One reason for their…at close range."
		10-13	"The okapi's rightful place within…tongue."
		29-22	"…okapis do not travel…forest interior."
		42-43	"…okapis engage in individual…foraging."
6. C	(GR, Must, AP)	15-43	"Because okapis were…foraging."

Passage #7: October 2000 Questions 20-27—page 130

20. E	(GR, MP)	All	
21. D	(SR, Must, P)	4-12	"Because of this assumption…have obscured."
22. A	(CR, Must, X)	Incorrect answer choices eliminated as follows:	
		40-44	"…the link between lipid…factors."
		22-25	"…researches found…distilled spirits."
		44-53	"We now know that…platelet adhesiveness."
		37-39	"…studies of wine drinkers…lipid levels."
23. A	(CR, Strengthen)	49-52	"Studies show that…adhesiveness."
24. C	(GR, Must, AP)	53-60	"One study demonstrated…alcoholic beverages."
25. D	(SR, Must, AP)	1-12	"Most scientists who study…have obscured."
26. C	(GR, Must, P)	All	
27. D	(GR, Must, X)	Incorrect answer choices eliminated as follows:	
		1-49	"We now know that…premature heart disease."
		1-22	"For example, alcohol…heart disease."
		34-37	"For one thing…victims of heart disease."
		49-52	"Studies show that…adhesiveness."

Passage #8: December 2000 Questions 15-22—page 132

15. C	(GR, MP)	All	
16. B	(SR, Must)	53-56	"In a warmer…decomposition rates."
17. A	(SR, Must, P)	11-15	"The increased vegetation…have predicted."
		36-59	"It is clear that…greatest temperature."
18. D	(CR, Must, SP)	25-27	"Patterson and Flint have…certain weeds."
19. A	(SR, Must, AP)	6-11	"…some research has…rate of global warming."
20. A	(CR, Must)	50-53	"Billings estimated…than it does currently."
21. C	(SR, Cannot)	16-35	"However, while…rangeland communities."
22. C	(CR, Must)	50-56	"Billings estimated…in decomposition rates."

Passage #9: June 2001 Questions 13-18—page 134

13. E	(CR, Must, SP)	46-50	"The new evidence…environmental agents."
14. C	(CR, Must)	15-22	"…if an experimenter…genes themselves."
15. E	(SR, Must, P)	46-58	"The new…hypothesis to be correct."
16. B	(CR, Strengthen)	39-45	"The case of…mutation and natural selection."
17. D	(CR, Must)	39-40	"The case of…to speed up evolution."
18. C	(CR, Must)	19-22	"This inherited…genes themselves."

Passage #10: October 2001 Questions 15-20—page 136

15. B	(GR, MP)	All	
16. D	(SR, Must, P)	20-25	"In formulating…the law of gravity."
17. E	(GR, Must, SP)	17-29	"Some evolutionary…factor in biology."
18. C	(CR, Must, SP)	30-41	"To illustrate the…gravitational field."
19. C	(CR, Must, SP)	17-20	"Some evolutionary…universal laws."
20. E	(CR, Must)	1-14	"Philosophers of science…in the first place."

Passage #11: December 2001 Questions 15-21—page 138

15. D	(GR, MP)	All	
16. C	(CR, Must, P)	1-7	"Discussions of how…sexual behavior."
17. B	(CR, Must)	37-58	"Thus, for example…deal with it physiologically."
18. A	(GR, Must, P)	All	
19. A	(CR, Must, X)	Incorrect answer choices eliminated as follows:	
		49-50	"This process…increased thirst…"
		47	"…stimulates the release of vasopressin."
		39	"…excretion of surplus body water..."
		16-22	"…homeostasis of body…narrow ranges."
20. B	(CR, Must)	42-44	"As might be expected…body fluids."

Passage #12: June 2002 Questions 8-13—page 140

8. B	(GR, MP)	56-60	"…not only is Curie's…later breakthroughs."
9. D	(CR, Must, AP)	24-27	"Some critics have…available to her."
10. A	(CR, Must)	36-40	"Furthermore, we must…components."
11. A	(GR, Must, P)	All	
12. C	(SR, Must, P)	1-19	"Spurred by the discovery…explain radiation."
13. A	(SR, Must)	15-19	"Furthermore…which to explain radiation."

Passage #13: December 2002 Questions 17-23—page 142

17. D	(GR, MP)	All	
18. E	(CR, Must)	41-42	"…like a volume dial…incremental settings."
19. A	(SR, Must)	13-22	"The major challenge to…originated elsewhere."
20. E	(CR, Must, AP)	48-61	"Soon thereafter…still in place today."
21. D	(GR, Must, X)	Incorrect answer choices eliminates as follows:	
		32-37	"Max Planck…blackbody radiation."
		48-61	"Soon thereafter, however…in place today."
		1	"With the approach of the twentieth century…"
		48-59	"…Albert Einstein…with Planck's speculation."
22. B	(SR, Must, P)	1-31	"With the approach…'ultraviolet catastrophe.'"
23. D	(GR, Must, P)	All	

Passage #14: June 2003 Questions 13-19—page 144

13. C	(GR, MP)	All	
14. B	(SR, Must, E)	All	
15. D	(GR, Must, AP)	50-57	"Nevertheless…universe together."
16. D	(SR, Parallel)	7-17	"…for decades …huge structures cohere."
17. A	(CR, Must, AP)	31-44	"But new evidence suggests…electron volts."
18. B	(SR, Must)	9-17	"…for decades cosmologists…cohere."
19. A	(GR, Must, X)	Incorrect answer choices eliminated as follows:	
		9-13	"…at least 90 percent…clusters of galaxies."
		31-34	"…new evidence suggests…oscillation…"
		47-49	"…even at the highest estimate…mass."
		14-17	"To account for this…structures cohere."

Chapter 6: Humanities Passages

Passage #1: December 1996 Questions 1-8—page 148

1. B	(GR, MP)	All	
		18-19	"Temperley's ambitious……this deficiency."
2. E	(GR, Must)	7-10	"general unavailability……historical consciousness"
3. D	(CR, Must)	10-13	"the sonatas……familiar enough"
4. A	(CR, Must)	42-44	"laws of……creative models,"
5. B	(SR, P)	51-54	"Beethoven did……for example"
6. B	(SR, P)	31-40	"To be……a 'school' "
7. E	(GR, P)	All	
		18-22	"Temperley's ambitious……in facsimile."
8. B	(GR, Must)	59-61	"perhaps the……it flourished,"

Passage #2: June 1997 Questions 17-21—page 150

17. A	(GR, Must, MP)	50-56	"Furthermore, while……public good."
18. B	(SR, Must, P)	46-49	"It is……industrial waste."
19. B	(GR, Must, SP)	33-36	"The economists'……maximize profits,"
20. A	(CR, Must)	50-56	"Furthermore,……public good."
21. C	(GR, Must, P)	All	
		25-28	"The economists……their profits."

Passage #3: October 1997 Questions 1-5—page 152

1. D	(GR, MP)	57-60	"The trouble…practices either."
2. D	(CR, Must, SP)	11-18	"Alpers argues…patronage system."
3. E	(SR, Must, P)	36-57	"Alpers' emphasis…native Leiden."
4. D	(CR, Strengthen)	45-47	"she argues…painting."
5. A	(GR, Must, AP/SP)	33-36	"Although there…market wanted."

Passage #4: October 1997 Questions 14-18—page 154

14. D	(GR, Must, MP)	1-4	"The debate……of views."
15. A	(SR, Must, P)	58-60	"The equilibrium……wilderness adored."
16. E	(CR, Must)	48-54	"Frederic Clements'……and stability."
17. C	(CR, Must, SP)	1-8	"The debate……environmental destruction"
18. D	(GR, Must, P)	1-4	"The debate……of views."

Passage #5: December 1997 Questions 21-27—page 156

21. C	(GR, Must, P)	All		
22. D	(GR, MP)	All		
23. C	(GR, Must)	1-2	"a fake…to deceive"	
24. E	(GR, Must X)	Answer choice (E) is proven by process of elimination.		
		The line references that eliminate each incorrect answer choice are as follows:		
		40-44	"in certain…its function."	
		25-26	"The modern…Italian Renaissance."	
		27-28	"a passionate…of antiquity."	
		40-41	"in certain…foreign concept."	
25. C	(GR, Must)	3	"the merit…separate issue."	
26. E	(SR, Must)	52-54	"only the…original function."	
27. D	(SR, Must, O)	3-8	"the merit…two extremes."	

Passage #6: June 1998 Questions 8-13—page 158

8. C	(GR, MP)	All	
9. B	(CR, Must, SP)	6-15	"During these years…peripheral issues."
10. A	(CR, Must)	48-50	"Appropriately…poetry as literary art."
11. C	(CR, Must, P)	15-26	"Scholars produced…Critical and Poetical."
12. D	(CR, Must)	37-44	"But after…can and cannot do."
13. A	(GR, Must, O)	All	

Passage #7: September 1998 Questions 1-5—page 160

1. E	(CR, Must, AP)	1-17	"Opponents of…community is protected."
2. A	(CR, Must, SP)	40-44	"Even the most…benefit to society."
3. A	(SR, Must)	9-13	"It is only in the context of…shared sacrifice."
4. E	(CR, Must)	18-23	"The responsibility…benefit of society."
5. B	(CR, Must, SP)	44-54	"Can the opponent…liberal democratic state."

Passage #8: June 1999 Questions 14-21—page 162

14. D	(GR, MP)	All	
15. A	(CR, Must, X)	30-36	"Neoclassical economists…unlimited growth."
16. E	(CR, Must, SP)	19-26	"According to…impoverish rather than enrich."
17. B	(CR, Cannot, SP)	50-55	"Conservation…in the amount of resources."
18. C	(CR, Must, SP)	55-59	"Onr measure of…producers and consumers."
19. C	(SR, Must, SP)	14-22	"Steady-state…rather than enrich."
20. D	(SR, Must, P)	37-59	"Some steady-state economists…consumers."
21. B	(CR, Must)	30-36	"Neoclassical economists…unlimited growth."

Passage #9: June 1999 Questions 22-26—page 164

22. A	(GR, Must, AP)	11-14	"…whetting the public's…art of storytelling."
		54-57	"…it appears that films…U.S. film industry."
23. C	(CR, Must)	43-57	"The new danger…in the U.S. film industry."
24. D	(SR, Must)	14-19	"The important feature…promotion of new films."
25. B	(GR, Must, O)	All	
26. D	(SR, Weaken)	35-57	"The problem with this…film industry."

ANSWER KEY AND LINE REFERENCE NOTES

Passage #10: October 1999 Questions 1-7—page 166

    1. B   (GR, MP)   All
    2. D   (SR, Must, SP)   12-23   "So fundamental is this break…interest and value."
    3. D   (CR, Must)   34-42   "…the clear impression…only to the eye."
    4. B   (CR, Must, P)   43-54   "It is also important…changes still to come."
    5. A   (GR, Must)   All
    6. E   (CR, Must, X)   Incorrect answer choices eliminated as follows:
                          37-41   "…they were primarily…to the eye."
                          12-19   So fundamental is this break…after the war."
                          21-22   "…break with traditional artistic techniques."
                          53-54   "…other artists who supposedly…still to come."
    7. E   (CR, Must, AP)   30-34   "But the forward-looking…social trends."

Passage #11: December 1999 Questions 7-14—page 168

    7. C   (CR, Must, AP)   46-48   "Agamemnon is indeed…victorious battle."
    8. C   (SR, Must, SP)   47-50   "But he also deeply desires…he says."
    9. D   (CR, Must, SP)   28-35   "These forces are…one choice over another."
    10. C   (CR, Point at Issue, SP)   24-55   "To A. Rivier…superhuman forces."
    11. E   (CR, Must, SP)   24-40   "To A. Rivier…there is only one real option."
    12. D   (SR, Must, SP)   15-23   "According to Snell..as a free agent.'"
    13. B   (CR, Must, X, SP)   Incorrect answer choices eliminated as follows:
                          13   "…each with grave consequences."
                          9-10   "..their prior notions…are dissolved."
                          11   "…reexamine their deepest motives…"
                          12-13   "They are given only two alternatives…"
    14. C   (GR, Must, P)   All

Passage #12: June 2000 Questions 21-28—page 170

    21. D   (GR, MP)   All
    22. B   (CR, Must, AP)   35-40   "For reasoned discourse…perspectives."
    23. B   (GR, Must, P)   50-61   "What would be required…the mind works."
    24. B   (CR, Must)   20-28   "But philosophers loyal…discerned objectively?"
    25. A   (SR, Must, P)   14-27   "With respect to features...objectively?"
    26. A   (CR, Must, P, X)   Incorrect answer choices eliminated as follows:
                          20-22   "But philosophers…gathered by introspection."
                          23-24   "Knowledge, they argue, includes…experience"
                          24-27   "Why should philosophy…be discerned objectively?"
                          8-14   "Scientists, they claim…any particular point of view."
    27. D   (CR, Must)   1-19   "Some philosophers find…any different?"
    28. E   (SR, Must)   41-49   "The situation may…themselves be sufficient."

Passage #13: December 2000 Questions 1-7—page 172

    1. C   (GR, Must, MP)   All
    2. A   (SR, Must)   Paragraph 1
    3. E   (GR, Must X)   All
    4. B   (SR, Weaken)   46-58   "In light……other nations."
    5. E   (SR, Must, P)   46-58   "In light……other nations."
    6. A   (GR, Must, SP)   19-23   "The economists……human indicators."
    7. B   (GR, Must, P)   All

Passage #14: June 2001 Questions 1-6—page 174

1. E	(GR, MP)	1-7	"Most authoritarian…to absolute power."
		56-60	"The more astute… political changes."
2. C	(CR, Must, AP)	50-51	Authoritarian rule…changes."
3. D	(GR, Must, E)	All	
4. B	(GR, Must, O)	All	
5. D	(GR, Must)	50-60	"Authoritarian rule tends in…changes."
6. E	(CR, Must, SP)	1-7	"Most authoritarian…absolute power."

Passage #15: June 2001 Questions 7-12—page 176

7. E	(GR, Must, AP)	42-56	"Working in this tradition…tragic and comic."
8. E	(CR, Must, X)	Incorrect answer choices eliminated as follows:	
		26-27	"Spirituals…longing or sorrow…"
		42-45	"Working in this…mastery of the performer."
		30-36	"In this regard…religious experience."
		29-30	"…both aim at…elation and exaltation."
9. C	(SR, Must, P, AP)	14-20	"the implication of…African American culture."
10. A	(SR, Must, P)	21-41	"Critics have noted…concept of self."
11. B	(SR, Must, P)	36-41	"These conditions are often…concept of self."
12. E	(CR, Parallel)	17-20	"Indeed, the blues…American culture."

Passage #16: June 2001 Questions 19-26—page 178

19. D	(CR, Must)	28-42	"The drafters of *The Convention*…determinations."
20. C	(CR, Must)	28-32	"The drafters of…unanticipated situations."
21. D	(CR, Must)	46-51	"…a 1985 UNHCR Executive…they live.'"
22. D	(CR, Must)	28-32	"The drafters of…unanticipated situations."
23. A	(CR, Must, AP)	21-32	"The original definition…unanticipated situations."
24. E	(SR, Must, P)	1-8	"When women are persecuted…protection."
25. C	(CR, Must)	52-55	"Such a pronouncement…international community."
26. A	(GR, Must, P)	All	

Passage #17: December 2001 Questions 1-6—page 180

1. D	(GR, MP)	All	
2. C	(GR, Cannot, AP)	44-47	"For example…conferences."
3. E	(SR, Must, P)	42-43	"it is true…supportive."
4. E	(GR/SR, Must)	1-4	"Traditionally…support."
		44-47	"conferences discriminate…conferences."
5. C	(SR, Must, P)	17-41	"What are…a loved one."
6. B	(SR, Weaken)	44-47	"conferences…access to conferences."

Passage #18: December 2001 Questions 7-14—page 182

7. E	(GR, MP)	All	
8. B	(GR, Must)	55-58	"the result…Renaissance England."
9. D	(CR, Must)	38-49	"English intellectuals…scholarship."
10. D	(SR, Must, P)	2-6	"the drama…England."
11. C	(GR, Must, SP)	33-37	"Binns argues…continent."
12. C	(GR, Must)	50-55	"These limitations…were written."
13. E	(CR, Must, P)	22-27	"The intellectual…scientist Newton."
14. D	(GR, Must, P)	All	

Passage #19: October 2002 Questions 21-27—page 184

21. A	(GR, MP)		All	
22. D	(SR, Must, P)		32-41	"The act of reading…moral principles."
23. E	(GR, Must, AP)		15-23	"Although training in ethics…as physicians."
24. D	(GR, Must, P)		All	
25. E	(CR, Must, X)		Incorrect answer choices eliminated as follows:	
			47-52	"It does not follow that…they arise."
			27-31	"Ethics courses drawing on…human events."
			11-14	"…aspiring physicians need…this."
			27-31	"Ethics courses drawing on…human events."
26. C	(CR, Must, X)		Incorrect answer choices eliminated as follows:	
			1-5	"One of the greatest…rigorous training."
			9-10	"…strictly scientific thinking is insufficient…"
			19-23	…theorizing about ethics contributes little…"
			27-31	"Ethics courses…world of human events."
27. E	(CR, Must, AP)		17-23	"Although the conceptual…physicians."

Passage #20: June 2003 Questions 1-5—page 186

1. E	(GR, MP)		All	
2. D	(SR, Must, P)		49-61	"This reassessment may…twentieth century."
3. A	(SR, Must, P)		24-33	"Zero-sum political and military…Cold War."
4. C	(CR, Must, AP)		56-61	"…the principal…of the twentieth century."
5. D	(CR, Must)		12-17	"Yet the constant…around 1815."

APPENDIX

Test-by-Test Passage Location Identifier

This section contains a reverse lookup that references every passage in this book according to the source LSAT. The tests are listed in order of PrepTest number, from PrepTest 21 (December 1996) to PrepTest 40 (June 2003). All other Law Services publication identifiers are also listed. Thereafter, the chapter, and page number where each passage can be found in this book is listed.

If you choose, you can use this lookup to find the four passages from an individual test and then do those four passages in order, re-creating that test section.

Passage   Book Location

December 1996 (LSAT PrepTest 21; 10 More Actual, Official LSAT PrepTests)

Passage #1: Chapter 6, page 148
Passage #2: Chapter 3, page 66
Passage #3: Chapter 5, page 118
Passage #4: Chapter 2, page 56

June 1997 (LSAT PrepTest 22; 10 More Actual, Official LSAT PrepTests)

Passage #1: Chapter 2, page 20
Passage #2: Chapter 3, page 68
Passage #3: Chapter 6, page 150
Passage #4: Chapter 4, page 100

October 1997 (LSAT PrepTest 23; 10 More Actual, Official LSAT PrepTests)

Passage #1: Chapter 6, page 152
Passage #2: Chapter 3, page 70
Passage #3: Chapter 6, page 154
Passage #4: Chapter 2, page 58

December 1997 (LSAT PrepTest 24; 10 More Actual, Official LSAT PrepTests)

Passage #1: Chapter 4, page 102
Passage #2: Chapter 2, page 22
Passage #3: Chapter 4, page 104
Passage #4: Chapter 6, page 156

June 1998 (LSAT PrepTest 25; 10 More Actual, Official LSAT PrepTests)

Passage #1: Chapter 3, page 72
Passage #2: Chapter 6, page 158
Passage #3: Chapter 2, page 24
Passage #4: Chapter 4, page 106

September 1998 (LSAT PrepTest 26; 10 More Actual, Official LSAT PrepTests)

Passage #1: Chapter 6, page 160
Passage #2: Chapter 2, page 60
Passage #3: Chapter 5, page 120
Passage #4: Chapter 2, page 26

December 1998 (LSAT PrepTest 27; 10 More Actual, Official LSAT PrepTests)

Passage #1: Chapter 3, page 74
Passage #2: Chapter 2, page 28
Passage #3: Chapter 5, page 122
Passage #4: Chapter 4, page 108

June 1999 (LSAT PrepTest 28; 10 More Actual, Official LSAT PrepTests)

Passage #1: Chapter 3, page 76
Passage #2: Chapter 5, page 124
Passage #3: Chapter 6, page 162
Passage #4: Chapter 6, page 164

October 1999 (LSAT PrepTest 29)

Passage #1: Chapter 6, page 166
Passage #2: Chapter 2, page 30
Passage #3: Chapter 5, page 126
Passage #4: Chapter 3, page 78

December 1999 (LSAT PrepTest 30)

Passage #1: Chapter 5, page 128
Passage #2: Chapter 6, page 168
Passage #3: Chapter 3, page 80
Passage #4: Chapter 2, page 32

June 2000 (LSAT PrepTest 31)

Passage #1: Chapter 4, page 110
Passage #2: Chapter 2, page 34
Passage #3: Chapter 2, page 36
Passage #4: Chapter 6, page 170

October 2000 (LSAT PrepTest 32)

Passage #1: Chapter 3, page 82
Passage #2: Chapter 2, page 62
Passage #3: Chapter 2, page 38
Passage #4: Chapter 5, page 130

December 2000 (LSAT PrepTest 33)

Passage #1: Chapter 6, page 172
Passage #2: Chapter 2, page 40
Passage #3: Chapter 5, page 132
Passage #4: Chapter 3, page 84

June 2001 (LSAT PrepTest 34)

Passage #1: Chapter 6, page 174
Passage #2: Chapter 6, page 176
Passage #3: Chapter 5, page 134
Passage #4: Chapter 6, page 178

October 2001 (LSAT PrepTest 35)

Passage #1: Chapter 2, page 42
Passage #2: Chapter 2, page 44
Passage #3: Chapter 5, page 136
Passage #4: Chapter 3, page 86

December 2001 (LSAT PrepTest 36)

Passage #1: Chapter 6, page 180
Passage #2: Chapter 6, page 182
Passage #3: Chapter 5, page 138
Passage #4: Chapter 2, page 94

June 2002 (LSAT PrepTest 37)

Passage #1: Chapter 3, page 88
Passage #2: Chapter 5, page 140
Passage #3: Chapter 2, page 46
Passage #4: Chapter 4, page 112

October 2002 (LSAT PrepTest 38)

Passage #1: Chapter 2, page 48
Passage #2: Chapter 3, page 90
Passage #3: Chapter 4, page 114
Passage #4: Chapter 6, page 184

December 2002 (LSAT PrepTest 39)

Passage #1: Chapter 2, page 50
Passage #2: Chapter 2, page 54
Passage #3: Chapter 5, page 142
Passage #4: Chapter 2, page 96

June 2003 (LSAT PrepTest 40)

Passage #1: Chapter 6, page 186
Passage #2: Chapter 2, page 52
Passage #3: Chapter 5, page 144
Passage #4: Chapter 3, page 92

LSAT Classification Notes:

1. The December 1993 LSAT was nondisclosed. It was later administered as the September 1995 LSAT and then released as PrepTest 16.

2. Starting in 1996, the February LSATs have been nondisclosed. In April 2000, the February 1997 LSAT was released as the Official LSAT PrepTest with Explanations, Volume One. In May 2004, the February 1996, February 1999, and February 2000 LSATs were released in The Official LSAT SuperPrep.

Contacting PowerScore

PowerScore International Headquarters:

PowerScore Test Preparation
57 Hasell Street
Charleston, SC 29401

Toll-free information number: (800) 545-1750
Website: www.powerscore.com
Email: lsat@powerscore.com

PowerScore LSAT Publications Information:

For information on all PowerScore LSAT publications.

Website: www.powerscore.com/pubs.htm

PowerScore Full-length LSAT Course Information:

Complete preparation for the LSAT.
Classes available nationwide.

Web: www.powerscore.com/lsat
Request Information: www.powerscore.com/contact.htm

PowerScore Virtual LSAT Course Information:

45 hours of online, interactive, real-time preparation for the LSAT.
Classes available worldwide.

Web: www.powerscore.com/lsat/virtual
Request Information: www.powerscore.com/contact.htm

PowerScore Weekend LSAT Course Information:

Fast and effective LSAT preparation: 16 hour courses, 99th percentile instructors, and real LSAT questions.

Web: www.powerscore.com/lsat/weekend
Request Information: www.powerscore.com/contact.htm

POWERSCORE LSAT TUTORING INFORMATION:

One-on-one meetings with a PowerScore LSAT expert.

Web: www.powerscore.com/lsat/content_tutoring.cfm
Request Information: www.powerscore.com/contact.htm

POWERSCORE LAW SCHOOL ADMISSIONS COUNSELING INFORMATION:

Personalized application and admission assistance.

Web: www.powerscore.com/lsat/content_admissions.cfm
Request Information: www.powerscore.com/contact.htm